Exam Secrets in Literature-in-English

What JAMB, WAEC and NECO Want from Candidates

For Senior Secondary Certificate and JAMB Examinations

Exam Secrets in
Literature-in-English

What JAMB, WAEC and NECO Want from Candidates

For Senior Secondary Certificate and JAMB Examinations

Volume 1

Mazi Basil Nwokorie

EXCELLER BOOKS™

A GLOBAL PRESS

Exam Secrets in Literature-in-English
What JAMB, WAEC, and NECO Want from Candidates
For Senior Secondary Certificate and JAMB Examinations

ISBN: 978-81-19524-10-5

First published in India in 2024 by Exceller Books,
An Imprint of GE Group
Address: G1, Dream Apartment, Degree College Road, Belgharia, Kolkata, 700056, India

www.excellerbooks.com

Dedication

This work is dedicated to the memory of my father, Ezinna Sylvester Nwokorie, to my wife, Ifeyinwa Juliet Nwokorie, my little ones: Chris, Hilary, Chinonye and Ezenwa, for whom I could write, and to a mother par excellence, Nneoma Roseline Nwokorie, for her love, unwavering patience, support, and practical desire that her children succeed in life.

Acknowledgements

I am immensely indebted to individuals and publishers who played significant and tremendous roles in the conception and production of this work. Foremost amongst them are my teachers in Literature-in-English, both at college and tertiary levels, particularly Mr. Frank Odua of Abia State University, Uturu. With brilliance and tenacity, he stirred up in me an interest in the subject, which led to the writing of this book.

I was greatly assisted by criticisms and suggestions from a fine gentleman, a friend, and a fellow advocate Sampson Eze, Esq, who saw this work in draft form.

I am grateful to Mrs. Chinwe Achonwa (nee Igwe), who, as a personal editor, waded through the manuscript and made suggestions that shaped the quality and outlook of this work. Madam, your efforts are highly appreciated.

I am highly indebted to Ms. Favour Onwumere of Glory to Glory Business Centre, Ogale Eleme, Rivers State, for her diligence in typesetting and organising the manuscript.

I appreciate my elder brother, Mazi Okechukwu Nwokorie, for his care and earnest desire that I do well in life. I am grateful to Engr. Uche Patrick Iwueze, my friend, and Engr. Chima Matt Nwaiwu, for their unalloyed support and for allowing me to use their facilities to proofread this work.

I am also grateful to Engr. Ugochukwu Chris Nwaodu and Mazi Chinedu Akubueze. I owe my love and respect to them. They, in many ways, influenced the success of this work.

I will always remain grateful to my uncle, Dr. E. E. Nwokorie (DVM), Associate Professor, University of Minnesota, USA, his lovely wife, and my auntie, G. N. Nwokorie, and their lovely family for providing me with one of the major sources for this work.

I appreciate Detoun Morawo (Maama Tee), CEO of DEVAT Books Publishing Ltd Ibadan, a woman of substance and publisher and editor, for her encouragement and meaningful contributions to the book's success.

Finally, in producing this work, I consulted and made use of the following books and copyrighted materials:

- A Glossary of Literary Terms (9th Edition) by M. H. Abrams & Geoffrey Galt Harpham
- Literature: Reading Fiction, Poetry, Drama and Essay (4th Edition) by Robert Di Yanni
- Literature: An Introduction to Fiction, Poetry, and Drama (9th Edition) by X. J. Kennedy & Dana Gioia
- The Language of Literature by McDougal Little, Elements of Literature 5th Course, by Holt, Rinehartand Winston
- Comprehensive Literature in English for Senior Secondary Schools by Martins Izuchukwu Amaechi
- Authority on Literature in English by R.O.C. Ilozue
- Galileo (Ramsed Publications Edition) by Bertolt Brecht
- Syllabuses and past exam question papers of Joint Admission and Matriculation Board (JAMB), West African Examination Council (WAEC).

I am also grateful to all copyright owners whose works or materials were referred to in this book. I made all the efforts to trace and acknowledge them. But if, in any particular case, I failed to give credit, the omission is highly regretted. Appropriate steps shall be taken to give due credit in subsequent editions of this work, especially where such omissions come to my attention.

Mazi Basil Nwokorie,
Author

Table of Contents

Words on Marble

'A secret is that which is unknown or known to some but kept away from others. It is the best way of doing something that many do not know.'

– Phemephe

Preface

Exam Secrets in Literature-in-English is a guidebook tailored towards assisting students and candidates in excelling in their senior secondary and university matriculation examinations in Literature-in-English across Nigeria and the four other anglophone West African countries: Ghana, the Gambia, Sierra Leone and Liberia. These rigorous examinations are administered by distinguished academic bodies such as the West African Examination Council (WAEC), National Examination Council (NECO), Joint Admission and Matriculation Board (JAMB) and other sister examination bodies.

The book is prepared and structured in strict compliance with the dictates and standards of WAEC, NECO and JAMB. It is written with the aim of addressing the challenges teachers and students face in the teaching and learning of Literature-in-English in the sub-region and perhaps elsewhere. It deals with the various aspects of the subject, including those that are regularly featured in the stated examinations. The author is aware that apart from the students and candidates preparing for O/Level WAEC, NECO, NABTEB and JAMB examinations, there are quite some others taking literature at introductory levels in higher institutions might be interested in this work. To this set, this book is nothing but an invaluable gift coming at a time when there are not enough books of similar background that meet their needs.

Drawing from personal experience, the author has endeavored to tackle the prevalent challenges that students and candidates encounter while preparing for their O/Levels and JAMB examinations. Additionally, the author has skillfully presented the subject as a vibrant art form, captivating the attention of both students and examiners.

The book is the culmination of extensive research aimed at uncovering the intricacies and enigmas that render the study of literature formidable. It is meticulously crafted to effortlessly aid students in their exam preparation.

The book possesses numerous distinctive features that set it apart from others in the subject.

- Firstly, it is meticulously structured in accordance with the scope and objectives of JAMB, WAEC, and NECO. This design promotes effective learning processes and is specifically tailored to aid students in examination preparation. It simplifies the teaching and comprehension of literature while maintaining the interest and systematic knowledge that literature offers.

- Secondly, the book delves into a comprehensive examination of literature, viewing it not only as an academic field but also as a valuable tool for instruction and entertainment. It explores strategies to enhance students' comprehension of the subject and the application of the requisite standard and knowledge expected of examination candidates. It makes a practical effort to unravel the challenges students face in grasping the subject and its significance in intellectual development, with a particular focus on the various elements that constitute literature.

- Thirdly, the book serves as a valuable guide for teachers by introducing a classroom approach to facilitate the teaching of literature. This innovative approach, which is distinctively novel, aims to simplify the subject matter while reigniting or reinforcing interest among both teachers and students.

- Finally, the book serves as an exposé on literary appreciation, presenting terms, principles, and techniques used in general literary discourse in an engaging manner. It also highlights key terms, principles, devices, and techniques prevalent in literature to showcase their application in literary works.

Moreover, the book endeavors to provide students with the essential knowledge required by examiners and offers guidance on how to approach the subject effectively.

By presenting the subject matter in a clear and simplified manner, it aims to assist students and candidates in excelling in their examinations. As a reference book for literature teachers, it includes a chapter on teachers' approach to teaching literature, with the intention of not only enhancing classroom instruction but also fostering active participation in the teaching and learning processes. By introducing relevant theories, models, and approaches for teachers to employ, the book aims to facilitate the delivery of the subject matter in a more effective and purposeful manner. Additionally, it provides a practical guide for answering exams, further aiding students in their academic endeavors.

Equally, a practical guide to answering examination questions was added to provide the students with the examiners' perspective and approach to answering examination questions in the subject. To this end, it is hoped that this book provides, in some measure, an answer to the perennial ill feelings held by some candidates against exam bodies when they fail or make undesirable grades in their exams. For one thing, the book guides the students into becoming masters in the subject even before attempting the first exam question.

Further, the inclusion of sample questions and their answers in both the essay and multi-choice tests drawn from past examination questions of WAEC, NECO, NABTEB and JAMB will, in no small measure, complement whatever advantage and progress the students will make after reading this book.

This book also contains the observations of the Chief Examiner of WAEC on the performance of candidates in Literature-in-English examinations in recent times. It also contains WAEC's Exam Scheme on the subject. Both were added to provide a guide for the students, candidates and teachers of the subject.

Essentially, incorporating the Chief Examiner's observations points at the main objective of this book—discovering what the examiners demand from the candidates. These observations are instructive and point out what the students and candidates need to do to prepare well for their exams.

In a nutshell, this work brings the knowledge and subject of literature from its perceived Olympian heights to such a level that the students and candidates can understand and use it in their studies and exams without much ado. This book will be found valuable by students who desire to do well in their exams and teachers of the subject, who bear the onerous task of preparing the students for the examinations and ensuring that they do well in them.

Further, I must say that this book is meant for students who place a high premium on their academic success. It is for those who desire to acquire the necessary tools and competencies for deeper communications, reading and writing. It is also for those motivated by the desire to explore the artistic and imaginative depths of the world created by writers in works of literature. To them, the coast is now clear and the voyage is theirs to make.

In Literature-in-English, there is a strong emphasis on immersing oneself, by way of reading, in literary works, particularly those recommended for subsequent examinations. This involves not merely skimming through the texts but rather engaging in a meticulous analysis that leads to a profound understanding of the underlying themes and significance.

For students to excel in their examinations, it is imperative that they partake in a comprehensive exploration of the texts and other pertinent materials related to the subject. This process is indispensable for achieving a thorough grasp of the intricate nuances and complexities embedded within the literary works.

Furthermore, the writer adds that this book is not, and does not pretend to be, an exhaustive discourse on literature generally or even on Literature-in-English as a subject offered in our secondary schools. It is a humble effort aimed at addressing the challenges students and teachers face while preparing for exams in the subject.

As a guide, the author asserts that this book holds the key to unlocking the examiners' repository and revealing their most closely guarded secrets and insights regarding literature-in-English examinations to students and candidates. The author foresees that students and educators will leverage this invaluable asset and other opportunities presented in this book to excel in their academic endeavours and preparations for the examinations. He exerted significant effort to intricately guide the students through the covert musings of the examiner to throw light on the effective approach to making productive and fulfilling use of the prescribed texts and materials for the examinations.

Finally, it should be noted that some of the materials used in this text were obtained from published works and materials on literature whose copyrights are hereby acknowledged. It was the author's responsibility to weave them with some unique expertise to create a readable piece fit for its purpose. This purpose, the author asserts, gravitates around assisting students in preparing for their examinations and teachers in teaching the subject with ease. The shortcomings via errors, omissions or inelegance of language that may be found herein are solely the author's. He completely and totally agrees with Thomas E. Patterson's idea that a text's strengths and weaknesses can only be fully understood by putting it to use. It is through the valuable feedback received from comments and critiques that future editions can address any shortcomings and improve upon them. Therefore, I warmly welcome any correspondence regarding this work, as there may be areas where further refinement or development can help the book move forward.

Mazi Basil Nwokorie,
Author

Chapter 1

Introduction

What Examiners Require from Candidates:
Examination is a process of evaluating learning outcomes. It serves as evidence that learning has occurred. In an academic setting, it measures the knowledge, skills, aptitude, or suitability of a scholar. It can take various forms, such as oral tests, written exams, or practical demonstrations of what the student must have learnt. Its purpose is not to prove students wrong in their learning, but to enable them to demonstrate their knowledge in writing or performance of specific skills.

Literature-in-English examinations are taken by students and candidates to appraise their comprehension level in the subject. Examination bodies require their candidates to demonstrate adequate knowledge of the respective subjects studied. The topics covered during exams are determined by examination boards, such as JAMB, WAEC, NECO, ETC, which outline the areas that candidates can expect to be tested on.

A quick review of Literature-in-English section of JAMB syllabus reveals that the examiners' objectives are aimed at achieving the following:

- Stimulate and sustain interest in literature.
- Create awareness of the general principles and functions of literature while appreciating the beauty and complexity of language.
- Appreciate literary works of all genres across all cultures.
- Apply the knowledge of literature to the analysis of social, political and economic events in our society.

On its part, the West African Examinations Council (WAEC) indicated that its syllabus for Literature-in-English was crafted to facilitate candidates in recognizing literature as a pivotal component of their comprehensive educational journey. Specifically, the syllabus is geared towards equipping students with the ability to develop critical acumen as a means to independently evaluate complex human dilemmas and themes.

The syllabus, therefore, provides for an examination that tests for candidates':

- Critical response to and awareness of how literature functions
- Familiarity with the terms and concepts necessary for the appreciation of literature
- Ability to distinguish between types of literature, their techniques of composition and mode of appeal
- Competence in understanding literary texts at their various forms and levels of meaning (e.g. surface and implied)
- Facility in responding imaginatively to literature through an effective and organised use of language

In Nigeria, this set of objectives drawn from the secondary education curriculum in the country was adopted, for the sake of uniformity, by sister examination bodies – NECO and NABTEB, for their respective examinations, hence, the much talked about Unified Syllabus.

Translated into details, these examination bodies require that candidates taking their exams exhibit a sustained passion for Literature-in-English and a deep understanding of the topics outlined in the syllabuses and curriculum for the subject. To meet these requirements, candidates must engage in thorough studies to acquire a comprehensive knowledge of Literature-in-English as stipulated in the examiners' syllabuses. More specifically, they need to be familiar with the diverse interpretations of literature by literary experts and its significance in national educational policies and strategies. Additionally, they should possess a thorough understanding of the various categories or genres that constitute literature, which are:

- Drama
- Prose

- Poetry

> **Drama**

In drama, students or candidates are expected to know and analyse the various types of drama studied and distinguish them from one another. Specifically, they are required to know the following: tragedy, comedy, tragi-comedy, melodrama and farce, among others.

Candidates are required to know the various dramatic techniques by which a story or action in a dramatic work is narrated or interpreted. These include but are not limited to characterisation, dialogue, flashback, mime, costume, music/dance, décor acts/scenes, setting, soliloquy/aside, style, etc.

Candidates must know the various styles used by writers in dramatic works and be able to identify them in the prescribed texts. They must be able to determine the themes of the prescribed texts, identify the plot, and be able to interpret the texts in terms of theme, plot, style, and socio-political context. They are expected to apply the lessons drawn from them to everyday living.

> **Prose**

Under prose, candidates are required to know what prose is all about and distinguish it from other genres of literature. To be precise, a candidate is expected to know the types or subsets of prose, which include:

- Fiction: Novel, novella and short story
- Non-fiction: Biography, autobiography and memoir

A candidate should be able to distinguish between types, classes, and subclasses of prose, analyse the components of each type and identify the category into which each of the prescribed texts falls.

Narrative Techniques/Devices

Candidates are also required to know the various narrative techniques and devices used by literary writers. Specifically, they must be able to identify:

- Point of View – Omniscient, first person and third person narrator
- Setting – Temporal, spatial/geographical, etc
- Characterisation – Round, flat, stock characters, etc
- Language/Diction – Choice of words and figurative language

Textual Analysis

This involves the general make-up of the work in terms of theme, plot, socio-cultural or political contexts or background. Candidates must be able to:

- Figure out the narrative technique used in each prescribed text
- Determine an author's narrative style
- Distinguish between characters
- Determine the thematic pre-occupation of the author of the texts and
- Indicate the plot and relate it to real-life situations.

> **Poetry**

Under poetry, candidates must understand what poetry is all about and the distinguishing features between the genre and other forms of literature. They must be able to identify the classes and the different types of poems and compare the features of the different poetic types, for example, sonnet, ode, lyric, elegy, ballad, panegyric, epic, blank verse, etc.

Poetic Devices

Candidates are expected to know the various poetic devices, including structure, figures of speech, imagery, symbolism, rhyme, rhythm, repetition, alliteration, personification, onomatopoeia, irony, hyperbole, diction, personae, rhetorical question, etc. They must determine the devices used by various poets and show how they are used to convey the poet's message or the aesthetic effect in each poem.

Poetic Appreciation

Candidates should understand the thematic pre-occupation of poems and their socio-political relevance. Candidates must be able to appraise poetry as an art with moral values and apply the lessons from the poems to real-life situations.

> **General Literary Terms and Principles**

Examiners expect candidates to know and identify the various literary terms and principles used in drama, prose, and poetry. Candidates are expected to know the distinctive features of the terms and principles, how they relate, and their appropriate usage. A proper understanding of these terms and principles helps the candidates give appropriate interpretations of the recommended texts and materials and respond well to questions based on them.

> **Literary Appreciation**

This is a concept by which literary works are analysed, interpreted and understood. It represents a conscious effort to understand literary works and their merits. It is usually done by reading and interpretation.

Candidates should understand that the business of literary appreciation is the analysis and interpretation of literary works. They should also know that acquiring the artistic skills necessary for doing this and reacting instantaneously to any literary work in the various genres of literature is essential for both their studies and exams. They must understand that the skills are either tied to particular genres or cut across all the genres of literature. Candidates must acquire these skills to be able to:

- Deal with the literary tools and devices used in a given work or extract and

- Provide meaningful interpretation and relate it to a real-life situation

To appreciate a literary work, that is, to understand and give it an appropriate interpretation, the readers must be ready to enter and flow freely into the world of the artist – writer or poet and to integrate, engage, and/or involve themselves in the artist's thoughts and feelings, and be able to read the author's mind dispassionately and as presented in work. This enables the readers to understand the work and fairly assess or evaluate it. In literary appreciation, the reader thoroughly considers the theme and style of the work, attempts an interpretation and makes an evaluation of it.

Interpreting literature is an art and skill that readers develop with experience and practice. The reader, usually a student or candidate, has to first understand the context of the text. The context of a text refers to the actual meaning and background put forward or conveyed by the writer. This meaning can be literal or metaphorical. The candidates must understand the structure of the texts, that is, the organisation, presentation, and diction, its effectiveness, and the devices used in the text. Adequate and effective reading of recommended texts – prose works, poems, and drama, allows the candidates to understand the work. It also helps them become skilful in the art of interpreting literary works. In the long run, they would become familiar with the import of the work or material. This guarantees better handling of questions and good performance in the exam.

Examiners also require candidates to know the various perspectives used in interpreting and analysing works of literature. These include historical, biographical, psychological, and sociological perspectives, each of which approaches the study of literature differently.

Again, at its inception, JAMB followed the Ordinary Level Syllabus of WAEC for its exams. However, later in 1990, it upgraded and introduced advanced-level topics to its syllabus, except in the Use of English. This upgrade and subsequent improvements in its policies gave rise to the highly competitive UTME examination that we have now. For one thing, the introduction of the Advanced Level topics enables it to select the best candidates to fill the few available spaces in affiliate tertiary institutions.

Again, JAMB examinations seek to separate 'the boys from the men' by selecting the best in terms of performance from the lot and presenting them to our universities, polytechnics, monotechnics, and colleges for admission. Therefore, the questions of JAMB examinations are not expected to be commonplace. In fact, it has ensured that 50% of its questions yearly are drawn from advanced-level topics. The questions deserve more than a casual or a passing glance. The answer options are deliberately structured to elude the shallow or hasty readers. Some of them can only be 'decoded' by candidates with the 'third eye' – the eagle's eye that misses nothing. This third eye can be acquired not by organ transplant or manipulation but by careful, vigorous, and effective preparation. This type of preparation forms the bedrock of this book and is aimed at revealing the best-kept secrets of examiners in Literature-in-English in Nigeria and beyond.

The examination is a test of knowledge, speed and accuracy consisting of 180 questions with a time frame of 2 hours (120 minutes). On average, this means that the allotted time for each question is 1 minute 30 seconds. The subject combination varies based on a candidate's desired course of study, with the Use of English being compulsory for all candidates. The Use of English has 60 questions, and the other three subjects have 40 questions each. The exam is a Computer-based Test (CBT), and all the questions are displayed on the computer at the exam centres. Candidates must submit their work within the specified two hours, or the system will log them out. It is, therefore, advised that the candidates should manage their time and finish the exam within the stipulated time.

Chapter 2

What Is Literature?

In ordinary parlance, literature is defined as an acquaintance with letters. However, as intended to be discussed in this book, it refers to the various creative and imaginative works that deal with the artistic creation, recreation, expression, or presentation of the thoughts and experiences of people for the purpose of information, instruction and entertainment. These thoughts and experiences of people that literature presents exist in various forms or genres, including drama, prose, poetry, etc. Engaging in literature is like a journey through life's experience as reflected and given prominence in the works of writers. To some, it is an art involving written works which, from a limited perspective, designates fictional and imaginative writings – poetry, prose, and drama. But in an extended perspective, and in the general view of a number of literary commentators, it also designates those other works both in the written and oral form, including philosophy, history, music, and even scientific works addressed to a general audience, distinguished in form, expression, and emotional power.

Literature imitates life by employing imaginative skills and crafts in the presentation of situations for a pre-determined purpose. It concerns itself with language, which is its sole tool. However, what makes the use of language literature is the method or manner of its expression. This method or manner of expression is usually deliberate with the aim of creating an effect, producing mental pictures and aesthetic beauty that engage our intellect. Therefore, one feels confident in saying that literature concerns itself not just with what is said but also with how it is said. Since literature is a method of expression, we agree with some writers that it involves skilful manipulation of the language to produce a desired or artistic effect.

Literature exists in oral forms, such as myths, legends, ballads, folktales, etc. and in written forms that include all written literary works. However, whatever form or description we can ascribe to a piece of literature, it is sufficient to say that borrowing the view of a literary commentator, that is a significant reflection of life and an imaginative extension of its possibilities. It centres on life and human experiences and has become a mirror through which we view the world.

Literature is considered the mirror of culture in society. This means that books written by a society are influenced by its happenings and life. Works of literature reflect society. Also, they serve as a testament to the human capacity for growth and redemption and have the power to provoke thought and inspire change; they are actually catalysts for change. Literature is, no doubt, a repository in which the artistic records of man's thoughts and experiences are kept for posterity.

> **Forms of Literature**

Literature has two major forms: fiction, which consists of works based on imagination, and non-fiction, which consists of works based on factual accounts or information. By this, we mean that whatever we have in literature is either factual or imaginary, made up by the writer, artist, or producer. However, it is evident that some literary works are partly factual and partly non-factual. This occurs when the creator borrows from factual events or happenings and combines them with their imaginative thoughts or creations to produce certain or specific effects in their literary works.

In language usage, literature has two major techniques – poetry and prose. Literature expressed in poetic form emphasises the aesthetic and rhythmic qualities of language, such as sound, symbolism, metre, etc., to evoke meanings in addition to ordinary or in place of ordinary meanings. Literature expressed in prose applies ordinary grammatical structure and natural flow of speech in the work. Drama, one will say, is not a language technique but can be expressed in either poetic or prosaic language.

> **Why Study Literature?**

Generally, we read literature for pleasure and the intellectual experience it provides. However, students in schools and colleges study literature because it is one of the recommended subjects in their academic programme or a course of study in tertiary institutions. Thus, they read literature to satisfy the academic requirements in their schools and colleges. Apart from being part of academic programmes in schools and colleges, literature affords students a lot of intellectual and moral development. In the first place, students learn core values, attitudes and morals embedded in recommended literary texts and works. They learn the customs and traditions of diverse people and places from the cultural and historical contexts in which the texts are produced. Through the study of literature, students develop skills in reading and writing. Students explore and apply their understanding of literature and the skills learnt through creative writing in the areas of poetry, drama, stories and essays. Students enjoy and respond creatively and critically to literary texts drawn from the past and the present from places of different historical and cultural backgrounds. They reflect on what these texts offer them as individuals and members of a larger society. Students also establish and articulate views through creative responses and logical arguments. They reflect on the qualities of literary texts, appreciate the power of language, and inquire about the relationships between personal preferences of texts, authors, audiences, and contexts as they explore ideas, concepts, attitudes, and values.

Second, the study of literature leads to the development of the human mind and skills in listening, speaking, reading, writing and viewing issues. It also helps develop the capacity to create texts for a range of purposes, audiences and contexts. We study literature to learn more about life and the human experience and to appreciate the dynamics of the human situation

– feelings, problems and prospects. According to a British scholar and novelist, C. S. Lewis, Literature adds to reality. In his opinion, it not only describes life but also enriches the necessary competencies that our daily life requires and provides. By this, one can agree that literature is a necessary tonic that turns human life around and makes it lively.

Thirdly, we read literature for entertainment, the pleasure it brings, and instruction. It delights and enlightens us through the various artistic creations, renditions and expressions of the imagination of people. In its depository are stories, epics, sacred scriptures and the classical works of ancient and modern times. As such, it is akin to a reservoir of entertainment, information, and knowledge, a sort of record of the works of a language, period or culture produced by writers and scholars. Through literature, people's experiences through the journeys of life are told, retold, highlighted and preserved.

The pleasures of literature are emotional as well as intellectual. Besides entertaining us, literature instructs us by showing us things of the world hitherto unknown or less comprehensible to us. For instance, some stories in literature, including children's stories in storybooks, are carefully contrived and scripted by their authors to teach morals and other didactic intentions to the target audience.

Literature allows us to move seamlessly and without limitations. It gives us the liberty to imagine ourselves in different places or times or periods and, in the process, enlarges and deepens our own perception of the world. While reading works of literature, especially fiction, we share the writer's imaginative vision and follow them into the world they create. We see the world as the writer perceives and presents it.

Literary works portray the thinking patterns and the social norms prevalent in a society at a given time. They depict the different facets of our lives and serve as a tonic and nourishment for our imagination and creativity.

Literature indeed reflects the society, its good values and its ills. In its corrective function, literature mirrors the ills of the society with a view to making the society realise its mistakes and make amends. It also projects the virtues or good values in society for people to emulate.

'Literature is the mere imitation of life.' There is a high correlation between literature and real life. Life gives the means through which literature develops in an artistic form.

What distinguishes literature from other disciplines is the use of creative imagination in the production of works of art. It is studied in schools and colleges because it exposes students to the realities of life drawn from different places and climes and at different periods of time.

To this end, we must distinguish between Literature-in-English and English literature since both are likely to confuse the general readers. Simply put, Literature-in-English is a subject in the secondary school education set-up in Nigeria and the English speaking West Africa. It is not about English literature, which is the literature of the English people of Great Britain, but about literature originating elsewhere but expressed in the English language. It is the study and exploration of texts and materials created or re-created in the English language from realms other than England or Great Britain as the case may be.

➤ **Origins of Literature**

The origin of literature may be traced to several sources that have existed from time immemorial. These include folklore, folk dance, customs and traditions, legends and myths, ancient rituals, festivals, etc. Essentially, these exist in oral forms and are rightly referred to as oral literature. However, with the coming of the art of writing, literary works were reduced to writing. Written literature, therefore, represents people's deliberate attempt at expressing their literary creativity and artistic thoughts in a more definite and permanent form.

➤ **Divisions of Literature**

Literature has three major divisions: poetry, prose and drama. These, together, make up what we call the genres of literature.

The word 'genre' denotes the classes, species and realms into which literary works are categorised.

Before the crystallisation of literary genres into these three major classes, other classes existed. At the time of Plato and Aristotle, the three divisions were known as lyric, epic or narrative, and drama. In their modern forms, they became better known and referred to as poetry, prose and drama. Each of these genres is further classified into other sub-family groups or classes discussed in detail in chapter 9 of this book.

> **Classification of Literature**

Literature can be classified into fiction and non-fiction. Broadly speaking, fiction is any literary narrative, whether in prose or verse form, which is non-factual but invented or created by the author or writer. In other words, fiction is a story or narrative that originates from a writer's imagination. It centres on 'invented' characters, situations, and events that did not actually happen or are based on factual events but have characters, dialogue, and settings created, contrived, or made up by the author. However, in a narrower sense, fiction denotes only narratives that are written in prose (novel, short story forms), which may not be a faithful record of reality. Sometimes, the word 'fiction' is simply used as a synonym for the novel, which communicates primarily through storytelling in prose. The purpose of fiction is to entertain, but it can also provide the readers with a deep understanding of life.

On the other hand, non-fiction is an account of factual (actual or true life) events presented in any of the genres of literature, especially prose. In non-fiction, a writer makes use of the techniques used in fiction to deliver their message. In other words, non-fiction refers to actual or factual events and incidents presented in the form of a novel-length story. It makes use of the techniques associated with fiction, including flashbacks, interior monologues, etc.

Non-fiction includes biography, which is a factual account of the life of a person written by another person based on information received on the subject. Example: Chinua Achebe: A Biography, by Ezenwa-Ohaeto. We also have autobiography, which is an account of the life of a person written by himself/herself. Then, we have essay, which is a short composition in prose that undertakes to discuss a matter, express a point of view, persuade us to accept a thesis on any subject, or simply to entertain. It usually has a single subject matter. We have expository essays, which are formal, have a scholarly tone, are tightly structured, are written in an impersonal style, and present or explain information and ideas. We equally have personal essays, which are non-fictional, less formal, and usually written in a conversational tone. They have looser structure, written in more personal style, and express the authors' thoughts and feelings about a single subject. We also have persuasive essays that are less formal and present arguments aimed at convincing readers to adopt a point of view. Essays, like fiction, include elements of character, setting and plot. We also have Criticism that defines, evaluates, analyses, classifies and interprets works of literature. Next, we have Travelogue and Adventure, which are narratives in prose form based on the experiences of an adventurer or traveller.

Literature can also be classified according to historical periods, genres, and political influences. Under historical periods, we have classical, medieval, renaissance, romantic, modern, contemporary and realist literature. Under genres, we have prose, drama and poetry. Under political influence, we have Elizabethan and Victorian literature representing literature during the reigns of Queen Elizabeth I and Queen Victoria of England. In Africa and some Asian countries, we have Pre and Post-colonial literature representing literature prior and after colonisation.

> **Prose**

This is a written discourse in ordinary and everyday language. This language is not patterned or expressed in the form of verse. It rather consists of writing that does not adhere to any particular formal structure other than simple grammar. It has no rhythmic regularity as in poetry but has logical or grammatical order with connected ideas. It resorts to the lavish use of words characterised by style and secures a variety of expressions through diction and sentence structure.

Prose is broken down into units – sentences, paragraphs and chapters. In prose, the story is told or narrated. The writer of a piece of prose has the liberty to use sentences of various lengths but is not free to use words like poets. The language of a prose work is comparatively clear, straightforward and direct. The work may be fiction or non-fiction. Examples include autobiography, diary, memoir, epistle, biography, allegory, essay, exemplum, fable, novel, parable, satire, short story, etc.

Characteristics of Prose

- As mentioned earlier, prose does not conform to poetic measure. Lines are not treated as single units, as in poetry. It is organised to run continuously according to the rules of grammar and punctuation and with no pre-determined line length.
- It does not have any specific rhythm or metre. Although, at times, it can be rhythmic, there are no set rules for metrical structure as in some forms of poetry.
- It neither rhymes nor uses a pattern of rhyme.
- It utilises some figurative language (for example, metaphor/simile) to engage the reader's interest, but it focuses more on telling a story.
- It uses a straightforward approach to presenting a story or information. It is a medium of expressing an idea or a point of view.
- It is written in paragraphs that can be accompanied by dialogue, graphics, headings and sub-headings.

Elements of Prose Fiction

- *Theme*

A literary theme is the main idea or underlying meaning a writer explores in a novel, short story, or other literary work. The theme of a story can be conveyed using characters, setting, dialogue, plot, or a combination of all of these elements.

- *Setting*

This is information about where the story took place and at what time. It also includes context beyond the story's surroundings, such as culture, historical background, geographical location, occupation, etc.

- *Plot*

A plot or plot structure is the sequence of events in which each event affects the next one through the principle of cause-and-effect. The causal events of a plot can be thought of as a series of events linked by the connector across the beginning, middle and end of a story.

- *Point of View*

Point of view is the writer's way of deciding 'who' is telling the story and to 'whom'. Establishing a clear point of view is important because it dictates how a reader interprets characters, events and other important details. There are three kinds of points of view: first person, second person and third person. (See Chapter 9 of this book.)

- *Characters and Characterisation*

Characters are the individual persons (usually humans or, at times, animals) who appear in the story. Characterisation is the act of creating and describing characters. It includes describing not only a character's physical attributes but also their personality. How the characters act, think and speak also adds to their characterisation. Characterisation is the method used by the writer to develop the characters.

- *Atmosphere*

Atmosphere is how an author uses the setting, objects, or internal thoughts of characters to create emotion, mood, or experiences for the readers. This is the condition and emotion in a story. In other words, it is the artful utilization of the setting, objects, or internal musings of characters to evoke emotion, mood, or experiences for the readers. It encompasses the ambiance and sentiment within a narrative.

- *Symbolism*

Symbolism refers to the use of representational imagery. The writer employs an image with a deeper, non-literal meaning to convey complex ideas. It is the use of a concrete image to represent an abstract idea or complex idea. For example, the heart is often employed as a symbol of love.

When creating a work of prose, the writer uses narrative devices. These devices are vehicles to convey their thoughts or messages to the readers. These include foreshadowing, flashback, monologue, point of view, dialogue, suspense and stream of consciousness. Chapter 9 dealing with literary terms and principles defines all these terms with examples.

In prose, the plot, which is the order or sequence of events or incidents in the work, begins with an exposition, which provides the background information on the action, describes the setting and introduces the major characters. We then have the conflict, which is the struggle between the opposing forces in the work, that is: the protagonist and the antagonist. It then develops a series of complications (that is, rising action), signifying the intensification of the conflict that leads to the crisis – the moment of tension. The conflict reaches a climax, which is the turning point or the moment of greatest tension that fixes the outcome. Then, the complications are sorted out, leading to the falling action or resolution (the denouement), which is the stage when the conflicts and crises are resolved and the story ends. Graphically, we can say that a plot is made up of exposition, rising action (complication), climax and falling action (denouement or resolution).

Most stories may not strictly follow this pattern or sequence due to the particular sub-class of prose to which they belong. What is illustrated here is a general sequence of plot.

Types of prose include narrative, argumentative, descriptive, expository, scientific and emotive prose.

Forms of prose include novelette/novella, short story, anecdote and novel. These have been explained elsewhere in this book.

> **Poetry**

It has not been easy to give a clear-cut and satisfactory definition of poetry. Writers like William Wordsworth, Samuel Johnson, Yeats, Samuel Coleridge, etc., had made notable efforts at defining literature. However, none of the definitions given by these writers was apt or comprehensive enough to rest the issue of defining poetry. The difficulty in defining poetry is often associated with the diversity in the poetic form and structure. However, it will be sufficient to give, in this work, an idea of what poetry is all about. Simply put, poetry deals with and is about poems. A poem is a piece of creative work in verse form arranged in metres and stanzas. It is a song-like composition in concrete language expressed rhythmically in an orderly or structured manner. It is a product of creative thought and the fragrance of language stimulated by emotion expressing deep feelings.

Poets dwell in the use of the aesthetic qualities of language to suggest meanings and evoke emotional responses. In so saying, we agree with R.O.C. Ilozue (Authority on Literature-in-English) that poetry has to do with emotional outbursts, imaginative thought, beauty and language. As such, I boldly say that poetry involves word engineering, whereon poets craft or weave special meanings and effects with and into words, or as Adaora Okoli, former staff of Nigeria Info, Port Harcourt, said, 'painting pictures with words'.

Unlike prose, poetry resorts to word economy and the use of high, elevated, noble and emotional language. This language may be simple and easily understandable or can be obscure: made complex by choice of words, figures of speech and other devices used. Although writers have their reasons and license for their diction, it is our opinion that poetry will be at its best if there are fewer impediments in the communication traffic between the poet and the reader. What is the essence of poetry if the reader cannot understand it due to complex structure or diction? The beauty of language is effective communication. Without this, all our utterances and writings are mere sounds and gibberish.

One distinctive mark or quality of good poetry is the imaginative use of language. To convey their message, poets make profuse use of figurative expressions, symbols and images. While some poets are concerned with the message they put across to their readers, others are more interested in the melody or the musicality of the words or expressions they use or the forms the poems take or come out with.

Pleasures of Poetry

Poetry offers us pleasures of sound and meaning, images and symbols, speech and feelings, and thought. It also offers intellectual pleasures and is often associated with learned minds and the noble. For example, noble characters in Shakespearean plays spoke in poetic language, while ordinary characters were made to speak in prose.

You may wish to reflect on the inner pleasure you experience as you unravel a poet's witty wordplay or the central idea in a poem. Consider how emotional you feel when you read certain poems by Shakespeare, Spencer, Milton, Wordsworth, Coleridge, R. Stevenson, R. Kipling, Gray, Soyinka, Christopher Okigbo, J. P. Clark, M.J.C. Echeruo, etc. Consider the feelings of joy, sadness, pity, fear, etc., that you experience after wading through an assemblage of words in poems by poets as though they are real.

Poetry improves our understanding and use of language since it involves words carefully contrived and placed in their best order.

Types of Poetry

We have chivalric, romance, emblem, epic, epigram, fabliau, lai (lay), light verse, lyric, idyll, elegy, dirge, lullaby, occasional poem, pastoral, rap, satire, sonnet, ballad, ode, rhapsody, etc.

Elements of Poetry

The key elements of poetry are:

- *Form*

This is how a poem appears or looks on the page. A poem's form can add to its meaning. Some poems have specific forms. For instance, we have *Limerick*, which has five lines with a rhyme scheme of aa bb a and lengths of 3, 3, 2, 2, 3 stressed syllables. We also have *Sonnet*, a poem of 14 lines that follows a strict rhyme scheme and specific structure with iambic pentameter. Poems are written in lines and structured in stanzas. They have a regular or repeated pattern.

Note: A poem without a regular pattern is called free verse.

- *Sound*

Poets, in their poems, use or arrange words to create sounds that appeal to the readers. Sounds are created by the use of rhyme, rhythm, repetition, alliteration, assonance, onomatopoeia, etc. The rhythmic structure of a poem is based on patterns of stress or patterns of different length syllables. These and more are discussed later in this book.

- *Imagery and Figurative Language*

Poems rely heavily on imagery and figurative language/ expression. Imagery is a language that appeals to the readers' five senses – sight, hearing, smell, taste and touch. It is that element in poetry that sparks off our senses as we read. It produces pictures in the mind of the readers or that of the audience listening to the rendition of a work in poetry.

Figurative language, on the other hand, is used where words and phrases make readers picture ordinary things in new ways. The three main types of figurative expressions are simile, metaphor and personification.

- *Speaker*

The speaker of a poem is the voice you hear in a poem. It is the voice that relates the story or ideas of the poem. The voice is not necessarily that of the poet but one adopted by the poet to deliver or render the poem. It is usually called the poet-speaker.

Features of Poetry

- *Theme*

This is the poet's pre-occupation or central idea or message which they intend to communicate to the readers.

- *Mood*

The mood describes how word choice, subject matter and the poet's tone convey an overall feeling that characterises the emotional landscape of a poem for the readers. In other words, it is the feeling the poet creates for the readers. It can be deciphered from the language or tone they use in the poem. The mood can be that of anger, happiness, sorrow, cheerfulness or jolly-like limericks. To determine mood, one may ask: Is the feeling evoked, mysterious, provocative, zany, ominous, festive, fearful or brooding?

Mood is the overall feeling or atmosphere of a poem, often created by the poet's use of imagery and word choice. Tone is the attitude of the poet toward a subject, or an audience conveyed through word choice and the style of their writing.
Simply put, mood and tone differ in the sense that mood is determined by the response of the readers to a piece of writing.

Tone, on the other hand, is the poet's attitude about the subject of the poem.

There are three categories of tone in writing: positive, negative and neutral.

Examples of mood in poetry are humorous, romantic, melancholic, whimsical, cheerful, light-hearted, pessimistic, optimistic, joyful, etc. Tone in writing is reflective of mood.

- *Poetic License*

This is the liberty of the poet to use words as arbitrarily (anyhow) as they desire without necessarily conforming to the rules of language or grammar. In doing so, the poet makes sense and communicates an experience despite breaking the rules of grammar or language.

- *Repetition*

Some poems contain repetition. Repetition may be of sound, syllables, words, phrases, lines, stanzas, etc. Poets often use repetition to draw attention to certain aspects in their poems and to create particular 'emphasis' that adds meaning to the poems. Repetition is found extensively in free verse, which does not have a traditional, recognisable metrical pattern. Repetition in free verse includes parallelism (repetition of a grammar pattern) and the repetition of important words and phrases.

Example 1:

"Bavarian gentians, big and dark, only dark darkening the day-time, torch-like with the smoking blossoms of Pluto's gloom, ribbed and torch-like, with their blaze of darkness spread blue down flattening into points, flattened under the sweep of white day Torch-flower of the blue-smoking darkness, Pluto's dark-blue daze, black lamps from the halls of Dis, burning dark blue, giving off darkness, blue darkness, as Demeter's pale lamps give off light, lead me then, lead the way."

- D.H. Lawrence, Bavarian Gentians

Example 2:
"Because I do not hope to turn again
Because I do not hope
Because I do not hope to turn..."

- T. S. Eliot, Ash-Wednesday

- *Refrain*

This is a poetic device involving the repetition of a line or a phrase at regular intervals in different stanzas of a poem. It usually occurs at the end of a stanza. It lays emphasis and creates rhythm.

For example, in Lenrie Peters' *The Fence*, the phrase: *there I lie* is repeated at the end of each stanza.

Refrain is a verse, a line, a set, or a group of lines that appears at the end of a stanza or where a poem is divided into sections.

- *Prosody*

Prosody is the study of the metrics, intonation and rhythms of a poetic work. It is a phonetic term that uses metre, rhythm, tempo, pitch and loudness in a speech to convey information about the meanings and structure of an utterance. In addition, prosody is an important element of language that contributes towards rhythmic and acoustic effects in a piece of writing. It includes different elements, such as sound, pace and meaning.

Example: Let us look at a line from the Christmas song: 'We wish you a merry Christmas.' We can see that emphasis is put on the word 'wish' while singing the song; the particular line is sung in a high and cheerful tone throughout the song.

- *Rhythm*

Rhythm is a strong, regular and repeated pattern of sounds. Poets use rhythm and metres to shape meaning. It is often useful to read poems aloud to be able to hear where different accents and different rhythms have been used. Consider these:

1. The long, slow, tedious Mathematics lesson

    Dragged on and on and on.
2. Square roots, sin and cosine, quadratics
    It's lunchtime!

If you read out loud each of the above, you will notice the rhythm. In the first example, the rhythm is regular (It does not change), while the rhythm in the second example is much brighter and snappier. What we learn from this is that in poetry, rhythm combines well with rhyme and metres to match the subject matter. They often influence the meaning of a poem. Rhythm and imagery have been recognised as the most important concepts in poetry.

- *Archaic Words and Spellings*

Poets often make use of archaic words and spellings. They use familiar words in unexpected contexts. They make use of figurative language and engage in wilful violation of grammatical rules to paint a particular picture or to drive their message home.

Classes of Poetry

- *Narrative Poems*

Narrative poems tell stories. The main pre-occupation of a narrative poem is to account for actions and events in a form similar to rendering or telling a story or describing actions. It gives a sequential account of events and people in the story it tells. Examples of narrative poems are epic, romance and ballad.

- *Lyrical Poems*

Lyrical poems were originally set to be sung with a lyre. Lyrical poets are interested in the musicality of the poems they write. To them, melody is the heart of verse, and poetry is at its best when it has music or musical undertone. Lyrical poems usually contain a regular rhythm with end rhymes. It usually expresses personal feelings. Examples: Elegy, epitaph, sonnet, rap and lullaby.

> ## ➢ **Drama**

This is the form of literary composition designed for performance on stage or theatre. It is an imitation of human life, actions and experiences. Dramatic composition is comprised chiefly of dialogue between characters and is usually aimed at theatrical performance on stage rather than reading. It has three necessary components: story, action and character. Of these three, action is the most important. It is intended chiefly for entertainment. It can also serve the purpose of instruction or education. In drama, we have actors who take the roles of characters to perform the indicated actions and utter the written dialogue. Being a synthesis of action and dialogue, drama cannot be fully realised unless it is acted on stage.

Drama has a long history rooted in folk dance, ancient rituals, festivals and other human activities. It is classified into tragedy and comedy. We also have tragi-comedy (which has elements of both tragedy and comedy), dance drama, melodrama, closet drama, history drama, pastoral drama, poetic drama, absurd drama, chronicle plays, epic theatre, folk drama, masque, miracle plays, morality plays, mime, pantomime, dumb show, opera, farce, problem play, satire, etc. as variants.

Plays are not written in paragraphs like in prose (novel or short story). Instead, they are written as lines of dialogue in the form of a script. In plays, the characters (represented by actors) are told what to say in the dialogue. The script is broken down into acts and scenes. Acts are major divisions of a play, while the scenes are smaller divisions within an act.

Elements of Drama

The following are the key elements of drama:

- Characters
- Plot
- Dialogue
- Setting
- Theme and
- Symbolism

Generally, they are used as in the case of prose; however, in drama, they are presented to the audience somewhat differently because, unlike novels or short stories, drama is meant to be performed on stage in front of an audience. The use of the key elements of drama must, therefore, conform to theatrical performance.

- *Characters*

These are the persons (personae) that perform the actions in the drama. They may be human beings, animals, or inanimate entities.

Characters are listed with short descriptions in the cast of the characters in the drama text.

In theatrical production of a play, the list of characters (cast) is usually given to the audience on a printed playbill as they enter the theatre so that they may be able to identify the major characters and the actors who will play them.

The difference between characters in prose and those in drama is that in drama, live people or actors represent the characters, while characters in prose works are not live. In the production, actors are chosen based on their physical and verbal ability to interpret the characters.

- *Plot*

The plot of a drama is the sequence of related events that take place in the work. It has an exposition, which introduces the characters and setting and also presents the necessary background of the drama. This is followed by a conflict or complication, which starts the rising action, in which the dramatic tension builds up or intensifies. This is followed by climax, the moment of highest tension. Then follows the falling action (resolution), in which all the loose ends of the story are tied up or resolved.

- *Dialogue*

By its nature, drama is almost entirely dialogue or conversations between characters. Dialogue reveals the plot and the personalities of the characters. Dialogue and action are the medium through which drama communicates. Dialogue takes various forms, such as the exchange between two or more characters.

- *Soliloquy*

In contrast to dialogue, soliloquy is a speech that a character in a play speaks aloud but can only be heard by the character and the audience. It is used as a way of expressing the inner thoughts and feelings of a character to an audience.

- *Aside*

An aside is a direct address to the audience that other characters are not privy to, whereas a soliloquy is the act of talking to oneself, regardless of who can hear.

- *Setting*

This tells us where and when the story in the drama took place. It also includes contexts beyond the surroundings of the story, such as culture, historical background, geographical location, occupation, etc. The setting is limited to what the audience can see on stage. Shifts in time and space are often indicated by the actors through their speech and movements. In setting, lighting plays an important role. It creates an illusion of time. Costumes and props are also involved in setting. While costumes portray and indicate a character's profession, status, age, ethnicity, etc, props are items used by the actors on stage to create an atmosphere of the play. Props include chairs, tables, writing materials, flowers, thrones, clothes, beds, etc.

- *Theme*

This tells what the play actually means. It deals with the main idea rather than what happens in the story and has also been described as the soul of drama. Theme is stated in the drama through dialogue or action. It can also be inferred from the entire performance. For a drama to give its complete output, the plot and the theme should be synchronised (that is, they should complement each other).

Features of Drama

These include stage direction, acts, scenes, setting, scripting, costume, audience, atmosphere, characters and characterisation, and deus ex machina (a literary device which uses a person or thing that appears or is suddenly or unexpectedly introduced into the play. Its purpose is to provide a solution for a previously un-solved piece of the plot), plot, theatre in the round, the three unities (unities of action, time and place), dramatis personae, cast, playwright, protagonist, antagonist, foil, denouement, conflict, catharsis, tragic flaw, dramatic irony, suspense, soliloquy, prologue, epilogue, chorus, flashback, mime, etc. All these features are not by any means expected to be found in any particular drama at the same time; it all depends on the sub-class to which it belongs. A good number of these features, sub-classes of drama, and associated terms are discussed in other chapters, including the chapter dealing with selected literary terms and principles. Although a lot can still be discussed in this chapter, we are mindful of the scope of the subject and are going to limit it to what the examination syllabuses provide.

- *Stage Directions*

These are instructions for the director, actors and stage crew for the stage production of a drama. Stage directions are notes printed in italics and enclosed in parentheses or brackets in the drama text. They tell the actors how to speak and move and describe the scenery to create the setting. They also describe the appearance and actions of characters as well as the sets, costumes, props, sound and lighting effects.

Chapter 3

Teaching Literature-in-English: A Classroom Approach

According to educational philosopher John Dewey, learning involves the acquisition of knowledge from both books and the wisdom of elders. In terms of formal education, this knowledge of necessity passes through teachers who bear the responsibility to effectively articulate and harness it in a way that enables their students to comprehend and utilise it for their growth.

While there is no definitive method for teaching Literature-in-English in our schools, it is my view and the position of this book that teachers should adopt approaches that best allow them to effectively deliver their lessons within the confines of the approved curriculum.

This chapter presents theories, models, approaches, general views and opinions based on experienced teachers' suggestions and academic research material aimed at providing guidance on teaching literature effectively within the classroom.

> ➤ **Theories**

Teaching literature, like other subjects, can be done in line with certain learning theories. These theories present different views and approaches to the teaching and learning of literature. Relevant to our objective here are the Transmission and the Socio-Cultural Learning theories. Let's attempt a summary of the relevant theories.

Transmission Theory

This theory has the teachers at the centre of the stage. They are seen as the sole source or dispenser of knowledge and the evaluator of learning. In a pre-determined order, they transmit or transfer their knowledge to students without seeking much from them. They try to literally empty themselves of the knowledge they have to enrich the students. They tell them all there is to know and what the subject entails. They assist them in reading and interpreting the recommended texts and materials. This theory has been largely criticised by researchers because it is teacher-centred and tends to give little opportunity for students' initiative. However, I posit that a wise teacher ought to know when to seek or allow students' initiative or participation in the learning process. They must engage the students in class activities and not spoon-feed them.

Social-Cultural Theory

This focuses on creating possibilities for students to learn by acquiring the skills and practices they need and then improving their use. In doing this, the teacher creates situations whereby students are able to interact with the materials to be studied. Both the teacher and students work together and contribute their individual bits of the teaching and learning processes to reach a common goal of understanding the subject. They also apply the resultant knowledge in solving their problems, particularly in their class exercises and exams.

This theory takes into account how learners are influenced by their peers in the learning process and how social scenarios impact their ability to learn. Teachers who apply this theory in their teaching plans are usually aware of how learners may directly impact one another. For this purpose, the teacher encourages the students to work closely with one another. The teacher also encourages the students to join literary clubs or associations that help them develop and improve their communication skills. Under this theory, students are often asked to share ideas, opinions and feelings while learning tasks and exercises with their peers.

By teaching literature in secondary schools in accordance with this theory, teachers can better promote life-long language learning than they can with transmission theory. This theory also exposes students to the benefits of shared responsibilities and the various ways they can help one another learn.

> **Models**

A study by Carter, R. in 1991 dealt with models used by teachers in teaching literature in secondary schools. Some of these models include cultural, language and personal growth models.

Cultural Model

This model represents the traditional approach to teaching literature and requires teachers to explore and interpret the social, political, literary and historical contexts of specific texts in their classroom presentations. This model reveals the universality of literature and encourages learners to understand different cultures and ideologies in relation to their own social, political, literary and historical backgrounds.

Language Model

This model allows teachers to employ strategies used in teaching language to deconstruct or interpret literary texts to serve specific linguistic purposes. Through this, students learn more about language and its relevance. It is the most common approach to teaching literature in schools. According to Carter and Long (1991), a language-based approach enables students to access a text in a systematic way to exemplify specific linguistic features. This approach has been somewhat criticised by researchers who described it as a reductive approach to literature. According to them, the learner is less engaged with the text than with purely linguistic practice. They see literature being used in a rather purposeless and mechanistic way to provide for a series of language activities orchestrated by the teacher.

Personal Growth Model

The focus here is on the particular use of language in a text and in a specific cultural context. In this regard, the teacher does the following:

- Present the students with the awareness, value, and pleasure of reading good literary works.
- Help the students appreciate or acquire a deeper understanding of important human concerns and relationships.
- Teach the students to appreciate values that enhance their understanding of themselves and their relationship with others.
- Teach the students how to effectively communicate their responses to texts and to support the same with reason.

➢ **Approaches**

Information-Based
This approach ensures that students acquire enough knowledge and information about the literary texts studied to expand their understanding of the subject matter. The teachers explain the content of the texts to the students in class and also provide them with background information on the texts.

Additionally, they ask questions to assess or evaluate students' overall understanding based on what they are taught and read.

Paraphrasic Approach
Here, the teacher retells the story of the texts in summary form (that is, only the storyline) to the students to help them understand the texts or refresh their understanding of their contents. The teacher then uses simple terms to explain what the story is all about to the students.

Ethical/Philosophical Approach
The objective of this approach is to utilise morals and humanistic values extracted from the texts for educational purposes. The teacher motivates students to recognise moral virtues or values incorporated in the texts and use them as models for their personal growth. The teacher raises awareness among students

regarding values derived from the texts while presenting and discussing ethical dilemmas presented in them that encourage students to adopt moral principles advocated by the author or to abandon certain behavioural tendencies deemed anti-social.

Stylistic Approach

In this method, the teacher assists students in comprehending a piece of literature by examining its language usage by the writer. The teacher urges the students to note significant linguistic features within the text beyond its surface-level meaning. This enhances language awareness as students are exposed to the various styles used by authors in their works. Stylistic exercises a teacher can adopt in this regard include:

- Identifying linguistic characteristics such as vocabulary and tense
- Extracting examples from written works that describe settings
- Recognising adjectives used to describe characters

However, neither approach alone is adequate. Therefore, it is recommended that teachers incorporate aspects unique to both methods into their lessons effectively so that literature not only becomes enriching, interesting, and enjoyable for students but also promotes their development.

> **General Views on Teaching Literature**

The acquisition of literary skills involves the development of listening, speaking, reading and writing capabilities. The teacher can utilise their expertise to help students excel in these areas.

In Literature-in-English classes, students have the opportunity to enhance their understanding of spoken and written English. They also develop skills such as interpreting context, using language strategies appropriately for different situations, and adapting language for various purposes and audiences. Teachers play a crucial role in imparting relevant knowledge and expertise to their students.

This segment examines the general approach teachers adopt while teaching literature. Studies show that interest in literature among secondary school students has been steadily declining over the years due to challenges they encounter with certain aspects of the subject. This includes reading through recommended texts, some of which are complex and voluminous.

With modern communication technologies readily available, many students face difficulties concentrating on their studies as more attention is devoted to these gadgets. Reading is essential to learning literature, but it is no longer easy or enjoyable for most students.

Teachers share similar concerns, too. The majority of the teachers in our schools find no motivation to teach anymore, while others who were qualified to teach have left the profession altogether, seeking better-paying jobs elsewhere and leaving quite a few behind who are struggling just because teaching is their sole source of income. They are forced to hold on, albeit with less than enough enthusiasm or creativity while teaching the subject.

To make matters worse, there is also a lack of requisite text materials in the hands of both the teachers and the students. Meaningful learning will become almost impossible unless these setbacks are addressed by the parties involved, especially the teachers who bear the responsibility of preparing the students for the exam, and there will be vilification if they fail in this regard.

Therefore, teachers must understand the subject thoroughly so that they can impart it to their students. They must understand prose fiction or drama texts before interpreting them to the students. During class time, teachers may highlight key elements such as storylines, characterisation, themes, morals, etc., rather than treating lessons like mere comprehension or memorisation exercises alone.

Examinations should not be viewed as the ultimate goal of learning. Emphasis must be placed on developing necessary literary skills and creativity within individuals rather than focusing on merely passing the examination. Teaching should not only focus on the prompt covering of the syllabus but also on creating and encouraging interest in practical activities geared towards enhancing retention levels long after the completion of the course.

For example, providing opportunities for individual students to share their creations with peers and explain their personal character themes, style of diction, and setting choices helps contextualise literary concepts and improves overall skill sets. In addition, participation in contests and events organised within or outside of schools provides creative outlets for expressing emotions and fears that are otherwise suppressed in traditional classroom settings.

Inviting local writers to meet with the students and read works aloud affords a chance to rekindle and sustain enthusiasm for the subject through interaction between writers and students. These experiences prove invaluable, especially given the current climate where technological advancements often distract from actual academic pursuits on a daily basis.

Finally, enacting scenes from plays recommended in textbooks is possible if resources permit efficient and effective visualisation of dramatic work and assist in retaining images, ideas, and dialogue whenever the students try to recall the scene/dialogue in the exam.

Chapter 4

Use of Recommended Texts and Materials

To excel in examinations, students must exhibit diligence and consistency throughout their studies. Furthermore, they must possess the recommended textbooks and materials as they serve as vital tools in this process. As such, examiners provide candidates writing Literature-in-English examinations with syllabuses that include works of prose, drama, and poetry.

Primarily, students and candidates should obtain these books and utilise them productively. Books are essential tools for preparing for exams; hence, their acquisition should not be taken lightly. Once acquired, it is crucial that students actually read them instead of merely using them as decorative items on their tables or increasing the weight of their school bags.

Apart from the recommended texts, students must also seek out other relevant examination materials such as past question papers, well-researched summaries (for revision purposes), marking schemes, and educational videos related to the subject matter or any aspect thereof. Furthermore, documented commentaries on candidates' performance during previous exams can be found (where available) within appendices of corresponding literature publications. These resources not only guide effective study strategies but also direct the course of preparation required for optimal exam performance.

Once prescribed books are obtained by students or candidates, it becomes imperative that they read through them thoroughly while familiarising themselves with appropriate approaches to each text's content.

One significant obstacle faced by many students while dealing with recommended texts is a lack of textual comprehension due to poor reading skills or environmental influences, which may affect concentration levels. Additionally, some texts may present challenges regarding diction/structure, further complicating matters. Textual comprehension requires understanding what writers intend to convey beyond mere surface-level descriptions presented within pages themselves. For example, George Orwell's *Animal Farm* is not exclusively about animals; rather, it serves as a political satire that highlights human nature under certain conditions.

Unfortunately, certain students depend solely on study aids and synopses provided by commentators rather than fully engaging with the original source materials. Although these commentator contributions can often be invaluable, relying on study aids without proper reference ultimately leads to shallow and hazy understandings of critical literary themes and concepts discussed therein. Although I do not recommend excessive reliance on synopses or summaries alone during revision periods, I am aware that there are individuals who struggle even while reading through these condensed versions. Instead, they opt for dishonest methods such as smuggling notes into examination halls, hoping to evade detection while committing academic malpractice.

This chapter provides the students with guidelines for effective reading, writing, and discussing prose, drama and poetry for Literature-in-English examinations. I adopt, with suitable modifications, the views of Robert Di Yanni in his book *Literature: Reading Fiction, Poetry, Drama, and the Essay* (4th Edition).

A. Reading Prose

- While reading prose, you imagine yourself entering into another world where the author is your guide. If you fail to follow them or get distracted along the line, you might never arrive at the desired destination. Unless you read the texts with adequate concentration, you might fail to follow them effectively. According to the author, you have to observe how the story opens. You should note the writer's language and sense of humour. You should also note their narrative technique and point of view.

- You need to have a notebook by your side to jot down important points or questions arising from the book that you will refer to later. The note can be of any kind, but it must help you keep track of your thoughts as you read.

- You must read the book with adequate concentration. You have to consider how the story's features guide your reading and direct your understanding of the work.

- Find time to read the story for the second time, concentrating on its plot and characters. The plot of a story is the particular arrangement in the book of actions, events and situations as they unfold in the narrative. During this second reading, pay attention to the subject matter and theme of the book, keeping in view their ideas and values.

- Take note of what the characters do or say and what happens to them. Characters are the personae in the work. This can be human entities, animals, or imaginary creatures used by the authors to tell their story. Usually, a story focuses on the events surrounding one character, the protagonist. Consider the technique of characterisation that the author employs.

- Consider the story using the elements of fiction: plot, characters, structure, setting, imagery, language, style, theme, symbolism, irony and point of view.

- While reading, be open-minded to the work, however strange, different, or difficult it might appear at first. Let not your peculiar prejudices hamper your appreciation of the story. Take the story as you see it. Relate what you have read to your experience of life, knowledge of literature and language.

- Consider the story's values as reflected in the dialogue of its major characters. Compare the values with current values and social issues.

- As stated earlier, ensure that you make notes on the texts. While keeping notes, it is advisable to make it periodic. Day-to-day account of points read-up is most advisable. A summary of the chapters read, and your reactions or response thereto may also be made. The advantage is that the readers can express their thoughts and feelings about the story immediately in their own words before they grow cold or forgotten. Such a record is most useful if kept up to date till the end of the story. It will serve its purpose well if read through at least twice a day and most advisably before going to bed and after waking up early in the morning. Regular revision of notes is as important as making them. This keeps the story or points noted down fresh in the readers' memory. There is no recommendation here as to how the note should look or be kept. What is important is that there should be a record of highlights or important facts read up. Let us consider three of such records:

Annotation

When you annotate a text, you make notes about the story at the top or the bottom of the pages, or both. It can also be in the form of underlining or circling words and phrases or bracketing sentences or paragraphs on the pages of the text. Annotating a work helps the readers note what they consider important and saves their time in re-reading the entire work in search of a particular point. The markings or annotations on the book thus serve as focal points or signboards at revision time. However, it must be noted that annotation makes the text look untidy, especially for a subsequent user.

Summarising

A summary is a precise account of an incident. It is a condensation or compression of a work's thought. Preparing a summary requires a careful reading of the work to ensure that the reader understands the text well enough to render its strong points briefly. As much as possible, this summary is done in the student's own words, restating the main ideas and important details. A summary should be shorter than the original work. It can be chapter-by-chapter or page-by-page summary. However, the chapter summary is better and more common. By this, the reader can, at a glance, tell what the book is all about.

While preparing a summary, students or candidates must avoid unnecessary details and elaborations and grasp the substance of the chapters. The concise account of the book, which is the positive resultant effect of this exercise, helps the candidates functionally during the exam revision. It saves their valuable time as they do not need to wade vigorously through the text again.

Paraphrasing

This is a written interpretation of a work, as far as possible, in the readers' own words. This may be line-by-line, page-by-page, chapter-by-chapter, or in the order in which the ideas or information flow.

> **Reading Strategies**

Predict

While reading a work of fiction, try to figure out what happened earlier, presently and next in the narrative and see if you can imagine how the story will end. Read on to see how accurate you are with your guesses.

Visualise

Visualise the characters, events and settings in your mind. This helps you understand what is happening in the story. It also helps during recall.

Connect

Connect yourself with what you are reading. Think about the experiences and feelings that you share with the characters or the writer. Connect any of the feelings, ideas and values to your own.

Question

While you read, ask yourself questions about the characters: What happened to them? Why is a character the way he or she is? What are the ideas raised in the work? As you read, look for answers to your questions. Searching for the reason behind events and the characters' feelings can help you feel closer to what you are reading and ensure comprehension of the text.

Clarify

Stop occasionally to review what you have read. Look for dates and signal words that clarify the sequence of events, such as before, during, after, next, last, etc. You may also wish to discuss the story with your classmates, who may draw your attention to parts or perspectives of the story to which you may have given lesser attention.

Evaluate What You Read

Evaluation means forming opinions about people, events and ideas. Try to form an opinion of the ideas, characters, issues, etc., about which you are reading in a text. Evaluate also the authors' purposes: Were they writing to inform, influence, or express an opinion or bias? Develop your own idea about the characters and events, and see if your feelings towards the characters change as you read. Determine for yourself how well the author told a story or used or developed an idea.

> ➤ **Practical Approach to Analysing a Work in Prose**

Writers concentrate lots of ideas in their works. However, they do not say everything they want to communicate to the readers. They sometimes expect the readers to fill in the gaps with information derived from elsewhere or to figure out some of the ideas or issues they cannot talk about. For the purpose of their exams, the students are expected to have first-hand information about the writer, their environment, and the historical and social contexts in which their work was created. This is so because literature is not an isolated field of study. Context reading provides background information about the author, the historical period in which the work was created, and the literary and artistic context of the work. These, more than anything else, shed more light on the message the writer wants to convey to the readers. For instance, Chinua Achebe's "A Man of the People" was written when Nigeria was at the threshold of political and economic corruption. The appreciation of this background information or context enhances the readers' understanding of the work.

To discover a writer's underlying idea in a work, a reader must analyse the story by breaking it into parts and examining how these parts work together to produce an overall effect. As stated earlier, first read the story as many times as possible to become familiar with the plot and to understand the significant ideas of the story or work of literature.

The readers are advised to analyse the specific elements of the story by answering the following questions:

- What happened in the plot? What is the central conflict or problem in the story? How was the conflict resolved? How does the outcome of the story relate to the theme?
- What changes took place within the main character?
- What mood does the setting convey? Does the setting affect the plot?
- What universal themes are addressed in the story?
- Does the story contain any symbols – that is, objects or characters that have meanings of their own yet stand for something else in the work?
- Are there any ambiguities – that is, things that can be understood in more than one way?
- What stylistic devices, such as figurative language or expressions, and sentence patterns were used by the writer? Are they appropriate for the story?
- What feelings are suggested by the story's imagery?
- How do the important characters in the story think, talk and act? In what ways do their actions or attitudes change the course of the story?

- What is the time and place of the novel? How does the setting affect the mood or the development of the plot?
- What point of view did the writer adopt? Is the story told by a first-person or a third-person narrator? What does the narrator think about the characters and events in the story?
- What universal truth does the story express about human nature, experiences, problems and relationships?
- Does any object or element show up repeatedly? Does any person, place, or thing seem to represent an abstract idea?
- Is the writer's diction/word choice straightforward, or is the language connotative? Is the diction elevated, neutral, informal or poetic?
- What is the novel's tone? How does the word choice affect the tone of the story?

The above questions will be answered easily by a student or candidate who has read the text and is conversant with the literary devices, concepts and principles used by the author, most of which have been dealt with in this book. The student or candidate must master these devices, concepts and principles to analyse the texts correctly and answer questions based on them.

B. Reading Drama

In trying to understand a work in drama, the students must bear in mind that drama is a staged art written essentially to be performed on stage. They must note that in general literary discourse, the term 'play' is often used interchangeably with drama. Some commentators have tried to draw some differences between the two. In fact, one stated that drama is raw action or theatrical performance on stage, while play is drama in written form existing on the pages of a book and yet to be performed. However, I believe that both are the same, an imitation of life.

Like fiction, drama relies on dialogue and description. Dialogue occurs when characters engage one another by means of conversation. It is what the characters say to one another.

Description in drama takes the form of stage direction. Stage directions are statements printed, usually in italics, in drama texts describing characters, scenes or actions to facilitate the stage production of a drama. In prose fiction, we have a narrator, but in drama, we are presented with the direct words of the characters. These come in the forms of dialogue, soliloquy, aside, etc. Stage direction helps the audience follow the actions of the play.

Drama shares certain features with poetry. Some plays are, in fact, written in verse. For example, most of Shakespeare's works were done in blank verse. Similarly, some poems contain dramatic elements. Robert Browning wrote dramatic lyrics and monologues exemplified by his poem, "My Last Duchess."

To better appreciate drama, it must be read with special attention to its performance elements. These include characterisation that implies aggregate performance of characters and an in-depth analysis of the characters in relation to their roles in the context of the drama. While reading, try to hear the voices of characters and distinguish one from the other. Take note of the tone and inflexions of the characters. Try to visualise how the characters look, where they stand in relation to one another, how they move about and their gestures.

Our experience of drama, apart from the intellectual understanding of the idea it conveys, includes emotional reactions to the plot and the interactions of the characters. These involve more than a rational and analytic understanding of the text. They include feelings, thoughts and emotional apprehensions regarding the context. They are what examiners demand in their questions. They coin their questions around them, and it takes attention and reading between the lines to uncover most of them. The earlier the students learn how to get around this, the better for them.

While reading drama, the students need to imagine that they are watching it on stage. They can do this by translating the script in their hands into a mental performance that they can visualise. They need to learn to look not only at what the words of the play mean but also at what they suggest about the characters' behaviours, movements, gestures and feelings. They need to learn to listen to the effects of their words on one another. They should try to imagine how the words might be uttered – gently or harshly, sarcastically or sweetly, loudly or softly, etc. They should also imagine where the characters are positioned relative to one another, the manner of their walk, the style of their physical gestures, and the alteration of their voices and facial expressions. They can do this by reading the drama patiently and deliberately.

Reading with adequate concentration leads not only to a proper understanding of the literal meanings of the dialogue but also to a proper understanding of its implications. The students may decide to read the work aloud or silently, read it with fellow students in a group (as in a discussion class), or discuss with others the mental reconstructions of the scenes of the text. However, they should not lose sight of the fact that drama, although reduced in book form, is literature, theatre and entertainment.

- ➢ **Guidelines for Reading Drama**
- • Read the opening stage directions carefully. This enables you to develop a mental setting for the drama. These stage directions are usually written in italics and enclosed in brackets or parentheses. They serve as guides and help performers, directors, actors and the rest of the stage crew put on the play. They describe the appearance and actions of characters as well as the setting, costume, props, sound and lighting effects. In fact, they help readers visualise the movements and actions of the characters. They tell you where and when a scene is happening and explain the settings and scenes. If you skip them, consciously or unconsciously, you will miss out on much of the play. If a cast of characters is listed, read it also carefully to understand the relationship of the characters to one another.

- Read the opening scene slowly. Refer to the cast of characters if you are confused about who is who. Read slowly and note the details that may assume prominence later.

- Keep track of the plot; like in fiction, the plot of drama centres on the main conflict that the characters try to resolve. Note the places in the action where the conflict develops most intensely. Look for the conflict and let yourself be involved in the story. Try to understand the nature of the conflict – what caused it and how it was or might be resolved. Pinpoint the crisis of the play and consider its implication in the story.

- Get to know the characters through the dialogue. Decide what values they embody and believe in. Consider what they may represent in the story. Visualise the characters as they move around, reciting their lines. Examine their relationship with one another, noting, especially, the effects on each other.

- Listen and pay close attention to the dialogue. Notice what characters say and how they say it. Hear the tones of their voices and imagine the pace and tempo of their dialogue. Consider what the characters' speeches reveal about them – honesty, arrogance, meanness, kindness, cowardice, etc. Note that dialogue takes various forms— for example, conversation between two or more characters, soliloquy and aside.

- Try to visualise the play's setting from the dialogue and stage directions. Take note of the visual details of the play and consider their functions and possible symbolic significance.

- Consider whether the play is a tragedy, comedy or tragicomedy. If it is a comedy, is it satiric or romantic? Consider the general mood and tone of the play.

- Try to summarise the central idea or ideas of the drama. This central idea, otherwise known as a theme, actually talks about what the play means or is all about. It deals with the main idea rather than what happens in the story. It is the soul of drama, so find out what point it seems to make. Find out where the playwright stands on the issues, attitudes, values and ideas raised or portrayed in the play. Note that the theme of the play can be revealed through dialogue or action or inferred from the entire performance. Also, note that the theme and the plot should be synchronised or complement each other to give a complete output.

- Consider the characters' actions in relation to your questions on experience. Consider the playwright's point of view in light of your own.
- Make a provisional judgement of the play and consider how effective it is as a literary and theatrical work.

It is of utmost importance to emphasise that to be able to effectively write on or about a work in drama or to deal with any questions arising from it, the students must make sure that they read the whole work, not just the dialogue. They should read everything in italics in the text: description of scenes, instructions to the actors in the stage directions, and, in fact, everything in print in the work. This point may seem obvious, but the meaning of a scene or even the entire play may depend on the tone or voice in which an actor is supposed to deliver a line. The directive on how to render this tone or voice is usually contained in the stage directions.

In this regard, students are free to make use of notes, commentaries and summaries on the recommended texts prepared by other writers and commentators on the subject. This is usually best done during revision time when the exam is knocking at the door. However, as noted in this book, these notes and commentaries should not take the place of the original texts. It is always better to refer to the original source that embodies the whole story than to rely on summaries or commentaries made by writers who might have approached the text from particular perspectives. Take note of memorable events or passages you might want to quote or refer to while writing or answering exam questions.

> **Interpreting Drama**

Interpretation of drama, as in other genres, involves careful analysis of what the playwright presents. This leads to a conclusion on its meaning and significance. While interpreting a drama, we try to discover what it might mean to us. We ask ourselves what the speeches and actions mean or signify and how the playwright used them to convey their message to the readers.

C. Reading Poems

Reading poems is like reading fiction and drama, where we observe details of actions and language, make connections and inferences, and draw conclusions. However, poetry requires much more attention to the words used, the sound and rhythm in the lines and stanzas, and syntax and punctuation. Yet, more than fiction and drama, poetry is an art of condensation and implication, requiring the readers to pay closer attention to the words used. One needs to read between the lines to discern what the poet is talking about.

Effective reading of poems involves learning how we experience, interpret and evaluate them. Poems present experiences in language which the poet creates. While reading poems, our experience involves more than considering the meanings of the words used. Also, it includes our comprehension of the poem's form, our appreciation of its patterns of sound and our understanding of its thought. To effectively understand a poem, one needs to ask and answer the following questions:
- What feelings does the poem evoke or convey?
- What ideas does the poem express?
- What worldview does the poet present?

While reading a poem, first, identify the type or class to which the poem belongs — whether it is a narrative, lyrical, didactic, sonnet, elegy, pastoral, etc.; identify the theme and/or the subject matter, and then look at the diction and determine how effective the poet is in their choice of words.

Note: To better appreciate a poem, especially its sound elements, you must read it aloud. Let your ears hear the sound.

➢ Interpretation/Appreciation of Poetry

Interpretation of poetry concerns itself with the intellectual processes that we engage in as we develop an understanding of poems. Our focus is usually on analytical and rational interpretations. We can learn to interpret and appreciate poems by taking the time to understand their basic elements. These elements include: the speaker, whose voice we hear in the poem; the diction, the language or the poet's choice of words as used in the poem; its syntax, the order of the words; its imagery, the details of sight, sound, taste, smell and touch; its figures of speech, the non-literal use of language such as metaphor, simile, etc; its sound effects, especially rhyme, assonance and alliteration; its rhythm and metre and its structure or formal patterns of organisation. All these work together harmoniously to convey meaning or feelings to the readers.

➢ Voice and Tone

Voice is what we hear when we read a poem. The voice does not necessarily have to be of the poet themselves or our own. It may be of a poet-speaker through whom the poet communicates their thoughts. This speaker may be a distant observer or the one involved with the experience expressed in the poem. The poet may create a speaker with a distinct identity to achieve a particular effect.

The voice conveys the tone of the poem. Tone is an implied attitude of the poet towards the subject matter. When examiners ask about the tone of a poem, they want to know the impression, feelings or attitude of the poet towards the theme or the subject matter. This raises the questions of whether the poet is affectionate, hostile, earnest, playful, sarcastic, satiric, serious, mock-serious, sombre, brash or teasingly humorous towards the subject matter or theme and whether the speaker admires, agrees with, ridicules or condemns the subject. Note that tone is not just attitude per se, but whatever a poem contains that makes the attitude towards the subject matter clear to the readers.

> **Diction**

This refers to the words a writer decides to use in a particular work. While reading any poem, it is necessary to know what the words denote. It is also important to know what they connote, imply or suggest. In poetry, connotation or secondary significance or meaning is very important. The students should look for words in the poem that connote or suggest particular meanings. These words convey what the writer has in mind. They are capable of changing the emphasis or the meaning of a poem. The students can underline words that they think are particularly relevant to the subject matter, theme or mood. They may also underline words that stand out to them, words that are striking and words that might be deliberately dull.

The students, therefore, should endeavour to know the denotative or root meanings and the connotative or secondary or associated meanings of the words used or of the entire text. The students should determine which of these meanings best conveys the poet's message as contained in the poem.

For poets, the best words are those that convey the actual message to the readers. These words convey feelings and sometimes indirectly imply ideas instead of stating them directly. The language of the poem may be simple or complex. The poet may stress certain sounds, such as pleasant sounds (euphony) or harsh sounds or letter combinations (cacophony).

The students must make good use of an appropriate English language dictionary to understand the diction of the poet and, more importantly, the actual message the poet conveys to their audience or readers.

> **Imagery**

In their works, poets include details that trigger our memories, stimulate our senses and command our responses. They create images that we can see with our mind's eye and feel with our senses while reading. They make us react in a particular way. These are concrete representations of a sense impression, feeling or idea. A sense impression can be pleasant, unpleasant or neutral. Images of light indicate knowledge, while those of darkness suggest ignorance, wickedness, deceit or death.

In poems, we see day and night come and go, as well as the various weather conditions and perceive the smell of things. All these are achieved through the creative use of words and expressions. Alluding to the nature of imagery, Paula Fox once said that great stories give us images that flash upon the mind like lightning flashes upon the earth. This points to the tangibility of imagery. Imagery adds flesh and bone to expressions, making them real, tangible and decipherable by our senses. Images may be visual (seen), aural or auditory (something heard), olfactory (something smelt), tactile (something felt) and thermal (heat). When an image forms a pattern of related details that conveys an idea or feeling beyond what it literally describes, we call it a metaphorical or symbolic image.

> **Figures of Speech**

Figures of speech are words or expressions used in a non-literal or non-ordinary sense. When we use figurative language, we make the words or expressions take up meanings other than their actual, natural, literal or denotative meanings; we make them express more than they mean ordinarily. The purpose of using figures of speech in writing and speech is to create graphic images or mental pictures that help the readers or listeners understand the message the writer or speaker wants to convey to the readers. They also deepen its significance and lay emphasis on incidents therein.

Commenting on the deviations from the usual day-to-day and conversational structure, style of speech or writing, or meanings of words and language, the Russian Roman Jakobson defines literature as organised violence committed on ordinary speech. Here, Jakobson is alluding to the figurative use of language, as exemplified by figures of speech in the English language. By this, words are made to deviate from their ordinary and natural meanings to meanings other than their ordinary, original or natural significance (that is, extended meanings).

Example: Go, jump into the lake!

Can we say that this expression requires one to actually jump into a lake? No! This expression suggests something else other than asking one to jump into a lake. It is a figurative expression that parallels: Do your worst! Come beat me! Go to hell!

Figures of speech are part of our everyday language. No writer sets out to include any particular figure of speech in their work. G. F. Lamb warned that we should not be tempted to regard figures of speech as ornaments to adorn our writing. According to him, writers use figures of speech unconsciously and express themselves naturally in certain terms because those terms best convey what they have in mind. This suggests that the figures appear in the works, as often as they do, as a matter of language and that such occurrences are often incidental and without premeditation. So, figures of speech are not deliberately fixed but flow naturally from the use of language and witty expressions.

Figures of speech are classified under the following:

- Figures of association and comparison: This group is made up of Simile, Metaphor, Synecdoche and Antonomasia.
- For transfer of qualities or relatedness: This group is made up of Personification, Metonymy, Synecdoche, Prolepsis and Hyperbole.
- For sounds: This group is made up of Alliteration, Assonance, Consonance, Onomatopoeia and Pun or Paronomasia.

- For contrasts and contradictions: This group is made up of Antithesis, Oxymoron, Euphemism, Irony, Chiasmus, Epigram, etc.
- For alarms or exaggeration: This group is made up of Hyperbole, Apostrophe and Climax.
- For understatement: This group is made up of Litotes, Anti-climax, etc.
- For word manipulation: This group is made up of Epigram, Paradox, Pun, etc.
- Figures of construction: This group is made up of Transferred Epithet (Hypallage), Rhetorical Question, Anagram, Syllogism, Prolepsis, Hendiadys, Zeugma, Syllepsis, Analogy, etc.
- Figures of redundancy: This group is made up of Parallelism, Tautology, Periphrasis (Circumlocution), Padding and Pleonasm.
- Figures of indirectness: This group is made up of Irony, Sarcasm, Innuendo, Euphemism, Litotes, Periphrasis, Transferred Epithet, etc.

These groups, sometimes and in some respects, interpolate with one another. That is why some of the figures appear in more than one group. We will examine these figures of speech with examples in the chapter dealing with literary terms. However, let's have a brief discussion of two of the figures, simile and metaphor, because of their special importance and relevance in poetry.

Simile and Metaphor

Simile and metaphor are figures of comparison. Both are used to make connections between unrelated things. Here, we see one thing in terms of another. For an expression to portray the true purpose of simile or metaphor, the two things being compared must differ in their nature or class but with striking similarity in a particular respect or attribute. Example: Man compared to an animal or an angel.

- *Simile*

This establishes comparison explicitly with the words like or as. Here, one thing is directly compared with another that shares a particular or similar attribute with it.
Examples: Susan talks like a parrot.
Uche is as strong as a lion.

- *Metaphor*

According to Aristotle, metaphor is an intuitive perception of similarity in dissimilarity. That is, finding a similarity between two things that have different natures. Metaphor employs no explicit verbal clue in the comparison as in simile. Its comparison is implied in such a way that the figurative term is substituted for another. It makes use of the 'to be' verbs, such as 'is' or 'was', to make the comparison.

Examples: *Hilary is an angel; Ekwesirike is the village's drum; Peterpan is a lion.*

A simile is more restricted in its comparative suggestion than a metaphor. In simile, the poet provides explicit clues that direct us to the comparative connection, while in metaphor, the comparison is implied, and one thing completely becomes another thing to indicate the comparison.

As stated earlier, in simile and metaphor, two things are involved. The comparison between the two creates a simile or metaphor. There must be a comparative connection between the two things. If this cannot be established, we will not have a simile or metaphor. Furthermore, not every sentence or expression that has the words *like* and *as* is a simile. In the same way, metaphor is not established in every expression where we have the 'to be' words of 'is' and 'was'. There must be a comparative connection between the two things that are apparently dissimilar or of a different nature. They are similar only in a particular attribute.

Take note that we have direct and implied metaphors.

Direct metaphor links two things more plainly.

Example: The hurricane was a steamroller. This comparison is direct and plain.

Implied metaphor, on the other hand, is a comparison that is not stated directly and can easily be overlooked.
Example: The hurricane steamrolled across the Gulf.

The verb 'steamrolled' is an implied metaphor that compares the storm and its power to a steamroller.

Note also that personification is a special kind of metaphor in which a writer gives human qualities to an animal, object or idea.

- *Extended Metaphor*

This is a metaphor that compares two unlike things, and the comparison continues throughout a series of sentences in a paragraph or lines of a poem. It often comprises more than one sentence and can sometimes consist of a full paragraph. For example:

> 'All the world's a stage, and
> All the men and women mere players;
> They have their exits and entrances;
> And one man in his time plays many parts...'

Here, Shakespeare compared 'earth' to a 'stage', and the comparison continued till the end of the series of sentences involved.

➢ **Symbol**

A symbol is any object, person, place, or action that means more than itself or represents something beyond itself in a literary work. A rose flower, for example, can represent beauty or love. A soaring bird can stand for freedom. Objects may represent things depending on how they are used in a poem or literary work. According to critics, symbols point at, hint at, or cast long shadows of something or an event in a literary work.

➢ **Syntax**

This refers to the grammatical structure and the rules that follow the deployment of words in sentences. It is the order of words in sentences, phrases or clauses. It is used to express or convey feelings. It determines the tone of a poem and also provides guidance to a speaker's state of mind.

➤ Sound

There are three kinds of sounds: Rhyme, Alliteration and Assonance.

When we read or listen to a poem being read, we hear sounds in the words used. Poets create sounds with words. The most familiar ones are rhyme, alliteration and assonance. Poets use these sound devices to enliven their poems. In humorous poetry, these devices are often exaggerated for comic effect.

➤ Rhyme

Rhyme is the matching of the final vowel or consonant sounds in two or more words in a line or lines of a poem. By this, we mean that two or more words in a line or lines of a poem may share similar or identical vowel or consonant sounds.

Rhyme improves the rhythm or musicality of a poem and makes it memorable.

Examples: queue-stew, schooner-tuner

When the corresponding sounds occur at the ends of the lines of poems, we have end rhyme as in the following:

> *"The depths are hot, the heights are chill,*
> *The streets are loud, the court is still."*
>
> *—Galileo*, Bertolt Brecht

When they occur within lines, we have internal rhyme.

Let us see the opening stanza 7 of Edger Allan Poe's *The Raven*, which illustrates both internal and end rhymes:

> *Once upon a midnight dreary, while I pondered weak and weary*
> *Over man a quaint and curious volume of forgotten lore*
> *While I nodded, nearly napping, suddenly, there came a tapping*
> *As of someone gently rapping, rapping at my chamber door-*
> *"Tis some visitor," I mutter, "tapping at my chamber door-"*
> *Only this and nothing more.*

- ***Exact or Perfect Rhyme***

This occurs when the words share corresponding sounds and stresses and a similar number of syllables.

Example: In Robert Frost's *Stopping by Woods on a Snowy Evening,* The first stanza reads:

> *Whose woods these are, I think I know.*
> *His house is in the village, though*
> *He will not see me stopping here*
> *To watch his woods fill up with snow.*

In the above, *know, though* and *snow* perfectly rhyme.

- ***Imperfect/Approximate/Slant Rhyme***

This is a less exact rhyme. The rhyming words do not completely share corresponding sounds and stresses and may not have a similar number of syllables.

Example: Slow-Low, Dizzy-Easy

- ***Masculine Rhyme***

This is where the rhyme consists of a single-stressed syllable.

Examples:

1. *The music in my heart I bore*
   Long after it was heard no more
2. *One, two, three, four, five, six,*
   Old Marina is a witch.
   At night, on a broomstick, she sits
   And on the church steeple, she spits

- ***Feminine Rhyme***

It consists of a stressed syllable followed by an unstressed syllable.

Example:

> *I conceive that the journey is not ending*
> *While the road kept on bending*

- *Assonance and Alliteration*

Assonance is the repetition of similar vowel sounds in the lines of a poem, while alliteration is the repetition of similar consonant sounds at the beginning of words.

Example:

> *He gives his harness bells a shake*
> *To ask if there is some mistake*
> *The only other sound's the sheep*
> *Of easy wind and downy flake*

Note the long /e/ sound of sheep, which re-echoes in easy
The /ow/ sound of downing, which re-echoes in sounds
The /s/ sound is repeated severally in the poem.

- *Rhythm*

Rhythm refers to the regular recurrence of the accent or stress in a poem or song. It manifests itself in the pulse or beat we feel in a line of poetry.

> Examples can be found in nursery rhymes like:
> *JACK and JILL went UP the HILL*
> *to FETCH a PAIL of WATer*

The upper case letters indicate stressed syllables, while the lower case letters indicate unstressed syllables. Poets rely heavily on rhythm to express meaning and feeling. In *The Sun Rising*, John Donne put the words together in a pattern of stressed and unstressed syllables thus:

> *BUsy old FOOL, unRULY SUN*
> *WHY DOST THOU THUS*
> *Through WINdows, and through*
> *CURTtains, CALL on US?*

➢ **Metre**

Traditionally, metre is the basic organisational device of poetry. It is the recurrent, regular and rhythmic pattern in verse. In other words, it is the recurrence, in regular or measured units, of a prominent feature in the sequence of speech sounds of a language. While reckoning the metre of a poem, we count the stresses we feel in its rhythm. By convention, the unit of poetic metre in

English is the foot, which is a measure of stressed and unstressed syllables. A poetic foot may either be iambic or trochaic, anapestic or dactylic. We also have spondaic and pyrrhic feet.

- ***Iambic Line***

An iambic line consists primarily of iambs. An iamb is defined as an unaccented or unstressed syllable followed by an accented or stressed syllable.
Examples: preVENT and conTAIN

- ***Anapestic***

Here, we have two unstressed syllables followed by a stressed syllable.
Example: /on the FOLD/

- ***Trochaic***

Here, a stressed syllable is followed by an unstressed syllable.
Example: /WOmen/

- ***Dactylic***

Here, a stressed syllable is followed by two unstressed syllables.
Example: /BELLS and grass/

- ***Spondaic***

It is composed of two successive syllables with approximately equal strong stresses.
Example: The first foot of this line: /Big, strong/reliable./

- ***Pyrrhic***

It is composed of two successive syllables with approximately equal light stresses.
Example: as in the first and third feet in this line /is to/begin/with the /

D. Structure of a Poem

Closed Form and Open Form

The structure of a poem refers to its pattern of organisation. The form of a poem depends on the pattern of sound, image, structure of syntax, and thought. Some poems have a closed form, such as a sonnet, while others have an open form, such as free verse.

> ➢ **Theme**

This is the pre-occupation of the poet, or the central idea a poet wants to convey in their poem. It is what the poet wants the readers to know. A poem can have more than one theme. To determine the theme in a poem, look for the subject matter. See whether it is, for instance, about youth, loss, renewal, patriotism, nature, love, hatred, etc., whether there are several themes and how they relate to each other, and whether the poet is merely teasing or entertaining or trying to teach a lesson.

> ➢ **Evaluation of Poetry**

This involves assessing the literary quality of a poem and deciding how good it is or how successfully it realises its poetic intentions. For example, we examine its language and structure and consider how well they work together to embody meaning and convey feeling. Second, we consider how significant the poem is for us personally and other readers, including the poet themselves.

E. Guidelines for Effective Reading of a Poem

The following guidelines are designed to guide the students in reading the prescribed poems and poetic extracts for the Literature-in-English exam. Our focus here is on understanding what poets express in their poems and how they do it.

- Read the poem carefully. You can repeat this a few more times, slowly and deliberately. The more you read a poem, the better you understand it. Each time you repeat reading a poem, you gain fresh insight into it. Also, repeated reading of a poem helps you become conversant with it. If possible, read it aloud so that you can appreciate its sound elements. Identify the speaker, the subject matter, the situation and the poet's tone.

- Make sure you understand the grammar of each line; pay attention to phrases or clauses used so that you can follow what each line literally says. Note any deviations from normal syntax and consider the reason for them.

- Attend to the words of the poem. Find both their denotations and connotations. Use a good dictionary to acquaint yourself with unfamiliar words and expressions and to refresh your memory of those you already know. A good dictionary is an ally you cannot do without while reading or analysing poems. Failure to use it leaves the readers on a strange and unfamiliar ground. Its use is key to unlocking the thoughts and the message of the poet lying hidden behind an assemblage of words. Words often shift in their meanings by virtue of context. The use of a good dictionary helps the readers find their way through. The students should not bother about the inconvenience of repeated interruptions in their reading while looking up for words and expressions used in the poem. Doing so makes for a better understanding and appreciation of the poem. More so, the students may, after their first reading, decide to make a list of the words and expressions they encounter for the first time and are not quite conversant with and look them up immediately or afterwards. They should do this before proceeding with further reading of the piece. They should look for the connection between the words and the images used. They should consider the connotations of metaphors, similes, images or symbols they identify in the poem.

- Listen to the poem's sound and rhythm. Notice where the rhythm and music are most expressive and try to explain why. Take note of where the tempo or language changes, alters or heightens. Relate the poem's sound to its meaning.

- Consider the poem's form and how its structure shapes its thoughts and emotions.
- Identify the socio-cultural and moral values that emerge in the poem. Consider how your own values influence your interpretation and evaluation of its worth.
- Consider the poem's beauty or aesthetic merit.
- Read the poem a few more times, and it will no longer remain the stranger it looked at the beginning.

Let us consider the following poems in light of our discussion:

1. The True Prison

It is not the leaking roof
Nor the singing mosquitoes
In the damp, wretched cell
It is not the clank of the key
As the warden locks you in
It is not the measly rations
Unfit for man and beast
Not yet the emptiness of day
Dipping into the blankness of night
It is not
It is not
It is not
It is the lies that have been drummed
Into your ears for one generation
It is security the agent running amok
Executing callous, calamitous orders
In exchange for a wretched meal a day
The magistrate writing in her book
Punishment she knows is undeserved
The moral decrepitude
Mental ineptitude
Lending dictatorship spurious legitimacy

Cowardice masked as obedience
Lurking in our denigrated souls
It is fear-damping trousers
We dare not wash off our urine
It is this
It is this
It is this
Dear friend, turn our free world
Into a dreary prison.

–Ken Saro – Wiwa

- **Poet's Background**

Kenule Beeson Saro-Wiwa was born on October 10, 1941. He was a writer, television producer, and environmental activist from the Ogoni area of the Rivers of Nigeria. He attended Government College, Umuahia, where he distinguished himself as an excellent student. He earned a scholarship and studied English at the University of Ibadan, Ibadan, Nigeria.

As an environmental activist, he led a non-violent campaign against environmental degradation of the land and waters of Ogoni and the Niger Delta by multinational petroleum companies, including the Royal Dutch Shell. He was also an outspoken critic of the Nigerian government. He criticised some issues bordering on environmental regulations, especially those that concern foreign petroleum companies operating in the country.

At the peak of his campaign, he was arrested and tried by a special military tribunal for allegedly masterminding the murder of some Ogoni Chiefs at a pro-government meeting. He was sentenced to death by hanging in 1995 by the government of Late General Sani Abacha. His execution provoked both local and international outrage with disturbing consequences.

His poems centre on the environment, especially the Niger Delta area of Nigeria, and the oppressive tendencies of military rule in Nigeria then. *The True Prison*, written around 1993, is one of Wiwa's prison poems that reflect his experience in the hands of oppressive authorities.

- **Thematic Analysis**

In this poem, the poet succinctly identifies fear as the bane of the society (Nigeria), which has, over time, become an assemblage of citizens who are scared to openly and with determination resist the oppressive tendencies of an undemocratic and dictatorial government.

For a better understanding of the poem, we will divide the poem into two movements. In the first movement of the poem (the denial), the poet denies that the penal complex (prison) where detainees are subjected to restriction and physical and mental torture against their will is the true prison. Drawing from his personal experience, the poet tells us that it is not what we suffer physically that makes us prisoners. To him, the leaking roof, the menace of singing mosquitoes, or the damp and wretched cell (normal features of our prisons) does not constitute the real prison. To him, the oppressive confinement by prison officials, the poor and inadequate food served in rations, and the dull and empty days transiting into hollow and dreary nights do not characterise true prison.

On the other hand, in the second movement, the poet subtly affirms that fear induced by the coercive influence of the military regime in the country then was the most pervasive prison in the lives of citizens. Fear instilled in the people gave rise to total and unquestioned obedience to oppressive measures of the military government under the pain of severe sanctions. The result is self-censorship, and considering this climate of fear prevalent then, the citizens were left with no other alternative than to accept oppression as though it were legitimate.

To gain the people's support, dictators deliberately adopt misinformation as part of their strategies. They do so by drumming lies into the people's consciousness over time. Where the lies fail, physical force becomes inevitable. The security operatives thoughtlessly accept to be used as tools in the execution of vicious orders in return for petty favours.

The poet indicts the justice system (represented in the poem by the magistrate) for pronouncing 'Punishment she knows is undeserved.' He lists her among those collaborating with the dictators in brutalising the people by meting out unjustified justice on persons, usually social activists, appearing before her (often on trunked-up charges sponsored by oppressive authorities and regimes).

The poet bemoans our moral decadence and mental laxity, which he feels holds the ground for oppressive leadership. He feels that citizens will no longer obey the government because they are sick and tired of its oppression and are planning for reprisals.

- **Poetic Devices**

Diction

The poet's choice of words is simple and uncomplicated. The words used are within the reach of an average student. They are appropriate and best convey the message of the poet to the readers. Words such as 'leaking roof', 'singing mosquitoes', 'wretched cells', 'measly rations', 'lies…drummed into your ears for one generation,' 'running amok', 'spurious legitimacy,' 'fear damping trousers,' are by no means difficult to understand.

Style/Structure

The poem is confessional. It expresses personal memories and experiences. It is a one-stanza poem, broken into two different thought parts or movements, which we shall refer to as the 'denial' and the 'affirmation.' In the first part (lines 1-12), the 'denial,' what can easily or generally pass for a prison, is denied by the poet because, in his view, it does not constitute true prison. In the second part (lines 13-31), the affirmation, he points out the real problem and that which converts our otherwise free world (lives) into a prison. The closing lines left a lasting impression by ending with a re-affirmation of what the poet conceived as the bane of society.

Mood/Tone

The mood of the poem is determined by the expressions: 'leaking roof,' 'wretched cell,' 'emptiness of day,' 'blankness of night,' 'measly ration,' 'wretched meal,' 'moral decrepitude,' 'mental ineptitude,' 'denigrated soul' and 'dreary prison.' All these paint a gloomy picture of despair or a not-so-happy situation, especially viewed from the background that the poet was writing from prison experience. The tone of the poet is earnest, sincere, solemn and grave.

Imagery

The poem is full of images, creating an oppressive and depressive mental picture. These include 'leaking roof', 'singing mosquitoes', 'wretched cell,' 'denigrated soul,' 'damping trousers' and 'dreary prison.'

Figures of Speech

- *Metaphor*

'It is lies that have been drummed into your ears for one generation' (lines 13-14)
'It is security agent running amok' (line 15)
'The magistrate writing in her book/punishment' (lines 18-19)
Gleaning from the poem above, one can see that lines 13-26 are metaphoric.
Onomatopoeia – 'clank…key' (line 4)

- *Alliteration*

'…callous calamitous' (line 16)
'lending …legitimacy'

- *Personification*

'Singing mosquitoes,' 'wretched cell,' 'wretched meal,' etc. (lines 3 and 17)

- *Hyperbole*

'Lies that have been drummed/Into your ears for one generation' (lines 13-14)

- *Repetition*

'It is not; it is this' (lines 10-12 and 27-29, respectively) for emphasis.

- *Transferred Epithet (Hypallage)*

Here, an adjective or descriptive phrase meant to qualify a person or a thing in a statement is transferred to another which it does not rightly or strictly qualify.

In line 16 of the poem, we have: '…callous calamitous orders.'

Also, in line 22, we have: '…spurious legitimacy.'

- *Rhyme*

'Decrepitude'/'ineptitude' (lines 20-21)

- *Theme*

'Fear' as society's true prison. What constitutes true prison is not the physical restraint or limitations but the fear-induced mental slavery we suffer as conscience and courage take flight from us.

2. The Dash Between

I knelt there at the headstone
Of one I love and cried.
Name, with dates of birth and death,
Was perfectly inscribed.
I pondered these two dates
And how little they both mean
When compared to the tiny dash

That lies there in between.
The dash serves as an emblem
Of our time here on the earth,
And although small, it stands for all
Our years of life and worth.
And our worth will be determined
By how we live each day.
We can fill our dash with goodness,
Or waste our lives away.
To ourselves, as well as others,
Let's be honest, kind and true,
And every day, live the way
We know God wants us to.
May we look for opportunities
To do a worthy deed,
And reach out with compassion
To those who are in need.
For if our hearts are full of love
Throughout our journey here,
We'll be loved by all who knew us
And our memory they'll hold dear.
And when we die, these memories
Will bring grateful, loving tears,
To all whose lives were touched
By the dash between our years.

–   *Ron Tranmer*

- **Poet's Background**

Not much is known about Ron Tranmer apart from the fact that he is a poet and actor. However, from his website (www.rontranmer.com), we learn that he was born in 1940 in Jerome, a city in Jerome County in the State of Idaho, USA. He was the oldest of seven children. He was 'married to an angel' with whom he has been living for 51 years.

He enjoys writing poetry. He wrote his first poem at the age of eight for the 'prettiest girl' in his class. He has written and copyrighted over 400 poems on many different subjects and on many occasions. Currently, he is working on his fourth poetic anthology.

His themes revolve around the supremacy and the importance of God, family, friendship, country, love, compassion and humour.

His poem, THE DASH BETWEEN, coming from his religious background, emphasises the need for man to fill his brief days on earth with good deeds in line with God's expectations. It emphasises the fact that man has a choice of living a worthy life or wasting it away on trivialities and deeds that will earn him eternal damnation. He feels that what matters is not when one was born or when he died or how long he lived on earth, but the quality of life he was able to place in the scale and sands of time while alive is what is sacrosanct.

- **Thematic Analysis**

This poem is a didactic poem wherein the poet seeks to persuade the readers to adopt a desired way of life. It is made up of eight stanzas of fairly equal lengths.

The poet speaker reflects on man's life as he visits the tomb of a beloved person (probably his wife). His attention is drawn to the inscriptions on the tomb, particularly the dates of the deceased's birth and death. He is fascinated by the short dash that separates these two dates and feels that the dash means more than the dates it separates.

To the poet, the dash between the dates represents the life and times of his late loved one (or that of all men) while alive. The dash represents our good and evil deeds from birth to death. In fact, it stands for our worth before God. To the poet, it stands for the sum total of our lives – our legacies, the objectives we met and the ones we failed to meet. He, therefore, urges the reader to choose to live a good life rather than waste it. He also enjoins us to be honest, kind, true and charitable in the way God wants us to be. He posited that if we do well while alive, we will earn the love of God and that of our fellow men in whose memories we shall remain evergreen even when we are no more.

- **Poetic Devices**

Diction
The language of this poem is quite simple and straightforward, filled with apt symbols and images that vividly present the poet's message to the readers. The grammatical structure is down-to-earth and simple, making it easy for an average reader to understand. The poet's choice of words is effective and easily conveys his thoughts to the readers.

Style/Structure
The poem is narrative or prosaic in nature. It has eight stanzas, each consisting of four short lines. The stanzas are arranged in stressed and unstressed forms without a rhyming scheme.

Tone/Mood
The tone of the poet is earnest as he seeks to persuade the readers to follow his advice. The poet seeks to impress upon the readers the need to spend their time on worthwhile ventures. The mood is sober and mournful as the poet:
> *'...knelt there at the headstone*
> *Of one I love and cried...'*

Imagery
The poem has quite a number of images that include 'headstone', 'dash', 'emblem', etc. These words form mental pictures in the minds of the readers, which helps them understand the poem more vividly.

Symbols
Certain words and expressions in the poem have extended meanings in the poem. The 'tiny dash' between the two dates stands for the short lifespan and activities of man on earth from birth to death – thus 'emblem of our time on earth.'
'journey' (line 26) stands for the spiritual movement from birth (life) to death.

'grateful loving tears' stands for the appreciation from those whose lives we have touched positively with our good deeds.

Figures of Speech

- *Personification*
  '…grateful loving tears' (line 30)
  '…lives…touched by the dash.'

- *Alliteration*

Many words alliterate in the poem.
Example: 'there at the headstone' (line 1)
'Worth… will' (line 13)

- *Consonance*

'…ourselves as well as others' (line 17)

- *Enjambment*

The poem is full of enjambments (run-on lines). Ideas in one line of the poem run into the next.
Examples: *'Name, with dates of birth and death,/Was perfectly inscribed'*(lines 3-4)
'The dash serves as an emblem/Of our time here on earth' (lines 9-10)

- *Paradox*

The expression conveys paradox in the following: 'and when we die, these memories will bring grateful loving tears, to all whose lives were touched by the dash between our years' (lines 29-32).

- *Theme*

The theme of the poem centres on the need for quality life and positive deeds while we are alive, the need to fill our days with good deeds so that we can be remembered even when we are dead.

Chapter 5
Preparing for Literature-in-English Examination

Give me six hours to cut a tree and I will spend the
First four sharpening my axe. Learning is not
Attained by chance. It must be
Sought for with ardor and attended to with diligence.

Students fail exams not just because they do not learn but also because they lack adequate preparation for them. While some start serious preparation only a few days before the exam, others adopt inappropriate study habits, such as cramming and passive learning.

Our focus in this chapter, particularly, is on the examinations conducted by West African Examination Council (WAEC), National Examination Council (NECO) and Joint Admission and Matriculation Board (JAMB) in Literature-in-English. As stated earlier, the purpose of these examinations is to assess or evaluate the overall knowledge or skills candidates have acquired over time and during their studies. This assessment, however, calls for preparation on the side of the students and the candidates. Without proper or adequate preparation, there is no guarantee that the students will perform well in the exam.

Exam preparation, therefore, has a direct effect on the outcome of the examination itself. Preparation, not chance, determines how successful a student will be in the exam. Even if success in an exam can be attributed to luck or chance, it must be stated, as observed by Louis Pasteur, that 'Chance favours only the prepared mind.' Chance does not write an exam or grant success; only those who prepare for it and perform based on their preparedness look forward to success. In this work, our cardinal objective is to introduce a practical approach to preparing for

Literature-in-English exams by exposing students and candidates to practical skills that enable them to achieve their goals. The test questions included here are designed to give the students or candidates a picture of what the examiner demands from them. Other relevant materials and preparation guides to assist them in navigating through the sea of the recommended texts and materials are also included.

What is tested in the exam includes the understanding of literature and its genres. It also includes textual understanding of recommended materials, such as books and poems. The study of literature involves the use of language and the appreciation of the art of writing. This chapter deals with some of the things a student is expected to know to effectively prepare for the exam. Good, adequate and timely preparation cannot be over-emphasised. This is the secret of academic excellence and the sole reason behind the production of this work.

Students' preparation and ability to practically demonstrate what they have learnt on paper determines their results. If they prepare well and are in line with the examiners' guidelines and expectations, they will do well on the exam. Adequate preparation begets self-confidence among the students, which, in turn, enables them to face the task of writing the exam squarely. Then, only the sky will be their limit. However, poor preparation begets a lack of composure in the examination hall, which, in turn, begets failure or, at best, lower grades that can hardly fetch the candidates good results or admission into the university or any of our higher institutions.

While preparing for the exam, it is important to bear in mind that adequate time and appropriate study materials are needed. Hence, the following are noteworthy:

- You must realise that you are studying not just to pass your exam and obtain a certificate or admission into higher school but to know and improve yourself. When you study to know, you will always pass your exam, obtain admission to higher institutions, and still retain the knowledge long after the exam or admission.

Remember, it has often been said that a certificate qualifies you, but the knowledge you have, more than anything else, distinguishes you. The knowledge you retain, utilise or practise within your daily affairs long after an examination is key and what matters most.

Learning, therefore, becomes the bedrock of academic activities through which one periodically acquires and updates one's knowledge. Therefore, preparing for an exam invariably becomes a necessary means to showcase what has been learnt.

- To pass your exam, you must invest in it. You must be prepared to invest time, energy and money in your studies. While preparing for exams, you need physical strength to read. Channel your energy to productive studies, use your time well, and apportion adequate time for your studies. You must spend money to buy textbooks, syllabuses and other materials necessary for the exam. You must also pay your fees and other outgoings.

- While reading, you must pay attention to details. Take time to look closely at the details provided by the author in the book.

- Organise your study space. Have enough space on your table to keep your books and other study materials. If you are highly organised, you will be less distracted. You must have adequate light and a comfortable seat. You cannot focus on your studies if your reading space or environment is not conducive to learning.

- Get rid of external and internal distractors while you read. You cannot allow yourself to be distracted by people or things around you and even by your own wandering thoughts. Curtail over-indulgence in the pleasures of television, mobile phones and computers (except where you are using them for the purpose of learning and the exam). Avoid watching movies, listening to un-educative radio programmes, visiting 'happening' places and joints, etc and face your studies squarely. After your exams, you can then go back to the pleasures, if they are properly so-called.

- Anticipate your physical needs, such as food, water, beverages, an airy environment, comfortable clothes, etc. If you anticipate these needs, you will make provision for them and thus be less likely to be distracted from your studies.

- Get Rid of Negativity: If you have negative ideas about studying Literature-in-English as a subject, or any aspect of it, for example, poetry, unseen literature, etc., you cannot focus well while studying the subject. Overcome the fear that you may not pass the exam or that the subject is too difficult. Unless you change this frame of mind, you will always get shut down as soon as you open your study materials on the subject.

- Revision: The essence of diligent studies is to be able to recall what you have learnt when needed, for example, during an exam. Revising what you have read as often as possible is one sure way of ensuring this. It is essential to review your notes after an hour or two of making them. You can also review them at the end of the day, the next day, or even after a week. This helps bring what you have learnt fresh back to your mind. Thus, it will be easy to recollect and retrieve what you have learnt during exams.

- Teach your friends what you have learnt. If you know a particular topic well, test your understanding of it by teaching your friends or people around you. By so doing, you can discover some of your weak areas in the topic or subject and improve on them since no one is an island. It will also help you master the subject or topic area much better.

Please remember that preparing for exams is not like cakewalking; the most important thing to do for students while preparing for exams is to read all the recommended books carefully and thoroughly. The students should take note of important incidents or events in the texts and highlight significant or challenging passages while reading. This will help them keep those incidents, events and passages fresh in their mind. They should also review them time and again, as it will help them gain a deeper understanding of the text. They may also include page numbers in their notes so they can return to those pages during revision.

> ➤ **The Right Time to Prepare for the Examination**

Exam preparation should not only be adequate but also timely. The syllabuses of the exam bodies in Nigeria (WAEC, NECO, and JAMB) cover the curriculum and scheme of work for the Senior Secondary Classes 1–3. Questions can be, and are usually, drawn from across the scheme of work for the classes. In view of this, it is opined that the right time to commence preparation for the examinations is not a few months before the exam, but at the time a student is entering Senior Secondary Class One. Knowledge obtained in junior secondary also forms an integral part of what is tested for in the exams.

It is risky to commence preparation at the Senior Secondary Class Three level or when the examination timetable is out, as the students may not be able to adequately cover the scheme of work or syllabus for the exam, bearing in mind that they have about eight (or three for UTME) other subjects to battle with.

For private candidates, it is assumed that they are not first-timers and, therefore, must have covered the syllabus for the exam. If this assumption is valid, they may not have as much work as first-timers. Their preparation will mainly be revision. However, if students or private candidates fall short of this requirement, they should nevertheless make haste and start serious work. They need not panic. They can still make it if they study diligently in the limited time they have.

If the students prepare well and early enough, they will have less work to do during the exam; if they fail to prepare well and on time, they will become vulnerable to the torrents of last-minute pressure that candidates experience when the exam is around the corner. This situation pays no student or candidate any good dividend but failure.

Daily commitment to studies is the bedrock of all efforts made at passing an examination. It will be a grave mistake, akin to an academic suicide mission, for a student to commence serious preparation for an exam late or after the announcement of the exam dates. Excellent results are often made long before the exam starts. This assertion, as preposterous as it may sound, underscores the need to commence exam preparations on time. Therefore, our recommendation is that the students or prospective candidates should make hay while the sun shines and commit themselves to serious studies on a daily basis before the announcement of the exam dates.

Related to the above is the need to choose an appropriate time of the day or night to study. Some people are better off at night, while others are effective during the day. Choose a time when you are at the peak of your brain power and least distracted or tired. This is because one tends to lose focus if one is fatigued and does not study with proper concentration.

Further, it is important to emphasise that candidates must read the recommended texts thoroughly to understand them or to be able to say enough of them. It has become a perennial complaint of WAEC, particularly the Council's BC Chief Examiner, for example, that candidates in Literature-in-English examinations demonstrate a hazy understanding of the recommended texts as they cannot meet the demands of the examiners. Although it is not practicable to understand a text inside-out, any effort made close to achieving this is good enough. Understanding a study material close to knowing it inside-out assures that the candidate will likely do justice to the examiner's questions when the chips are down, all other things being equal. Knowing the book well entails reading the book as many times as possible with concentration. It is not important how many times you read or revise your texts to become conversant with them. What is important is that you read them with full concentration and know their contents well enough to easily handle questions based on them.

It must be noted that knowing the text well enough does not call for cramming the whole text or any part thereof. Cramming a text or attempting to do so is a tedious task that may not help the candidates in the long run. In the first place, the candidates may not be sure that the materials they crammed can be used well in the exam. Second, there is no guarantee that the students can perfectly recall the crammed materials. In fact, recalling crammed materials may be affected by a person's physical or mental condition at the time of the recall, and during the exam, which is usually a period of tension and anxiety for many candidates, things can get even worse. Besides, cramming is a gamble. If the topic or area crammed does not, as is usually the case, feature in the questions, the time and efforts expended for the crammed work would go in vain. We, therefore, recommend that students first thoroughly read the texts to understand their contexts clearly and then memorise them.

Again, reproducing the information from a text verbatim from memory does not mean you comprehended the text well. A candidate does well if they can adapt and apply the information from the book well enough to answer questions based thereon in an examination or discussion.

Note the saying about cram work that goes like this: 'When the deed (exam) is done, the knowledge is gone'. This is true because knowledge obtained through cramming does not last long but disappears shortly after the exams. Then, what will be the essence of such knowledge if it is lost shortly after the exam as if the examination is the end of learning?

It must also be noted that examiners seek a particular approach and expect the candidates to adopt the same in handling the demands made by the questions. Candidates, therefore, should be able to analyse a piece of literature under discussion and make relevant and thoughtful inferences or comments on it. The skill tested here is the candidate's ability to understand the given text by analysing its thematic content, evaluating its style and effectiveness, and the candidate's ability to answer test questions based on it.

If a candidate reads a recommended text sufficiently, they will be in a position to demonstrate in the examination that they can effectively deal with literary and linguistic concepts, techniques and forms in the book. They will also be able to interpret and evaluate the literary text relying on information or evidence from the text itself. To ensure this, the candidate must be familiar with literary techniques, terms, concepts, principles and devices and understand how they were used by the writer in the context of the book. They will help them not only in textual analysis but also in the critical discourse of the book. The candidate should be able to point out, for instance, in poetry, the use of poetic devices such as rhyme, metaphor, simile, imagery, symbolism, sound, structure, etc., and appraise how effectively the poet used them to convey their message or meaning.

When the discussion is on prose fiction, it is essential to be familiar with the terms used in narrative works, which include: atmosphere, plot, structure, point of view, style and imagery. A student should be able to interpret these literary devices as they are used in the text. With drama, the candidate should be able to discuss the text or answer the questions with terms such as dramatic conflict, catharsis, tragedy, comedy, setting, and so on. They should be conversant with key scenes, the theme and dramatic styles presented in the text. The candidate must know these terms and concepts and look for them in the text while reading. Identifying them as used in the text will help them understand and interpret the work correctly.

The students should know which genre a particular set text belongs to. Such genres are tragedy, comedy, satire, farce, history, romance, etc. They should know the name of the writer (real or pen/assumed), the protagonist, and at least the other major characters of the work and their roles in the story. They should also be able to quote from the text to buttress their points or arguments and prove that they actually read and understood the writer's message.

In essay questions, the examiners examine how well the candidates understood the mechanics of the language. They scrutinise how the candidates present their answers in terms of expression, spelling, punctuation, style, grammar and paragraphing. However, in objective questions, the examiners seek to know the candidates' speed and, perhaps, accuracy because they want to know whether the candidates can attempt all the questions within the given time.

Further, the students must have a collection of past question papers. This will help them self-assess themselves and determine how well they are prepared for the exam. For this purpose, a chapter on tests and past exam questions is included in this book. Apart from providing the candidates with the kind of questions set by the examiners, it gives them an opportunity to assess their preparedness, speed and ability to attempt all the questions within a specified time.

➢ Use of Examiner's Syllabus

As mentioned earlier, to prepare well for any exam, the students or candidates need the necessary work tools. A syllabus is one of them. Now, apart from having the prescribed texts, the candidates must also acquire and use the examiner's syllabus. A lot of our students and candidates do not know the importance of this material and, hence, do not ask for it while registering for the examinations. Even when the examiners make it available, students hardly make any use of it. Only a few just cast a passing glance at it, while others just use it to decorate their reading tables or increase the contents and weight of their school bags to impress their parents and friends and show them they are studious. They do not understand the need to read the recommended texts and topics using the syllabus as a guide. As a result, most students and candidates end up reading irrelevant materials and topics on which no examiner will examine them.

A syllabus, by its nature, is a reading guide or map to the students, confining them within the prescribed limits. In fact, it is a rule book, and neglecting it jeopardises the chances of effective preparation for the exam by the students or candidates. Therefore, preparing for an examination with an examiner's syllabus is essential and a sine qua non to pass the examination. Preparing for an examination without the syllabus can only be compared to a blind man trying to find his way home at a crossroads unaided. The syllabus guides the students to read, interpret, and evaluate the texts based on the recommendations of the examiner. The syllabus also encourages them to explore wider and universal issues and promotes a better understanding of the topics.

We, therefore, recommend that teachers and instructors of this subject should emphasise or re-emphasise the need for their students to acquire and make effective use of the examiner's syllabus while preparing for exams. It will not only enable them to have a controlled direction in their studies but will also save them valuable time that would have been dissipated or spent wandering rudderlessly in the sea of topics in the subject or recommended texts, some of which may never show up in the examination.

Note: A candidate may not do well in an exam if they use the wrong syllabus. For instance, a candidate should never use WAEC syllabus for JAMB examination even though the two bodies share common topics in their syllabuses. JAMB has a few recommended texts and poems that are different from those of WAEC, NECO, and NABTEB. Therefore, we must give Caesar what belongs to Caesar.

> **Memory Improvement**

Learning activities centre on memory. Therefore, the learner must improve their memory capacity to attain the academic excellence they pursue.

Memory Improvement Skills: *Reading Skill*

Reading means going through what has been written with the aim of understanding it or refreshing one's memory of it. The written material may be made by the readers themselves or by another person. Good reading skill is essential for memory improvement. It enables the students to fully understand and interpret what the writer is trying to convey to them. The skills a student can acquire through reading include: skimming, scanning, browsing, perusing, etc. While the first three skills can be used in quick or shallow reading, especially during revision time, perusing, which is deeper reading, is essential for a thorough understanding of a text.

Improving Reading Skill

The most effective strategy for improving reading skill is to practise reading. Reading consistently ensures improvement in vocabulary, knowledge, ideas, insight, focus and attention span. Developing good reading skill is a gradual process that thrives on consistency. It helps improve a student's understanding capacity while making them familiar with what a writer writes.

To improve your reading skills, do the following:

- Read in context. Focus on words in clusters rather than individually. This is because words do not often have definite meanings except in context.
- Read more with the eyes than with the lips, except when absolutely necessary. For example, reading a poem aloud helps the readers appreciate the vocal or sound elements and devices in the poem.
- Use the dictionary, encyclopedia, or thesaurus, as the case may be, to look up unfamiliar words and expressions. This increases word power and vocabulary building. Ensure regular use of the new words and expressions in both writing and conversation. Otherwise, you may soon forget them, or they may disappear from your memory in no time.

- Identify topic sentences while reading. This helps in note-making and in summarising the key points read up.
- Use appropriate speed (not too fast, not too slow) that ensures full understanding of what you are reading. Vary your speed in line with the nature of what is being read. No doubt, some materials are too technical to understand if read in a hurry.
- Read regularly to improve your speed, assimilation and understanding of what is read.
- Read voraciously. Read wide and cover vast areas in the subject or recommended texts. Read also different texts by different authors on the same subject or topic. This will help you get a variety of perspectives on the subject or topic. Do not depend only on what your class teacher teaches or hands down to you. Find out more from other sources and teachers, and gain a fresh perspective.
- After reading, close the book and your eyes and reflect on what you just read. This will help you internalise what you read and make it easier for you to recall.
- After reading, try recalling what you just read. Do this with your book closed. Ask yourself: what have I learnt from the passage, chapter, or topic?
- After recalling what you read, you may want to recite it to yourself or a fellow student or write it down somewhere. You need not recite or write it word for word. It is enough if it contains the main point of the subject, topic, or idea the writer is trying to convey.
- Review what you read by taking a brief look at the subject or topic read.
- Sometimes, it is not easy to study alone, and it can get boring. So, form or join an academic discussion group, as it can help maintain concentration. Present or explain to the group what you read (which the other members of the group may have also read) for discussion. The discussion will help refresh your memory of what you read. By this, you stand the chance of seeing the topic

and subject matter from other perspectives, which you may not have imagined or focused your mind on earlier. This may also highlight the areas where you need more work or improvement. Also, you can learn one or two new things from your friends if this opportunity is utilised properly.

- Keep away from junk food: What you eat or drink may affect your energy level and focus. Eat brain food. You need nutritious food that helps boost your memory and concentration. Experts in the food industry suggest foods such as yoghurt, fish, seeds, etc. On exam day, eat good food that will slowly release energy throughout the exam period and drink plenty of water to remain well hydrated.

Focusing the Mind

This is keeping one's mind on what one is doing. This helps the students channel all their attention towards what they are reading with less distraction. A person with a focused mind is most likely to have a sharp and clear picture of what they are reading. They are less likely to forget what they read.

Understanding Skill

The students should avail themselves of all the skills that engender a proper understanding of what they read. Cramming is not recommended. It is like loading the stomach with indigestible food substances. Cramming is not actual learning, as the person cannot categorically prove that they understood what they crammed. A crammed item does not last long in the memory, and there is no guarantee that the crammer will recall all the items they crammed. Encoding or registering information in the memory cannot occur without understanding. If the information obtained during the course of studies is not registered in the memory, the students cannot recall it during an examination.

It has been discovered that stimulating the brain helps one remember easily what is stored therein. If students desire to remember or recall something more easily, the first thing they need to do is bring it to life in their imagination. They have to find an exciting or stimulating way of reviewing what they studied or read in their minds. They can transform these into mental pictures and make them funny and exciting in their imagination. This will help them easily remember or recall what they read.

Rumination Skill

In the academic field, rumination is a process of carefully reflecting on information acquired through learning. It leads to assimilation, which, in turn, leads to understanding, and the understood information crystallises into knowledge. The students must, therefore, make time to go through what they read. For instance, revising their notes will help them recall or retrieve information from memory.

Repetition of Information

Repeated reading of a particular topic makes it stick to memory, the same way nursery rhymes stick in children's memories. Therefore, students are advised to read their texts as many times as possible so the contents or points they read stick to their memory.

➢ **Exam Preparation Guide**

Do Not Cram, But Make Notes!

Students should avoid cramming the recommended texts or whatever text they are relying on for their exams. Instead, they should make short notes while studying. Cramming everything can overload the brain and cause health implications. It is also possible to forget crammed work, especially in an exam, due to tension. Making brief notes and reading them over and over during revision helps one remember the points read up.

Try to maintain concentration during learning classes. Do not struggle to write down all the teachers say, but make simple notes, capturing the essence and important facts of what is being taught. Good notes bring the learnt lessons back to life and help the students remember what the teachers said long after they had left the classroom. Write down only the key points or essence of what is being taught. The purpose of attending classes is not to make perfect notes but to listen to and grasp what the teachers are saying. The need for notes is to remind us of what we learn during our studies.

Time to Study

Time is possibly the most important factor in preparing for exams. According to researchers, the human brain is in its most active state between 5 a.m. and 8 a.m. and between 7 p.m. and 11 p.m. Therefore, students who study during these hours, all other things being equal, are most likely to have high retentive memory.

Where to Study

It is good to study in a place where you feel comfortable and relaxed and where you are assured of high concentration. If you can, rise early in the morning and study. Go to the library or any other place where you can find quietness to study. Understand your study topics in your own words and ensure you can translate the passage you are reading in your own words. Doing so will help you understand your notes. Try to understand what you read or study. Do not just cram, but make sure you understand the topic thoroughly.

Ask Questions

Ask your teacher questions on any topic or aspect of the subject you find confusing or difficult to understand. Do the assignments given by your teacher. Their assessment of the assignments at the end will help you find your strengths and weaknesses in the subject. Your fellow students or candidates can also help you when necessary. Ask questions even if it sounds stupid. Doing so will help you clear your doubts and fill in blank spaces in your knowledge base.

Organise Study Groups with Friends

Never hoard knowledge. Get friends together for group study or discussions. You may have questions that they have answers to. Share what you have with them, including your notes, time, information and other study materials. Let your friends improve along with you as long as you do not lose focus over time. In the discussion class, your friends may share a different but important perspective or interpretation of what you already know, which they picked up from anywhere, including the study material you had extended to them. This may be one of the most effective ways to challenge yourself; this, I think, will also be a worthwhile effort.

Trust God and Yourself

Students and candidates should meditate and pray well before an exam. This will provide immense energy and give them peace of mind. It will also help them gain self-confidence, knowing that they are not alone.

Eat and Sleep Well

The biggest mistake some students make during exams is that they do not eat and sleep well. They assume that they have much to cover and, therefore, feel that sleeping is a waste of time. However, studies have shown that students need 6 to 8 hours of sleep a day. They also need to take care of their diet, as what one eats directly impacts learning and retention ability. They should avoid junk foods and instead have foods that will continuously supply energy to their brains.

Reading the Text

We have severally stated in this book that the students should read the recommended texts. They must not place undue reliance on study aids, summaries, hand-outs and synopses while preparing for the exam. They must be aware of websites that offer summaries and analyses of literary works. Some of them are very good and helpful while some are created by mediocre people whose only aim is to brisk money from helpless and clueless candidates. While some of their materials are unworthy research-wise and glaze over key concepts, others contain outright misinformation that damages the chances of the candidates.

Most Literature-in-English exams feature what the students are meant to cover in the recommended text. For instance, a story in a prose text may have several themes, but due to lack of adequate time for diligent reading or deep research, lack of space in the material, incompetence, or inadvertence on the part of the person who prepared the study aids or summaries, some of the themes may be omitted or given less attention. The ones omitted or neglected in the study aids or summaries may then be the ones to feature in the exam questions to the peril of the students who relied on the materials.

While reading prose texts, the students need to concentrate on the background of the work and memorise the plot points, characters, and context presented in the book. In poetry, they need to read the shorter poems several times over. For the longer ones, they must read them diligently between the lines as many times as possible. In all, they must concentrate on the well-known or pivotal lines, literary devices and the context of the poem.

Theme

The students must ensure that they remember the theme of the texts they studied. The theme is the main message the writer shares with the readers. The message might be a lesson about life or an insight into human nature. The students must know that themes are often not stated directly. Therefore, they must infer them from the details and events of the story. A theme can be revealed by reflecting upon the meaning of the title of the story. It can also be deciphered from key phrases and sentences about strong ideas in the book, such as courage, freedom, honesty, love, hate, discrimination, etc. They can examine how the main character grows or changes and what he or she learns about life and from his or her environment.

While writing about themes of the recommended texts or considering them in unseen passages, it is necessary to state them concisely in words. To discover the theme of a particular work, let's do some exercise: Locate the central point of the story. Jot down everything you associate with it. For example, 'man's inhumanity to man', 'the hopeless situation of man amidst trials and troubles', 'man against nature', 'dander', 'bravery, courage in the face of danger and adversity', etc. After completing the list of associated points, circle the two or three most important from the list and try to combine them in a sentence. If you locate the accurate central point and choose your associated points carefully and correctly, you will get an appropriate theme of the story.

Setting

Setting is the time and physical location in which the action of a story takes place. The time may be past, present, or future; daytime or night-time; any season of the year; or historical period. Setting can be temporal or spatial. It is temporal when it involves the period when an event took place. For instance, the temporal setting of the poem *Boy on a Swing* by Oswald Mtsali is the apartheid period of 1943-1993 in South Africa. It is spatial when it relates to space and position. This is the physical environment where an event takes place. The physical or spatial setting of the poem *Boy on a Swing* is the entire South Africa, where the white overlords reigned with terror.

In Achebe's *Things Fall Apart*, the temporal setting is the pre-colonial period in Igboland, while the spatial or physical setting is the geographical location known as Igboland or the South-Eastern part of Nigeria.

The events in a story can unfold at a place, real or imaginary. Setting can, however, include the mood that the location evokes. The students should take note of a setting that raises the pitch of excitement and makes the story more foreboding, tense, or cheerful.

While writing about the setting of a story, it is essential to ask and answer the following questions:

- When did the story take place?
- Is the time of the year of any importance?
- Does the weather play any meaningful role in the story?
- Where did the story take place?
- Does the location suggest anything about the characters' lives?
- Do different characters become associated with different locations?
- And finally, does any external element of time or place suggest something about the protagonist?

Characters

The students should pay close attention to the characters and the role each of them plays in the development of the story. They should know the names of the major and the minor characters in the texts. It gives a poor impression of the students or candidates if they fail to demonstrate that they know the names of the characters in a recommended text on which they are to be examined. To avoid this, the students/candidates must review the names and roles of the characters before the exam day so that they are fresh in their memory. Besides knowing the names of the characters, the candidates must identify their nature and relationship with one another. The true nature of characters is not only revealed by what they say but also by their appearance and what they do.

Know and Identify the Protagonist and the Antagonist

The main character of a story is called the protagonist. This character may be a hero. Typically, the protagonist will face a challenge in the form of an antagonist. The antagonist is the person, thing, or force that acts against the protagonist and tries to prevent them from achieving their goal or dream. Bear in mind that the action of the story usually grows out of and is about the personality of the protagonist and the situation they face. A close examination of these actions unravels the entire story.

Note: If you want to understand a protagonist or, indeed, any other character in a story, first consider their personality. Find out what makes this individual different from other characters in the story. While reading, note the physical, mental, moral, or behavioural traits the character displays in the story. See if any of these traits is significant in the story. Find out if any of these qualities foreshadows or foretells the action of the story. Note what motivates the character (what makes them do or act as they do). Figure out if this motivation is as reasonable to the readers as it is to the character. These salient points excite most examiners and motivate them to test candidates thereon. This is one of the secrets; grab it.

Plot

Plot, as described in this book, is a linear sequence of events in a story. It is a pattern of actions, events and situations. In well-written works of fiction, this narrative pattern is carefully organised by the author to create a certain effect or set of effects on the readers. Examples include suspense, sadness, humour, excitement, terror, etc. Plot also suggests a relationship among characters, events and situations.

The students must ensure they can explain the plot of a recommended text in one sentence. If they can make a synopsis or summary of the plot or recreate it in their mind, they will be able to remember or recall greater aspects of the story while answering the exam questions. If they cannot summarise the plot of the novel, short story, or drama in one sentence, then they are not well-prepared for the exam as far as that particular text is concerned.

Turning Point

Almost every story has a turning point for the main character or characters. Most times, there is at least one significant question on the turning point of a story. The students should, therefore, make sure that they can identify and explain what happened at the turning point and show how it changed the main character or characters in the text. This is one of the secrets.

Symbolism

Most stories have some level of symbolism embedded in them. Often, examiners feature questions on symbols used by a writer, demanding that candidates relate them to modern-day realities. Simply, a symbol is a person, place, or thing in a narrative that suggests meaning beyond its literal or ordinary sense. We have political, religious, geographic, economic symbols, etc. Writers often, in their works, adopt symbolic elements relating to rebirths, purifications, forgiveness, vengeance, initiation, death, prosperity, etc. Therefore, the students or candidates should endeavour to identify them and know what they stand for in the narrative, play, or poem.

Conflict

Most plots centre around conflict. The action of a plot is usually set in motion by a central conflict, which is a struggle between opposing forces. We also have external conflict, which is a struggle between a character and an outside force – another character, a physical obstacle, nature, or society. We equally have internal conflict, which is emotional conflict within a character. For example, a character who struggles against their fears. Note that conflict exists in literature to add excitement to the story. In fact, it may be the central or focal point around which the story is woven. Therefore, the students or candidates must mark this out and be able to discuss its role in the development of the story. This is one of the secrets.

Practice Tests

While preparing for the exam, find time to test yourself on what you have read and try to replicate exam conditions as much as possible. Practise tests are the single most important strategy for preparing for any exam. It familiarises the students with the timing, flow of the exam, the format and the kinds of questions they will meet on exam day. It ensures that the candidates spend the right time on each section of the exam paper. In practice mocks or test exams, the candidates become their own examiners. During revision, practise with past question papers and answer the questions within the time stipulated for the paper and allocated for each question. Be sincere to yourself and work as if you are actually writing the exam. Try to answer all the questions before looking up the answers. The more the students exercise with the past question papers, the better they become for the exam.

Writing

After mastering how to read and prepare for the exam, it is only natural to learn how to write and apply, or express on paper, the knowledge we have obtained in our studies. The actual writing of the examination is as important as preparing for it. Since our focus in this book is on passing the exam, our aim would be defeated if, on exam day, despite the effort committed to preparations, the candidates fail to deliver or deliver poorly. Therefore, besides preparing for the exam, equal attention should be given to writing. Writing is the ability to use the written words to create a clear message. It is the best way to communicate or show the examiner what you have read or learnt. Therefore, no matter how intelligent and smart a candidate may be, they may not be able to convince the examiner that they know the subject if they fail to communicate their knowledge well in writing.

Note that most of the candidates fail in exams not because they lack substantive knowledge in the subject but because they lack practical delivery skills on exam day. This situation is serious and frustrating and often leads to the wrong belief by some candidates that examiners are sadists who take joy in failing candidates. This is unfair. If a candidate is brilliant yet fails an exam or gets a low grade, their problem may be that of delivery rather than that of knowledge. Let them sit back and reflect on how they actually write during exams. Let them work on themselves in the area of writing and the skills needed for it.

You must have observed that most people tend to speak far better than they can write. Therefore, the students must work on themselves in the area of writing. They must acquire good writing skills. Let them learn from the authors or writers of the various books they read. They will do better if they also engage in mock exams using past question papers and hand their scripts to their teacher for assessment. The teacher then will, among other things, identify their shortfalls with writing and suggest ways of improving on it.

The irony of the exam is that despite the length of time and energy you invest preparing for it and the volume of work you cover, you are only going to be judged by what you are able to put down on your answer script in an exam of a few questions that usually last for a few minutes or hours. This calls for seriousness and diligence on the part of the candidates because once you finish writing and hand over your script to the invigilator, you cannot rewrite or modify your answers. You will then be assessed and graded based on the contents of your script. In other words, you will either pass or fail on the strength of what you have written in that script. Therefore, whatever error or shortfall in grammar, writing skill, spelling, punctuation, style and diction you make during the exam will cost you valuable marks and will ultimately determine your grade in the exam.

Remember, in written exams, you do not have the luxury of checking spelling and grammar. Candidates will either pass if they write well or fail or score low grades if they write badly.

The written part of the examination is often graded based on the organisation of ideas, clarity, cohesion, style, and how persuasive it is. The candidates must be highly organised in their answers, ensuring that facts are presented well – one leading to the other. The candidates must endeavour to show explicitly, in their answers, how the ideas they write about relate to the question asked. Poor presentation or delivery begets poor marks. To succeed here, the candidates must learn how to write and express themselves well on paper. What the candidates write represents what they know about the subject, and the examiner assesses them based on that. Therefore, they must let the examiner know what they know by presenting their answers well and coherently.

The students must write in a clear and narrative style: The essay must move in an obvious sequence and direction. They must vary their sentence structures, employ a wide range of vocabulary, and organise the essay into a logical thought or structure. The ideas must flow logically in paragraphs. The examiner must not struggle from point to point, trying to make meaning out of what you write. In fact, the examiner is interested in seeing how the candidate organises their facts or points, as well as their expression and mechanical accuracy. A candidate must avoid annoying the examiner with bad English, illegible handwriting, wrong spelling and grammatical blunders. They will be penalised for such errors.

Therefore, when you write, do not heap empty phrases or disjointed sentences devoid of the points the examiner expects on your answer script. Do not blabber like a child or beat about the bush (the offence of circumlocution). Get to the point and address it squarely without mincing words. Do not be bombastic. Remember, it is an examination and not a pleasurable composition. Those who adopt bombastic composition often aim to impress the examiner with their big, high-sounding words. They think they can score more marks by showing off prowess in the use of 'big' words or grammar. Do not do it because the examiner requires only simple English and well-structured sentences for the answers.

There are plenty of instances of what careless and inordinate use of 'high-tech grammar' or big words in an examination can lead to. This has been exemplified by an interview between one grandiloquent honourable and a Punch Newspaper reporter. This honourable gentleman is famous for his flamboyant use of high-tech, high-sounding and rare words and expressions.

Excerpt

Reporter: Did you write exams in school in these big words?

Honourable: I used such words very freely in my exams both at secondary school and in my university, and little wonder I had the misfortune of my English results being seized intermittently in my O'Levels. WAEC released my results for the other subjects and withheld my English results. This happened for about three years. Twice, I passed the University Matriculation Examination but I could not proceed to the University because of my English results that were not released. At the end of the day, it was released after the third attempt.

In my view, the Honourable's result may not have been seized but withheld to afford the examiner time to re-examine the script before publishing the result. The question is: Can a candidate afford to wait for a good three years for their result as did the Honourable on account of the use or misuse of the so-called high-tech grammar, words and expressions? Your answer is as good as mine.

Let the answers be concise and less time-consuming for the examiner to mark your script. Do not waste their time with long, windy and repetitive sentences when a short and simple one can do the job for you. It is essential to break up the answers into short sentences and paragraphs to avoid boring the examiner. Try and say exactly what you mean and nothing more.

Avoid using slang and colloquial expressions – informal words and expressions that are not part of the Standard English Language. They are used more in spoken language than in written and are restricted to particular contexts or groups of people. They are often regarded as glaring misuse of words or phrases and considered inappropriate in formal writing or academic contexts, such as in exam essays.

Examples:

1. 'I was supposed to be in a party with my friends, but they flopped on me.' In this sentence, the slang term being used is 'flop', which means a planned event that does not happen.

2. 'I got a job promotion even though I don't go to work half the time. I'm so sick.' Here, the slang term used is 'sick', which literally means ill. However, in slang, it refers to something being awesome or cool.

3. 'I can't believe my life has passed so quickly; now that I am in the hospital, I guess I will just kick the bucket here.' The slang expression used here is 'kick the bucket', which means to die.

'My legs are killing me.' Killing me is a slang that means 'really hurting.'

For this reason, children should be discouraged from using slangs. Those who use them end up using them while writing in school exams, whereas it is discouraged in the academic world.

Do not use abbreviations, including the ones now prevalent in mobile phone text messaging. Do not use symbols such as: '&', '%', '>', '@', '#' and other mathematical signs that have crept into modern casual writing. Do not use clichés (phrases or ideas that are overused and no longer have the meaning they used to have). Examples: 'There are plenty more fish in the sea,' 'I've got my plate full.'

Ensure you correctly spell the names of characters, cities and other proper nouns that appear in the text. Numbers should be expressed in words, especially when they are less than ten or when they are used to start a sentence.

Quotation marks should be used or placed where appropriate around any directly quoted speech or text and titles of publications.

Learn how to write by reading the works of different writers. Reading and writing are intertwined. When you read what published authors have written, you are immersed not just in their ideas but in the way they write, the pulsing of their sentences and the aptness of their diction. The more you read, the more you imbibe the rhythm of the author's language. This rubs off on you and influences your writing. Reading is not a substitute for writing, but it helps to lay the foundation that makes good writing possible.

As you read, consciously observe the author's writing styles and, if possible, adopt them while writing.

To write well, you must learn the rules of grammar. You must spell and punctuate correctly, and ensure you edit your write-up as soon as you are through with writing.

Note that lack of close textual reference, neglecting to refer to authors, poets and playwrights by their names, poems, books and plays, or by their titles, and failure to include even one quotation from the set texts, poems or dramas in your essay is an infringement for which the examiner can penalise you by awarding low marks. Use specific examples and illustrations from the texts in your essay. Although you are encouraged to write in your own words, infuse the message of the writer. In other words, construct and tailor your argument using what you have read in the text. Unless otherwise required, let your analyses of the examples given be more focused on the ideas of the author or their message to readers. Do not bring extraneous facts, especially those not likely to feature in the marking scheme.

Finally, organise your writing into paragraphs that observe the four elements of paragraphing: unity, order, coherence and completeness.

Paragraphing

A paragraph is a section or segment of a piece of writing. It is usually made up of different sentences revolving around a particular subject. Paragraph writing demands focus and complete attention on that subject.

How do we write a good paragraph? We do this by ensuring that the four essential elements of a paragraph – unity, order, coherence, and completeness are present.

In each paragraph of the essay, one particular idea or topic is presented, developed and explained. To successfully do this, the paragraph must be written in a unified and coherent manner.

- ***Unity***

Unity in a paragraph begins with a topic sentence. A topic sentence contains the main idea of a paragraph. It establishes a direction for the paragraph with other sentences supporting and developing it. It often appears at the beginning of the paragraph, where the main idea of the paragraph appears first, followed by other sentences bearing information supporting or developing this idea. A topic sentence can also appear in the middle or at the end of the paragraph, depending on the writer's style.

To be effective, a unified paragraph must follow the idea in the topic sentence and not deviate from it. It is effective because all the sentences effectively relate to the topic sentence at the beginning of the paragraph.

- ***Order***

Order refers to the way one organises one's supporting sentences. Order can be achieved by organising the flow of thought in the paragraph in numerical sequence. This directs the readers from one point to the next.

Order can be in line with importance, chronology or logic. A genuine paragraph always has organisation. In a well-organised paragraph, the readers read through the lines and transit smoothly from one point to another. A paragraph can also be structured in patterns: from general to particular, particular to general, whole to parts, question to answer or effect to cause.

- ***Coherence***

This is the quality that makes your writing clear and understandable. The sentences are connected to one another in terms of subject matter. A coherent paragraph has sentences that logically follow one another and do not contain isolated thoughts. Coherence can be achieved by using transitions that help connect ideas from one sentence to the next. There is coherence where there is a flow of thought or ideas in the sentences of a paragraph. Using coherence, the writer presents their sub-topics in an orderly fashion that the readers can easily follow.

- *Completeness*

This is self-explanatory. This occurs when we have a well-developed or well-designed paragraph. The sentences are vivid and strongly support the main idea or narrative. They contain enough information, phrases or sentences to cover the idea. It involves three supporting sentences along with the topic sentence and a concluding sentence. The concluding sentence summarises the central idea by strengthening the topic sentence. For the paragraph to be complete, it must have enough sentences so that the main idea in the topic sentence is completely developed. The writer gives themselves enough space to develop the topic. They give reasons to accept their argument and incorporate some examples to give those reasons more validity. Generalisations are supported with examples or illustrations. They give details and descriptions that help the readers understand what they are writing about. It would be tragic to assume that the readers will understand what you have in mind. You have to be specific and develop your ideas thoroughly, and at the same time, avoid repetition.

For further reading on this, see Strunk, Wiliam Jr., and E. B. White's *The Elements of Style,* 4th ed., Allyn and Bacon, 2000.

Chapter 6

Tackling Literature-in-English Exam Questions

In essay questions, candidates are required to write answers that fulfil the demands of the questions asked. Essay questions test complex learning objectives, and the processes and skills candidates use in answering them.

> **Use of Good English**

To do well in Literature-in-English examination, candidates must have a good command of the English language. Language is an essential part of literature. In fact, it is the only tool and medium with and through which literature is expressed. Both are inextricably linked and complementary to each other.

In view of this, candidates are expected to use good and correct English expressions that best convey their knowledge in the essay exam questions. In fact, examiners often express on their question papers their willingness to award high marks to candidates who write their answers in good English. This underscores the need for the students to improve their writing skill, ensuring that they express themselves well and correctly. This skill has to be acquired well ahead of the exam date. They can achieve this through competent teachers of the English language and constant practice with the aid of good study textbooks on writing skill.

During the exam, they are expected to make use of simple and correct English in presenting their answers to the questions asked. As stated earlier, the candidates should avoid the temptation of trying to show off their knowledge of English vocabulary and flowery or bombastic language. I have often come across candidates bragging, after their exams, to their friends how they 'gave WAEC assignment on vocabs'.

Unfortunately, the use of the so-called 'vocabs', high or big grammar does not impress most of the examiners, nor does it portray good command or mastery of English language. However, there is no rule against the use of 'big' grammar, flowery, or even bombastic language in exams. What is important is using them well and appropriately and avoiding the sin of malapropism.

What examiners mean by good English is nothing short of good expression: the right choice of words or expressions at the right time and place. It also includes the correct use of punctuation and tenses. As much as possible, avoid ambiguity and do not confuse the examiner. They may not be patient with your script.

Further, candidates writing Literature-in-English exam must bear in mind that the subject Literature, like others, has its own language and that using such language in written or theory exams will showcase their wisdom. Candidates must make use of literary terminology and principles while answering the questions. For example, words like 'form', 'style', 'symbol', 'structure', etc., must be used where appropriate. It is for this purpose that we have added a chapter, a form of glossary, on the terms, concepts and principles used in Literature and literary discourse. Therefore, candidates who desire to get good grades on their Literature exam must avail themselves of these terms and their usage in literary discourse. A student becomes conversant with the terms and principles by reading them up and using them constantly in literary discussions and pre-exam writings, including class tests and assignments. In the long run, this helps them present arguments and answers to questions in the appropriate literary language. They must aim for intelligent clarity in their essays with words and expressions that know their meanings and usage.

Candidates must also realise that Literature exam has its own unique demand for the presentation of facts and points in the exam questions. In view of this, the Exam Ethics Project in Nigeria recently counselled teachers of Literature to step up their efforts in drilling students and candidates along this line and to ensure that students understand what examiners want them to do. This is to prevent the recurrent situation where candidates state what they think rather than what the examiners want.

It is suggested that model questions and answers, especially for essay exams, should be made available to students to give them a glimpse of what the examiners expect from them. I totally align myself with this call, bearing in mind the saying that 'example is better than precepts.' It is better to teach with concrete examples from which the students can learn. If a student does not know how to tackle exam questions while preparing for it, it is not likely that they will know what to do when faced with the exam in the real situation in the exam hall. For this reason, past essay questions for exam purposes and their answers have been included in this book.

➢ **Explicating, Summarising, Comparing and Contrasting**
The written aspect of Literature-in-English examination revolves around explicating, summarising, comparing and contrasting. The understanding of these and how to go about them is very important and key to doing well in the exam. Let us consider their importance and the demand they make on the candidates.

Explicating
This is a form of literary analysis whereby literary works or issues therein are explained. It is an essay that proceeds with a careful line-by-line or word-for-word examination of a passage – a poem, story or play. It discloses and explains the importance of the work or passage. Explication requires close reading of the text to uncover the meaning, message or lesson the writer intends for the readers. To be successful in this, the students must closely examine the language of the passage to explain its significance. All the details in the passage are explored and given in-depth attention.

Explication is effective when used to illustrate the meaning of the work. It is useful for unravelling the meaning of a complex passage or drawing the readers' attention to a particular point missed while reading in the first place.

Summarising

A summary is a short or succinct account of a work. It is a condensation or compression of its thought or idea. To be able to summarise a work, you must read it carefully. You are required to wade into the details of the work or passage, extract the key thought or idea from it and render it accurately, fairly and as much as possible in your own words. In summarising, two skills are involved: the ability to identify the main idea and the ability to recognise the evidence that speaks in favour of the idea in the text being summarised. You can do this by looking for the sentences or groups of paragraphs that convey the writer's meaning. It does not involve evaluation or passing of judgement on the worth or merits of the writer's idea. The candidates must succinctly present the point(s) conveyed by the work as the writer sees them.

Comparing and Contrasting

This is an interpretative approach to literary analysis. Here, significant elements in a single work are compared and contrasted with one another. Similarly, a particular aspect of two different works can be compared and contrasted. You may also be required to compare and contrast the speeches and actions of two characters in a work. This comparative analysis has the potency of sharpening your perception of the work(s) under consideration. In comparing and contrasting, you highlight the similarities and differences between the two things being compared. For example, in comparing two poems, you might see that one contains rhyme and the other does not; that the action is external in one poem or story and internal in the other; that one story contains much dialogue while the other has little; that the settings, tone etc. differ in significant ways. In comparing and contrasting two works, the focus is usually on elements such as style, language, theme and content.

➢ **Common Terms Used in Essay Questions**

A close look at past WAEC and NECO essay question papers reveals the regular use of certain operational words or formats such as analyse, comment on, compare, contrast, compare and contrast, give an account of, account for, criticise, describe, evaluate, define, interpret, justify, review, explain, summarise, distinguish, discuss, etc., in the questions.

These operational words are used by examiners to get what they want from candidates in the exam. They vary in their formats and demands on the candidates. They require a particular approach. Mastering them and, indeed, the nature of the questions to be encountered in the exam, therefore, should be an important aspect of a candidate's preparation.

To do justice to a question, candidates must carefully read and understand it and know what demands it makes on them. They must endeavour to understand what the examiner wants before attempting to answer the questions. Let us have a brief discussion of these words and expressions to demonstrate what examiners expect from the candidates and how they should answer them.

'Analyse'

To analyse means to take things apart to see what they are made of or how they work. In academic discourse, analysis involves breaking up an idea or argument or taking it apart to identify its strengths and weaknesses. This requires the candidates to describe the main ideas, relationships, assumptions and the significance of a particular thing or issue. It also requires them to examine the nature and structure of the thing or issue, especially by considering its component units or aspects. It requires the candidates to organise their thoughts, look for evidence, interpret or make generalisations. They identify motives and causes or make deductions or inductions. A question beginning with this word requires the candidates to make use of information (evidence) drawn from the text and as portrayed by the writer.

The personal opinions of the candidates are not required other than what the writer puts forward.

'Comment On'

To 'comment on' requires giving or saying one's opinion or perspective on a subject matter. Examiners require the candidates to express their views on a particular point or issue raised in a given work. This gives the candidates ample opportunity to freely speak their minds on the subject, independent of the opinions expressed by the writer. By doing so, the candidates can freely explain what they understand of the issue as contained in the text and, in the process, air their opinions. They outline the positive and negative aspects of the topic or issue. They are required to reach some conclusion or reasoned judgement based on the balance of what they had identified as merits and demerits of the issue(s).

To succeed in this, the candidates must understand the story, point, or issue they are required to comment on. In other words, they must read the book or passage with close attention to details.

'Compare'

This requires the candidates to discuss the pros and cons of two things and show how they are similar or related to each other. The two things are placed side-by-side, and their similarity is pointed out. Examiners often require candidates to examine two characters, incidents, themes, etc., in a particular work or different works and to compare them with each other. Candidates are expected to interpret the said characters, incidents or themes and point out the areas of similarity. While comparing two characters, the candidates may choose to dedicate the first half of their answer to one and the second half to the other character or thing compared. They may still use an alternating structure whereby they consider each side-by-side. They may focus on characteristics such as the physical appearance of characters, their interaction with other characters, and their behaviour at critical moments of their actions.

'Contrast'

This is an instance of comparison between two things where the two are shown to be dissimilar in nature or any particular way. The focus is on the differences. Two characters or incidents in a work may be in contrast with each other, and the candidates are required to focus on those things that make them different rather than their common grounds or similarities. We can contrast the character of the hero with that of the villain in a work.
Example: The character of Ezeulu and that of Ogbuefi Nwaka in Chinua Achebe's *Arrow of God.*

In contrast, we talk of the dissimilarity between two things. The two things compared together do not complement each other; rather, they both exist in separate worlds of their own. In Shakespeare's *The Merchant of Venice*, Antonio's character contrasts sharply with Shylock's. While Antonio's life is full of human kindness and love, Shylock's life is full of hate and vengeance. To find the contrast between two things or attributes, the candidates need to furnish adequate details of the contrasting elements. The contrasting elements can be eloquence, fearlessness, height, integrity, honesty, etc.

'Compare and Contrast'

Here, significant elements in a single work or two different works are compared and contrasted with each other at the same time. Candidates may also be required to compare and contrast works in two genres of literature: poetry and drama, prose and essay, etc. For example, in contrasting two genres of literature, say poetry and essay, one can make the following observations: Poetry is thought to be sublime and often difficult to understand, whereas essays are intentionally structured to be clear. However, in comparison, it can be observed that both poem and essay fundamentally aim for the same end – to effectively convey an idea, argument or message.

In comparing and contrasting, you focus on the similarities or likeness and dissimilarities or differences in the two elements or works being compared and highlight them. For example, in comparing and contrasting, you might see that one poem contains rhyme while the other does not; that the action in a story is external but internal in the other; that one story contains much dialogue while the other has little; that a play contains more action, while the other does not; or that the settings, tone, themes, etc. resemble or differ in significant ways. Candidates are expected to identify, highlight and discuss the similarities and dissimilarities between the two works given.

While comparing and contrasting two works of prose, drama, or poetry, the focus is usually on forms, imagery, symbolism, diction, sound, characters, effects, subject matters, or aspects of technique such as metres or points of view. Equally, significant features common to the two works, such as authorship, style, genre, historical background, period, and situation, can also be compared and contrasted.

To handle the question properly, candidates need to take the comparison first and then the contrast. One is not entitled to greater marks than the other, so both should be dealt with equally. A comparative analysis should lead the readers to a conclusion or an evaluation of the merits of the literary works.

'Give an Account of'

To account for or give an account of an incident in a work is to give details or a written or spoken description of that incident. It is also an explanation of an incident or situation in the work. Candidates are required to narrate the story of the incident in detail, using illustrations from the work that will help convey the story.

'Criticise'

To criticise a work, argument, or anything is to comment on the strengths and weaknesses (merits and demerits) contained therein. We match the positive and negative aspects and draw conclusions that must be objective or fair. In criticism, we look at the work as a whole and consider the success or failure of the author in adequately conveying their message to the readers.

'Describe'

This requires the candidates to present an accurate picture of an event or phenomenon.

It requires the students to describe a character, an event, a subject, etc., as clearly as possible so that the readers can have a vivid mental picture of what they are reading about.

'Evaluate'

This requires the candidates to weigh up or give an assessment of someone else's opinion, citing its positive and negative features, advantages and disadvantages and evidence for or against it. In other words, they are required to judge the quality of ideas, values, and works of art and give rational opinions on issues or controversies. The position or stance which a writer takes in a work can be evaluated vis-a-vis the general position or stance. Evaluation gives rise to the formation of personal opinion after due consideration of given views. It encourages candidates to give reasons for their judgement.

'Interpret'

This requires the candidates to explain the meaning of something or an event. Candidates can use examples from the work to present their opinions and then describe and evaluate them.

'Justify'

This requires the presentation of the basis for a particular event, phenomenon or stance and why you think it is so. Candidates are expected to present evidence drawn from the work to support their views and conclusions. They have to state adequate grounds for the position they take. 'Justify' is similar to 'assess' and 'support' because a reasoned judgement on the candidate's part is called for.

'Review'

This requires the candidates to present a kind of summary of the important aspects or parts of an event or an attitude in a work and to comment critically where appropriate.

'Explain'

This requires describing a situation or event to somebody to enable them to understand it easily. It also involves giving reason for something or an event. In an examination, where candidates are asked to explain a point or issue, it is assumed that they already know the story and, therefore, should be ready to supply the details of it. Candidates supply these details as if they are addressing somebody who has no facts of the story or is ignorant of the event. Answers here are usually long and expected to meet the point.

'Distinguish'

A question asking a candidate to distinguish between two works or characters demands that the candidate points out and discusses the difference between the two. It is similar to 'contrast'.

'Summarise'

As the name suggests, candidates are required to discuss concisely the main points or issues in a work or passage. The question requires no examples or embellishments of the answers. All irrelevant details are avoided for the gist.

'Discuss'

This requires candidates to write or talk about something in detail, demonstrating the idea or opinion expressed by the writer in the work. It involves objective analysis that leads to a position. Answers here are usually longer than those in 'Explain'.

'Define'

This requires that you give the meaning of the subject. This meaning is usually specific to the course of the subject. Determine the precise limits of the term to be defined. Explain the exact meaning. Definitions are usually short.

'Illustrate'

This requires the candidates to give concrete examples of the subject matter, which can be theme, diction, tone, or topic in issue. They provide actual examples of the ideas they are writing about. They should also cite examples of earlier and later incidents in the book or work supporting their answers.

'Outline'

Describe the main ideas, characteristics, or events. This does not necessarily mean writing a numbered outline.

'Trace'

Here, you show the order of events or progress of a subject or event as presented by the writer.

> **Context Questions**

Context questions demand that you know items such as theme, characterisation, style, and structure as used in the prescribed texts or poems. Questions on drama test candidates' knowledge of the plays as works of art meant for the stage. Questions on poetry test candidates' ability to recognise the various means through which a poet communicates their feelings and ideas.

Cultural and historical context questions require the candidates to identify and explain specific literary, cultural and intellectual history or backgrounds of the text.

In a nutshell, context questions tend to probe into when the text was written, what society was like when it was written, what or who influenced the writer, what political or social influences there were, and what influences might have been in the genre that might have affected the writer. When the text was written and when it was set might also have an important part to play in what was written.

Themes come from experiences that writers go through in their lives while writing. For instance, why did Chinua Achebe write *A Man of the People*? Why did Ayi Kwei Amah write *The Beautyful Ones Are Not Yet Born*? How does the context of the play *Trials of Brother Jero* affect the text's meaning?

Also, it is essential to acquire and use the recommended Poetry Anthologies containing the set poems. A list of the poems is contained in both the JAMB and WAEC syllabuses. A good number of them run commentaries and analyses on the poems; these will be of immense assistance to students and candidates.

Paper 3 of the exam comprises the African and Non-African Prose grouped into two sections: A and B. In these sections, two questions are set for each of the recommended texts, and candidates are required to answer one question from each section. Questions on prose test candidates' firm grasp of the structure of the texts and the various means by which the writer dramatises the experiences of the characters to make the work look real.

> **Multiple Choice Objective Questions**

This constitutes Paper 1 of the examination. This paper tests candidates' knowledge of the prescribed Shakespearian texts and literary appreciation. 50 compulsory questions will be answered by candidates.

The questions test a candidate's overall knowledge of the subject. They test many levels of learning and a candidate's ability to integrate information. They do not allow the candidates to demonstrate knowledge beyond the choices provided in the options. The candidates do not have the chance to explain anything. They either choose the correct answer or the wrong one. This, in any case, encourages guessing or approximation due to the presence of at least one correct answer in the options. While guessing may not be an appropriate or safe way to demonstrate knowledge, a candidate may resort to it when they have no alternative, as they are faced with the dilemma of choice. Faced with this situation, they need to make what some people choose to call an 'educated guess'. They do this by using the elimination method. By so doing, they narrow down the options to a number they can safely choose from.

Candidates have to read the questions carefully because the way they are framed is bound to confuse a shallow or hasty reader. Be wise and conscious that the questions are not as simple as they may appear at first sight. Always read a question more than once and between the lines to understand its demands before choosing your answers.

The paper demands complete coverage of the syllabus. The candidates have no opportunity to choose which questions to answer, explain their answers, or express any view. They either get it right or wrong.

In answering the questions, the candidates must apply logical reasoning to their choices. They must not choose an option for the sake of choosing; they must be convinced that the option chosen is the correct answer.

Below are strategies that may help handle multiple-choice questions in an examination.

- Observe the Rules and Regulations of the Examination Body: Take the oral instructions of the invigilators in the exam hall. Observe the rules and regulations of the examination body. Take no part in any form of exam malpractice.
- Track Your Time: Estimate how much time to spend on each question and ensure that you maintain it. For instance, JAMB allocates 45 minutes for each subject except Use of English. This means that you have 54 seconds to answer each question. Do not be too fast, as you may overlook some important facts or features of the questions. Do not be too slow, as you may end up not attempting all the questions. Judicious allocation and use of the time allotted to each question matter a lot. Aim to attempt all the questions within the prescribed time.

- Master the Directions: Read the instructions or directions in the questions carefully to understand exactly what the questions require and how to tackle them.
- Study the Questions: Read the questions carefully and become absolutely sure of the demand they make on you. Be careful in choosing the options. Make sure you understand what the examiner wants before setting out to write. Watch out for words like 'not' and 'except.' They tell you to look for choices that are false, different, or opposite of what appears to be the answer.
- Answer by Elimination: In multiple-choice questions, the candidates should anticipate the answers. They may close their eyes and imagine the answer before reading the choices. If they understand the question but still get confused about the answer, they have to eliminate the choices they think are wrong or odd. This will help them narrow down the answer field and also save valuable time. Then, they can make an educated guess. They must avoid distractors. These are answer choices that are true but do not correlate with the question.

  However, while using the elimination method, candidates occasionally encounter a situation where they are left with two options that seem equally correct. In this situation, typically, the most specific (unambiguous) option is usually correct. Therefore, candidates must be careful before selecting an option.
- Questions on Tone or Mood: These questions demand that you infer the writer's attitude towards the subject of the question. While reading, it is necessary to pay close attention to the descriptions of the subject of a work or passage and see if they are positive, negative or neutral. Find out if the writer is hopeful, sad, admiring, wishy-washy, sarcastic, etc. It is good to know the meanings of words like sanguine, melancholy, reverent, ambivalent, hilarious, sardonic, and other similar descriptive words

and expressions that were regularly featured in past exam questions.

- Questions on 'Main Idea or Best Title': Answering such questions requires you to consider the big picture created in the work or passage. You need to consider what the subject is, what aspect of the subject the writer addresses, or what the writer wants you to understand about the subject.

- Questions Based on Evaluating the Writer's Craft: Answering such questions requires you to look at the organisation, logic and argumentative techniques of the writer.

- Questions on 'The Odd Item': Answering such questions demands a careful examination of the items in the options given. The candidates must consider all the options one by one and eliminate the items that do not fit into or fall under a group or class to which the rest belong. The class may be based on the genre, for example: prose, drama and poetry. It may be based on a class made up of figures of speech, literary devices or their sub-classes. It may be based on a class of authors – Africans or non-Africans, playwrights – Africans or non-Africans. A question may be based on whether the items are novels, short stories, African or non-African, male or female authors, poets or playwrights. The class can be infinite. However, what is important is the ability of the candidates to point out the odd item from the options. They will be able to do this if they are conversant with the classes to which the items belong, the majority of which have been dealt with in this book.

- Questions on identification require a candidate's recognition of the author and recalling content materials such as particular elements of the plot.

- Multiple-choice questions: Here, examiners sometimes use the same letters for correct answer options for several questions in succession. This is often deliberate and makes the candidates uncomfortable, worrying that their answers might be wrong. The answer may not be wrong because examiners usually play this psychological game on the candidates to make them doubt themselves, falter, and choose the wrong option. They intend to test the candidates' firm understanding of the subject.

- Pay attention to choices such as 'all of the above' or 'none of the above.' To eliminate them, all you need to do is to find the answer that does not fit.

Chapter 7

Unseen Literature

Unseen literature usually forms part of the Literature-in-English objective test exam. However, it can still take the form of a theoretical question, whereby the candidates are expected to supply their answers just as they do in Comprehension questions in their English Language Paper 1 examination. Unseen literature is based on the form of literary criticism, which deals with the analysis and appreciation of the techniques used by writers to convey meaning in their works. It requires, for success, an inquisitive mind that demands to know, for instance, why the writer makes certain lexical, setting, and title choices.

Unseen literature is presented in the form of extracts or passages from literary works outside the ones recommended for the exam. Candidates are required to answer questions thereon. It calls for a good understanding and interpretation of literary techniques and styles used to produce specific effects on the readers. It requires an open mind and sound argument – a situation where a reader freely follows what they are presented with, allowing all shades of opinions expressed by the author. The readers read and absorb the message they are presented with and answer the questions based on the facts of the extract presented by the author. In other words, the analysis of the extract or passage is done based on the evidence provided in the extract or passage itself. The readers take the passage as they see it and are not expected to introduce personal views, judgement or expectations into the analysis apart from those that are universal or specifically demanded. In analysing or interpreting the extracts, the candidates are required to make use of the right argument and ensure that it is not out of context.

> ### **Unseen Passages**

As stated earlier, unseen passages are extracts culled from texts other than the ones prescribed by the examination body. It is referred to as 'unseen' probably because candidates had no opportunity to study the passages or extracts or the texts from which they were taken while preparing for the exam.

These passages are drawn from works in drama, prose and poetry. To do well in questions on unseen literature, the candidates must avail themselves of good study materials treating this aspect of the exam. These include textbooks that deal with unseen literature, such as the one right in your hands now, and past exam question papers of JAMB, WAEC, NECO, and other examination bodies. These past exam question papers present the questions first-hand to the candidates as examiners want them.

Strategy

Questions on unseen extracts and passages examine candidates' ability to appreciate the written literature. The questions gravitate around the central theme, mood, tone, setting, figures of speech and other language devices used in the passage. The most important strategy used in dealing with questions on unseen literature is understanding the passage itself. This involves efforts to read carefully and understand the overall meaning of the passage or the central theme/idea, issue, purpose or message of the passage or extract. Focus or emphasis should be directed on key areas of plot, narration, characterisation, the tone or attitude of the writer or poet, and their language or diction.

Candidates can do well if they understand the message the writer or poet puts across, the mood and the attitude of the writer, the characters and the effects of the techniques used. Candidates are required to give appropriate interpretations of the passage in terms of idiomatic, symbolic, metaphorical and literal use of language.

Narration

Candidates are required to make use of the narrative techniques, most of which have been dealt with in this book, in the appreciation of unseen passages. A narrator's perspective and personality can greatly affect how a story is told. The narrator is the character used by the writer to tell the story. In poetry, the persona (voice or poet-speaker) takes the place of the narrator. The narrator is the mask or identity used by the writer to bring across the message. Proper understanding of this and other techniques used in the narration makes the work easier for the candidates.

The point of view used by the writer must be identified. It is essential for the candidates to be able to distinguish between the various aspects of point of view and know how they are used in literary appreciation. Worthy of note are the following: the age of the narrator (age being an indicator of wisdom and maturity); the narrator's background – social status, level of education, etc.; their character – whether personal, distant, formal, informal, humble, or arrogant. However, all these do not always feature in a passage at the same time. However, the candidates need to pay close attention to the passage to be able to identify the ones that feature.

Character Analysis

Characters in literary works are creations of the writer. The writer tells the story through the characters. It is, therefore, essential to understand the characters as the writer portrays them in the book. The areas to look out for in character analysis are appearance, behaviour, background, relationship with others, and language in words and thoughts. A character can be determined by what they say or do or fail to do or what other characters or the author say about them. The candidates must be observant here.

Appearance

Characters' physical appearance often gives a hint of their background and personality. Consider the characters' facial features, demeanour, physique, dress, etc. These speak volumes of the characters. For example, consider the appearance of clowns and jesters in Shakespearian plays and what it suggests of them in the development of the plays. Consider also the appearance of native rulers, oracles, doctors, witches and wizards, and occult members in African literature and see what colour it adds to the story. The candidates should not overlook these while reading them, as they are vital and contributory to the essence of the literary work.

Behaviour

Expressed or repeated behaviour, habits, or mannerisms often hint at a character's inner personality. The candidates must, of necessity, understand and interpret the behaviour and point out its significance in the text.

Background

History or background information about a character, or even the writer themselves, may provide useful hints about the character's social status and behaviour. For instance, the issue of corruption in post-independent Ghana formed the background of Ayi Kwei Armah's *The Beautyful Ones Are Not Yet Born*. It gave useful hints about the lives of the characters in the book.

Relationship with Others

The character qualities of an individual usually manifest when they interact with other people. The way other people relate to them equally points to their personality. The writer can impose character qualities: positive, negative or lukewarm, on a particular character in contrast with other characters.

Words and Thoughts

What a character says to other characters, to a large extent, reveals who they really are. A character's interior monologue – the extended or outward presentation of their thoughts – often hints at their inner self, and one can correctly predict or interpret their actions or character based on that fact.

➢ **Unseen Poetry**

The poetry section of the unseen literature exam requires the candidates to analyse a poem they probably had not come across before the exam. As such, they are expected not to have had a prior contextual (historical, cultural, social and biographical) understanding of the poem or the poet. In unseen poetry, the focus is usually on identifying and evaluating the formal elements of a poem, including point of view, language, poetic devices and form/structure. From these comes an examination or discussion of the poem's main theme and significance.

Procedure

- Read the poem at least twice. Read it aloud, if you can, but do not disturb other candidates.
- While reading, jot down or underline every observation, question, or feeling you get from the poem. Pay special attention to how the poem begins and ends.
- Ask yourself what elements in the poem lead you to a particular observation or conclusion and how the poet achieves this effect.
- Remember that the poet uses poetic devices to achieve particular effects. Breaking up the poem into formal poetic components enhances your understanding of its overall theme, tone, and/or general purpose.

Framework for Analysis

In analysing an extract, look out for the following:

- *Point of View*

Point of view can be identified by looking at the poet speaker (the voice or persona) and describing any part they play in the events of the narrative and any limits placed on their knowledge about the subject of the poem.

- Identify the characteristics of the speaker/poetic persona.
- Find out whether there is anything to suggest about the historical, cultural, or social background of the speaker/poetic persona.
- Find out the tone of the speaker's voice.
- Find out whether the perspective the persona takes in the poem is objective or subjective.
- Find out whether the persona suggests an omniscient or limited point of view.

- *Language*

Look closely at the language of the writer and determine whether it is descriptive or figurative.

- Descriptive Language: These are words or phrases that are descriptive or reportorial in nature. The readers are meant to interpret the language literally and determine why the poet chose to employ descriptive language.
- Figurative Language: These are words or phrases that depart from their literal or ordinary meanings. Figurative language employs metaphors, similes, symbols and a host of other poetic devices to communicate meaning to the readers. The candidates have to determine how the poet employed figurative language in the poem. They also have to determine the kinds of figures used (i.e. metaphors, similes, symbols, etc.) and how they relate to the poem's main theme.

- *Imagery*

This refers to a set of related images in a poem or the totality of images in the poem. Images are mental pictures created with words by poets in their poems. They are created through words or phrases that refer to sensory perceptions; it may be a visual picture, a sound, a tactile sensation, a taste or an odour/smell. Look closely at the passage and identify images (if any) in the poem. You can determine the kind of imagery used in the poem – visual, auditory or taste and the kind of emotions and experiences the imagery evokes on the subject.

- ***Patterned Nature of Language***

These are patterns in language created through rhyme, repetition, sound and metre (stressed and unstressed syllables). Identifying patterns is central to understanding how sound creates meaning in a poem. Determine how the patterns created through the language contribute to the meaning of the poem. Look closely at the passage and see if the poet made use of rhymes, repetition, alliteration, etc.

- ***Poetic Devices***
- Alliteration: Repetition of initial consonant sounds.
- Allusion: Direct quotes or indirect references to other poems.
- Assonance: Repetition of vowel sounds.
- Caesura: A pause in a line of verse dictated by sense or natural speech rhythm rather than by metrics.
- Enjambment: It is the continuation of a sentence without a pause beyond the end of a line, couplet or stanza. Often forms of the 'to be' verbs are used, such as 'is' or 'was', to make the comparison.
- Onomatopoeia: The use of words with kp sound.kkk abilities.
- Repetition: Using words, phrases, lines, or stanzas over and over.
- Rhyme: Similarity of ending sounds between two words.
- Simile: A comparison between two objects using a specific word of comparison such as 'like' or 'as.'

- *Form and Structure*

Poetic Forms: Look closely at the form of the poem. Poems are often written in a conventional form with pre-established structural rules. Some of these forms include: ballad, dramatic monologue, elegy, epic, free verse, haiku, idyll or pastoral, light verse, limerick, lyric, ode, narrative, sonnet and villanelle.

Rhyme Pattern

This is the sequence in which the rhymes occur. The first end sound is represented by the letter 'a', the second is represented by the letter 'b', etc. It also determines whether the rhyme is a couplet, triplet, quartet, etc.

- *Metre*

This is the recurrence of a pattern of stressed and unstressed syllables.

- *Stanza Structure*

This is a grouping of two or more lines of a poem in terms of length, metrical form, or rhyme scheme.

- *Formal Layout*

This is the shape that the poem takes on the page.

- *Motif*

A motif is a recurring type, object, setting or place in a literary work. It often creates a unifying association. It is not a theme but rather a symbol or an idea that is linked to the theme.

- *Theme*

The theme of a poem is its controlling idea. Readers find themes by reading or viewing a poem in a particular way. This way of reading or viewing involves looking at specific details in the poem and treating them as a general subject of interest. The themes we often see in literary works include but are not limited to the following:

Love	Power	Courage	Betrayal
Intolerance	Lust	Freedom	The Human Spirit
Greed	Innocence	Pride	Jealousy
Fate	Choice	Illusion/Reality	Prejudice
Hate	Cowardice	Fear	Chance
Corruption	Pride	Guilt	Wisdom
Ignorance	Loyalty	Faith	Deceit

Finally, it must be stressed that to do well in this aspect of the exam, candidates have to master the processes involved in interpreting, evaluating and analysing poems and passages.

> **Sample Questions and Answers on Unseen Literature**

I

'Such drizzling can go on for many days', she said in a dull voice. They both relapsed into silence, making a picture of bereaved children from whom life suddenly lost warmth, colour and excitement. There was no fire in the hearth.

The mood captured in this passage is one of:
A. Excitement
B. Warmth
C. Hopefulness
D. High Spirits
E. Sadness

Analysis

Mood refers to the atmosphere or the overall feelings aroused by words and sounds of a story, play, or poem. To identify the mood of a story, start with the setting, pay close attention to details of time and place, and ask yourself how the setting makes you feel. Look carefully at the writer's choice of words. Find out whether the story ends happily or whether it presents a sad, bitter or tragic outlook on life. Find out whether the passage makes you feel sad, amused or thoughtful. Mood can also be identified as gloomy, romantic, threatening, etc.

Now, from the above passage, consider the expressions: 'dull voice', 'relapsed in silence', 'a picture of bereaved children from whom life suddenly lost warmth, colour and excitement', and the last sentence: 'There was no fire in the hearth.' Can you figure out the overall feelings created by these expressions? Whatever you get is the mood of the passage. The choice of words by the writer can create a sorrowful or a not-very-happy mood. Option E, therefore, best captures the mood of the passage.

II

That year, the harvest was sad, like a funeral, and many farmers wept as they dug up the miserable yam. One man tied his cloth to a tree branch and hanged himself.

The mood conveyed in this passage is one of:

A. Excitement
B. Sadness
C. Joy
D. Elation
E. Triumph

Analysis

In trying to answer this question, the readers must consider the overall impression the passage makes on them. They may ask: How did the writer portray the subject? What mental picture did he create in the passage? Now, look at the writer's choice of words. He specifically used the word 'sad.' He also used the words 'funeral,' 'wept,' 'miserable,' and the phrase 'hanged himself.' Take a look at the words and see what picture they evoke in your mind. It cannot be that of excitement, joy, elation, or triumph. The author's words, both individually and when taken together, created a mood of sadness. Option B, therefore, best captures the mood of the passage.

III

The woods decay, the woods decay and fall.
The vapors weep their burthen to the ground.
Man comes and fills the field
And lies beneath,
And after many a summer dies
The swan.

The theme of these lines is:
A. The falling of leaves
B. The ground on which leaves fall
C. Man as a farmer
D. The power of death over every life
E. The flight of birds in certain seasons.

Analysis

In answering this question, the readers have to refer to the definition of theme as noted in this work. We stated that theme is the pre-occupation of the writer, or the central idea they want to convey to the readers in their work. Theme is what the writer wants the readers to derive from their composition.

Now, if you look at the above passage, you can see that the operative words from the lines are 'decay,' 'fall,' 'ground,' 'beneath,' and 'dies.' What do they suggest? Can you see a progression into nothingness or depreciation of the subjects: woods, vapors, man, and swan? The words suggest an end to the subjects. Therefore, the pre-occupation of the writer in the passage is the power of death, which overcomes every life or thing as stated in option D in the question.

IV

And the promised pleasure
Will never ever be found
In the face of vanished treasure,
In the face of plundered pound

Hidden beneath roots of greener grasses
In a land far from the masses.

The tone of the poem above is:

A. Interrogative
B. Persuasive
C. Optimistic
D. Pessimistic

Analysis

Can you recall our discussion on tone? We stated that it is an implied attitude of the poet or writer towards the subject matter. A question on the tone of a poem or passage demands to know the impression or attitude of the writer towards the theme or the subject matter of the passage. The issue raised is whether the writer is affectionate, hostile, earnest, playful, sarcastic, etc., towards the subject matter or theme. Whatever in a passage makes an attitude towards the subject matter clear to the readers. From the above passage, the operative phrase that sets the tone is: will never ever be found. What does it suggest regarding the attitude of the writer to the subject matter: the promised pleasure? Considering the overall word choice, we can undoubtedly say that the poet's tone is pessimistic, especially when the subject matter is placed side by side with the phrases: vanished treasure, plundered pound, hidden beneath roots, and a land far from the masses. Option D is, therefore, the correct answer.

V

My heart is a quiet drum;
Sometimes, it flares like a
Quiet drum
Cracking through a damask sky;
It lifts me in its fired spectacle.

The imagery in the excerpt above is:

A. Auditory and Visual
B. Tactile

C. Olfactory and Visual

D. Olfactory and Tactile

Analysis

As discussed in this work, images are details in a passage that trigger our memories, stimulate our senses and command our response. They may be visual (something seen), auditory or aural (something heard), olfactory (something smelt), tactile (something felt), thermal (heat), etc. A writer's words create images we can see with our mind's eye or feel with our senses. These images make us react in a particular way. Images are concrete representations of a sense impression, feeling or idea. Now, from the above piece, we have the expressions: *quiet drum, Cracking through,* which created auditory or aural images, and *flares like a damask sky, which fired spectacles* that created visual images. Therefore, option A is correct.

With these few instances and the analysis thereon, the students will be in a better position to appreciate the approach to overcoming the problems posed by unseen passages.

Chapter 8

Guide to Answering Essay Questions

Stay Composed
It is common to experience a sense of emptiness and anxiety in the days leading up to the examination despite thorough preparation. Do not succumb to panic, even if you encounter a moment of mental block during the test. Take a few deep breaths, compose yourself, and gather your thoughts before commencing the writing process. Have faith in your abilities, and your recollection will soon resurface.

It is imperative for candidates to unwind their minds a day or two prior to the examination. They should steer clear of anything that induces stress or apprehension. Being restless or agitated can undermine all the diligence and dedication invested in preparing for the exam. The following suggestions may prove beneficial:

Read Through the Questions
Take a few moments to carefully read the questions. Pay close attention to discern precisely what is being asked of you. Most essay questions are meticulously phrased, containing explicit instructions on what to write and how to structure your response. Address the questions as presented rather than veering off course.

Refrain from including irrelevant details that add no value but merely consume time.

Keep in mind that you are not asked to explain every aspect of the subject or the storyline of recommended texts. The question is focused and necessitates a response directly pertinent to it.

While scanning the question paper, potential answers may spontaneously come to mind. Jot them down promptly so you do not forget them. It may be beneficial to underline or highlight keywords or phrases in the question paper that point to the answer. This guides your thinking during the writing process.

Brainstorm regarding the question and the probable answer. Jot down everything you can recollect about the question asked. You may want to put these jottings down in brief or shorthand form, without any specific order, to prevent losing any valuable thoughts that can translate to an answer to the question. You can later arrange them in a more coherent manner. Upon reviewing your notes, consider organizing them in a structured manner.

Arrange your thoughts into a well-crafted essay by structuring the information you have gathered.

When composing your essay, start by outlining the key points and then elaborating on them in separate paragraphs. Even if you are unable to fully develop the outline later due to time constraints, some examiners might still award marks for the outline. In essence, plan your answers before putting them into writing. Take a moment to do this. Begin with the questions you feel most confident in addressing thoroughly, followed by those you are less certain about. This approach will help boost your confidence and maintain a steady pace.

Manage Your Time Well

To effectively manage time, candidates must hone their time management skills by practising with past exam papers regularly before the actual exam. The ability to think and write quickly is crucial in this context. Candidates can demonstrate fast thinking and writing only if they possess a comprehensive understanding of the subject matter. This is due to the fact that it typically takes less time to articulate thoughts on familiar topics compared to unfamiliar ones. This underscores the importance of having a deep understanding of the subject or text, as previously highlighted.

Developing the proficiency to write swiftly during an examination necessitates diligent and timed practice. Timed practice is typically executed using past question papers where candidates condition themselves to address all questions within a specified timeframe as if they were taking the actual exam. Candidates must engage in repeated practice sessions until they enhance their efficiency in addressing all questions promptly. Candidates are advised to allocate a few minutes at the commencement of each question to outline the essential points for their answers. Additionally, they should allocate some time at the conclusion to meticulously review and refine their answers.

Essay questions do not allow for guesswork but necessitate candidates to showcase their knowledge, writing prowess, and impeccable spelling and grammar. The candidates require ample time to tackle the stipulated number of questions in the paper and craft their answers well. However, time constraints often plague them during exams, resulting in written answers inadequately as they feel rushed and unable to organize and proofread their answers thoroughly.

Despite operating under pressure, candidates must allocate a few minutes to strategize their time effectively. Swift thinking and writing are essential to address all the required questions within the examination's time frame. Proficiency in time management is paramount. Crafting a time schedule is crucial to determining the allocation of minutes to each question based on the total examination duration.

The distribution of time is typically predicated on the complexity of the questions and the total marks assigned by the examiner. Candidates must allocate more time to questions with higher mark values or those demanding greater effort. In cases where questions carry equal marks, equal time must be allotted to each to ensure comprehensive coverage. Candidates should not neglect one question at the expense of another. Prioritizing questions they are most adept at is advisable. For instance, if four questions must be answered within an hour, allotting 10 minutes to each question is prudent. Upon completion of the time allocated to a question, candidates must move on promptly to the next one. Upon completion of the final question, twenty minutes might remain, enabling candidates to revisit partially answered questions and finalize or fine-tune their responses to them.

Good Writing: Write Neatly and Present Your Answers Well

When students or candidates write neatly and present their answers well, they have more chances of scoring high marks. Good writing is writing well and leading the readers clearly into one's thoughts. The main characteristic of good writing is clarity. It requires telling in a written form what you know or have in mind in short, lucid and logical sentences. In an examination, writing well involves expressing your answers clearly on paper in such a way as to help the examiner fully appreciate your knowledge as expressed.

Another aspect of good writing is having good handwriting. Candidates must have good and readable handwriting. Your handwriting must be legible so the examiner does not need to strain their eyes to be able to read your script. This is because there are other scripts waiting to be attended to by the examiner, and they may not be prepared to allow extra time for your script. You will lose marks if the examiner is unable to read your script due to bad or illegible handwriting. Your handwriting should be English and look like it, and not look like Chinese or Arabic to an English examiner.

Note that the examiner reading your script does not see through your mind. They can only see what you have in mind by what you have written in your script. You must, therefore, spell out what you have in mind by writing it clearly and legibly and explaining what you mean in your script. Be clear, develop your points, and do not assume that the examiner will understand what you have in mind or want to write. Lead them not only through your argument but also by convincing them that you are sure of what you are saying by backing it up with evidence drawn from the text. This makes your argument stand out and more forceful, and your script becomes worthy of high marks.

Note also that your first sentence must catch the examiner's attention. It should bear some relation to the issue in the question and indicate the direction of your argument.

Write in short and direct sentences. Each sentence should carry one point so that the meaning moves along in clear-cut steps. Do not introduce unnecessary points or phrases that add nothing to the desired answer.

Choose your words well and carefully. Use the right words that say what you have in mind. Do not ramble. Do not carry excess baggage; do not use unnecessary words; elaborate, but not unnecessarily or excessively, in order to impress your examiner. Go straight to the point. Say enough to make yourself clear.

Effective Argument

Remember that what is important is not just what you write but how well you write or present your points. The use of the right and effective argument is essential in your answers. An effective argument is one that drives your points home. This involves proper blending and adaptation of your personal view with that of the writer in answering a question. By this, we mean stating a point or an idea you picked up from the text while adding or offering your personal opinion or interpretation through proper analysis. However, where the question demands that you contrast the argument of the writer, be sure that you present a clear contrasting argument in opposition to the writer's. Say succinctly all you need to say on not agreeing with him.

Put down your thoughts carefully and ensure you do not miss important points while answering the questions. Present your points in sequence, each logically connected to the other and leading up to a conclusion.

Note again that you must back up analytical points with appropriately selected information and evidence from the text. The examiner needs to be convinced that you read the texts and that you were prepared for the exam.

Effective Communication

Effective communication is closely related to good writing and effective argument. A candidate can only communicate to the examiner what they know about a question through writing. How well they express their thoughts on paper matters a great deal. Communication between a candidate and the examiner cannot be said to have taken place just because the candidate had written something. The examiner needs to understand what the candidate has written. If there is a dislocation here, no communication will take place; the question will remain unanswered, and vital marks will be lost. The late literary icon Chinua Achebe alluded to this fact when, in his book, *There Was A Country*, he stated: "The triumph of the written word is often attained when the writer achieves union and trust with the reader..." Union and trust with the reader here refer to effective communication between the writer and the reader (and, in our case, between the candidate and the examiner). This requires the candidate to write well in terms of constructing and punctuating their sentences well and correctly. They must be clear, simple, and to the point. Thus, the writer writes, and the reader understands, and in our case, the candidate writes, and the examiner understands. Candidates must choose their words carefully and appropriately. The words they use in their essay questions may either make or mar their chances of success on the exam. Any word or expression they are not so sure of its meaning or its correct usage should be avoided. They must also keep their sentences short and simple.

Demonstrate Understanding

Candidates write essay exams in Literature-in-English to demonstrate their knowledge and writing skills. They not only convey information but also prove to the examiner that they have mastered the subject and the texts and that they can use the knowledge derived from the text skillfully in writing. In other words, their purpose should be both informative and persuasive. Candidates must demonstrate an understanding of the texts and literary skills through personal and creative interpretation and analytical criticism. To do well in this regard, they must avail themselves of all the skills and competencies necessary for the interpretation of the texts relevant to the exam. Wrong interpretation of the texts not only begets wrong answers but also presents them as poor candidates and the ones unworthy of the examiner's pass or high marks. Interpreting the questions correctly ensures that they will not write out of context but to answer them correctly.

A candidate's answers need not be 'yes or 'no' at times. It can be a 'maybe' or 'it depends on' or 'partly yes' and 'partly no'. It can still be 'yes but' or 'yes unless' or a variety of other responses and their backup argument. The key thing is to demonstrate an understanding of the question asked and answer it well enough with evidence drawn from the text and with a proper argument.

Use good writing skills and strategies while answering the questions. Make your main points stand out by keeping them in distinct paragraphs. Keep in mind that your purpose is to persuade the examiner that you know the subject.

Make your answers clear, concise and coherent. Be sure of your facts while answering the questions. When you are in doubt, drop the point.

Ensure your answers are direct, to the point and satisfactory to the examiner.

Use of Present Tense

In the exam, you will often need to write about a poem, a novel, a short story, an essay, or a play. In doing so, you may use present or past tense. You may write either in the present or in the past tense but not in both at the same time. You must be consistent with your tenses unless you have good reasons to vary them. It is conventional to use present tense in describing what happens within a literary work (that is, the actions of characters) and past tense to describe actions that took place in the past and what the author did or said. For instance, in answering a question based on

Achebe's work, *The Problem with Nigeria,* candidates can present their answer thus:

'Chinua Achebe's *The Problem with Nigeria* reflects on the failure of leadership and emphasises that unless our leaders get it right, the nation will for long remain in its present state of hopelessness and want. The writer portrayed public officeholders as individuals lacking the statesmanship necessary to put the country on the right track.'

The present tense was used to describe the narrator's actions of 'reflecting' and 'emphasising', while the past tense 'portrayed' was used to describe the action of the author.

'Bertolt Brecht's *Galileo* points to a preference for scientific evidence and reliance on the senses over dogmatic assumptions that rely on imagination and reasoning. While displaying a strong conviction that the new cosmology gives man only peripheral importance, whereas the old cosmology had given him a central role, some of Brecht's characters reveal a deep-rooted preference for the former. Brecht made use of characters sharply contrasted along the divides of sense and imagination.'

The verbs describing what the play did were in the present tense, while those describing what Brecht did were in the past tense.

Good Punctuation

Punctuation in the English language helps the readers understand a sentence through visual means. It structures the written language graphically by means of a set of conventional marks. It creates sense, clarity and stress in a sentence. It makes our point in a sentence stand out. A good understanding of the use of punctuation marks is essential, and the students or candidates must master them. Without punctuation, or with poor punctuation, the real or intended meaning of a sentence may not come out well or at all. Consider these sentences:

You need not engage only in sports music business politics etc to be famous in today's Nigeria i think ill flirt with info-tech broadcasting and movie making.

Now, let's see the difference after punctuating the above sentence!

You need not engage only in sports, music, business, politics, etc., to be famous in today's Nigeria. I think I'll flirt with info-tech, broadcasting, and movie-making.

The difference between the two sentences is clear. Without punctuation or with poor punctuation, our sentences will scarcely make any sense. No examiner awards marks to candidates whose sentences make no sense because of bad or no punctuation. Good punctuation gives credit to mechanical accuracy.

Avoid Using Contractions

Contractions such as don't', 'can't, 'won't, 'wouldn't', etc., which are normal in speech-language, are not appropriate in written exams and formal writing. Always write and spell them in full.

Revision of Written Answers

Take time to read through your script at the end before handing in your script. Usually, while writing in a hurry, as we do in exams, we tend to misspell words, omit words, punctuations, articles, prepositions, verbs, etc., forget to answer parts of a question, mistake or misstate dates and omit figures. It is good to take some time to revise all your answers. No matter how time-pressed or how sure you are with your answers, try and go through your work a second or even a third time before handing your script to the exam invigilator. This is to forestall surrendering your vulnerable script to the examiner when you have not fully satisfied the demands of the questions asked or when it is replete with errors and omissions that could have been corrected had you taken time to go through your work before submitting it to the invigilator.

Candidates must realise that there is no prize, additional mark or incentive for those who finish the exam or submit their scripts earlier than others. The first to submit exam scripts is not necessarily the most intelligent one. What the examiner cares about is what they see on your script and what you have put down correctly on your answer script, and not what you intended but failed or inadvertently omitted to write. Therefore, be sure to read through your answers carefully. The errors can be wrong grammar or expression, spelling, tenses, omissions of words, prepositions, punctuations, and non-use or misuse of capital letters. Check if you completely answered all the questions and their sub-units or numbers required of you. It is better to go back and check for these rather than hurrying out of the exam hall earlier than others to your own failure or detriment.

For instance, the omission of verbs such as 'is', 'was', 'are', 'were' etc.; prepositions such as 'in', 'from', 'to', 'out,' 'of,' 'on' etc; articles such as 'a', 'the,' 'an'; conjunctions such as 'and', 'but', 'or,' etc. can gravely alter a sentence and thus, rob it of the intended meaning it was meant to have. Therefore, unless you have time to go through your work and correct the errors and omissions, your write-up will be meaningless, and all your efforts will be rendered futile as you are bound to lose marks. In the long run, this jeopardises your chances of success at the exam.

Further, confirm that you spelt the author's names correctly. Also, confirm that you stated the poem or book titles correctly before moving to the next question or submitting your script to the invigilator. At the foot of every answer, you may leave some lines or space to which you may return later to squeeze in points you might have omitted earlier. This can boost your marks.

In the case of multiple-choice questions, go through the questions and their answer options again. Check whether there is a need to change any of the chosen options, especially those for which you are not very sure of their answers. Make up your mind whether to retain the answers or to change them and respond accordingly.

Never Cheat in Exam Hall

Students and candidates are strongly advised against taking part in any form of exam malpractice. It is harmful to the image of the student. If, for any reason, the candidate is not ready for the exam or does not know the answers sufficiently, they should nevertheless attempt the questions as much as they can. They can also decide to withdraw from the exam. It is more honourable to fail or withdraw from the exam and repeat it later than to pass by fraudulent means. Again, it will be a disaster if they are caught and disgraced by the invigilators for indulging in exam malpractice. Instructively, we must always remember Nelson Mandela's famous statement, which posits that destroying any nation does not require the use of atomic bombs or the use of long-range missiles. It only requires lowering the quality of education and allowing students to cheat in examinations.

To ensure high marks, you must prove to the examiner that:

- You have comprehensively addressed all questions asked.
- Your answers are derived from the recommended texts.
- You have provided supporting evidence for your responses through quotes from the texts; if you paraphrase, it must be done convincingly to demonstrate familiarity with the texts.
- You possess a thorough understanding of the writer's ideas and/or message(s).
- Your essay is predominantly written in your own original language rather than relying excessively on quoted text.
- Your analysis is logically structured and coherent.
- The style of writing adopted in your essay remains objective and analytical throughout its entirety.

- The evidence presented in support of your arguments is appropriate and relevant to the question asked.
- Your essay demonstrates proficiency in English language usage, clarity, and coherence.

If these criteria are met consistently across your write-up, you can expect to receive an excellent grade on your exam paper!

Chapter 9

Selected Literary Terms, Concepts and Principles

Literary terms and principles are used in the realm of literature and general literary discourse. They are used in a specially defined or understood sense. They are used to express, classify, analyze and interpret works of literature.

The entries included in this chapter are some of those that commonly feature in Literature-in-English examinations of WAEC, NECO and JAMB in Nigeria and elsewhere in English-speaking West Africa. They include:

1. Absurd Literature

This term applies to literary works that portray the human condition as essentially absurd. Writers in this aspect of literature feel that this condition can be adequately represented only in works of literature that are themselves absurd.

Examples: Alfred Jarry's *Uburoi (Ubu the King), 1896*, Camus' *The Myth of Sisyphus, 1942*, Samuel Beckett's *Waiting For Godot, 1954*.

According to Martin Esslin, these works project their rationalism, helplessness and absurdity of life in dramatic or prosaic forms that reject realistic settings, logical reasoning, or a coherently evolving plot. See *Theatre of the Absurd* (New York: Doubleday, 1967), pp.-7.

For absurdist dramatists, man is not understandable, and life is disorderly and chaotic. To them, experience is meaningless, and existence is purposeless. They portray human beings as irrational, pathetic figures and helpless against life's chaos. To them, man's absurd conditions can best be captured and presented only in works equally absurd.

According to Robert Di Yanni, absurdist plays rely on and even go beyond abrupt changes of direction and tone to create their effects. The dominant theme of many of the dramas is the inadequacy of language to serve the ends of human understanding. They illustrate the breakdown of language as an instrument of communication.

2. Act and Scene

An act is a major division in the action of a play. A scene is a sub-division of an act. It consists of units of action in which there is no change of place or break in the continuity of time.

3. Action

This refers to what characters do in works of drama or play or on stage.

4. Adventure Novel

This is a novel where exciting events are more important than character development and sometimes theme. It emphasizes adventure above every other purpose or end of literary works. **Example:** Alexander Dumas' *The Three Musketeers*.

5. Aesthetic Distance

This is used to define the detachment with the actions and fortunes of characters represented in a work of literature.

6. Affective Fallacy

This is the error of evaluating a poem by its effects, especially its emotional impact on the readers.

7. Allegory

This is a narrative, in prose or verse, in which the agents and actions, and sometimes, the setting, are cleverly made to make coherent sense literally and at the same time to communicate a second, correlated signification. It is a literary work in which characters, settings and events stand for abstract ideas or moral qualities. Allegorical characters are often one-dimensional since they are meant to represent only a particular aspect of human nature. An Allegory can be read on one level for its literal meaning and on a second level for its symbolic or allegorical meaning. **Example:** In *Pilgrim Progress* (1678) by John Buyan, Christian, on his journey to the Celestial City, meets personages such as Mr. Worldly Wiseman, Hopeful and Giant Despair and travels to places such as the Slough of Despond, The Valley of Humiliation and Doubting Castle.

Other examples are John Dryden's *Absalom and Achitohel* (1681), Edmund Spenser's *The Faerie Queene*, and John Milton's *Paradise Lost.*

8. Historical and Political Allegory

In this type of allegory, characters and actions are made to represent historical or political personages and events.

9. Allegories of Ideas

Here, literal characters represent concepts, and the plot represents an abstract doctrine. The central device here is the personification of abstract entities such as virtue, vice, state of mind, mode of life and type of character.

10. Apologue

This is a moral fable, usually involving personified animals or inanimate objects which act like human beings to allow the author to comment on human conditions.
Examples: George Orwell's *Animal Farm*, Rudyard Kipling's *The Jungle Book*

11. Allonym

A literary work published under a name other than the author's name (penname).
Example: Eric Blair's *Animal Farm* was published with the penname George Orwell.

12. Autonym

A literary work published under the real name of the author.

13. Parable

A short narrative about human beings presented as an analogy stressing or highlighting the lesson the narrator is trying to bring home to their audience.

Example: Jesus Christ's parables of *The Good Samaritan,* and *The Prodigal Son, etc.*

14. Examplum

This is a story told as a particular instance of the general theme in a religious sermon.

Example: Chaucer's *The Pardoner's Tale*

15. Proverb

This is a short, pithy statement of widely accepted truth about everyday life. It is allegorical in nature because the explicit statement is meant to have, by analogy or by extended reference, a general application.

Examples: *A stitch in time saves nine, People living in glass houses should throw no stones.*

16. Alliteration

Alliteration is a technique in poetry involving the repetition of consonant sounds at the beginning of a sequence of nearby words, for example, two words on the same line of a poem. The emphasis is usually on sound rather than on the letter itself.

Example:

In a somer season, when soft was the sun – The consonant "s" alliterates in the line.

When to the seasons of sweet, silent thought

I summon up remembrance of things past

And with old woes new wail my dear time's waste…

s, th and w consonants alliterate in the above Shakespeare's Sonnet 30.

17. Consonance

Also called slant rhyme, it is a kind of rhyme in which the linked words share similar consonant sounds but different vowel sounds.

It is the repetition of consonant sounds anywhere within words.

Examples: Live-love, lean-alone, pitter-patter, reason-raisin, mink-monk, gloomy-woman.

Sometimes, only the final consonant sound is identical, as in fame-room and crack-truck.

18. Assonance

This is the repetition of two or more identical or similar initial vowel sounds in successive words (close to each other), which creates a kind of rhyme. This repetition occurs within syllables with changing consonants. It is a direct opposite of alliteration.

Example:

All the awful auguries.
Watch your stopwatch.
The tide rises, the tide falls
The twilight darkens, the
Curlew calls.
Please bake me a date cake.

19. Allusion

Allusion is an inexplicit identification and passing reference to a literary or historical person, place, event, or another literary work in a literary work. It is a reference, in a literary work, to something outside the immediate scope of that being presented. The reference is either direct or indirect and to someone or something well-known from history, literature, religion, politics, sports, science, or some other branch of culture outside a literary work. It may refer to another work of literature or events or persons in history, art, or contemporary life. When writers make allusions, they expect their readers to recognize the reference.

Example:

In Thomas Nashe's *Litany in Time of Plague:*
Brightness falls from the air,
Queens have died young and fair,
Dust hath closed Helen's eye.
In the above, "Helen" in the last line alludes to Helen of Troy.

Types of Allusion

- Biblical Allusion: This is a reference, in literary works, to stories or materials from the Bible.
- Literary Allusion: This is an allusion to a literary work.
- Classical Allusion: This is an allusion to classical works – i.e. works by ancient Roman and Greek authors or their themes.
- Historical Allusion: This allusion is derived from history. To be effective, the object alluded to must be notable.

20. Anachronism

This is the deliberate placing of an event, a person or a thing outside its historical era or period.

Example: In *Julius Caesar,* set in ancient Rome, Shakespeare introduced a clock that strikes the hour, when for sure clock was not invented at the time of Caesar.

21. Anagnorisis

This is the discovery or recognition by the protagonist of something of great importance hitherto unknown to them.

Example: In the drama *The Gods Are Not To Blame,* this happened when King Odewala suddenly discovered that he was the cause of the calamities that befell his kingdom.

22. Anaphora

This is a deliberate repetition of a word or phrase at the beginning of each line of a sequence of sentences, paragraphs, lines of verse, or stanza.

Example:

Tell them that proclaim untimely death,
Tell them that upset the pillars of hell
Tell them that they are not home yet with
The dispatch of him the god's worship…

–   Echoes of Vengeance, Basil Nwokorie

23. Anecdote

This is an unelaborated narration of a single incident or episode. It differs from a short story, which, in contrast, organizes the action, thought and dialogue of its characters into the artful pattern of a plot directed towards a particular effect on an audience. Anecdotes are often humorous and can either be real or fictional. Anecdotes can be incidents whose focus is primarily on the course and outcome of events.

24. Ballad

Traditionally, a ballad is a song or verse that tells a story. The story is told in monologue or dialogue form and usually has a simple, steady rhythm, a simple rhyme pattern, and a refrain, all of which make it easy to memorize.

The stanzas are short. Sometimes, the last line is repeated from verse to verse.

Folk Ballads are usually transmitted from generation to generation or performer to performer without being written down.

Literary Ballads are written to imitate the sounds and subjects of Folk Ballads.

Long ago, all ballads were sung. While many ballads were sad and eerie, others were funny.

25. Antagonist

This is an important opponent of a central character or protagonist in a work of prose or drama.

Example: In *Hamlet,* Prince of Denmark, King Claudius is the antagonist to Hamlet, the protagonist.

26. Villain

This is an antagonist that is evil or capable of cruel and criminal actions.

27. Foil

This is a character in a literary work which, by sharp contrast, serves to stress or highlight the distinctive character or temperament of the protagonist. This character or temperament is usually weak and demeaning on the public image or perception of the protagonist.

Example: In *Pride and Prejudice,* the gentle and compliant Jane Benet serves as a foil to her strong-willed sister, Elizabeth. Note that a foil is not an antagonist, but their attributes contrast those of the protagonist.

28. Intrigue

This is a scheme by a character that depends on the ignorance or gullibility of the person against whom it is directed.

29. Suspense

This is a state of uncertainty and curiosity on the part of a concerned reader or audience about the future course of events and actions or what is going to happen next to the characters with whom the readers or audience have established a bond of sympathy. It has been described as one of the hooks a writer uses to keep the audience or reader glued till the end of the story.

30. Surprise

When a certain event surpasses our expectations about a story or plot, it is called a surprise. It is also referred to as the shock of the unexpected.

Dramatic irony is a special kind of suspenseful expectation when the audience or reader foresees the impending disaster or triumph, but the concerned character does not.

31. Sub-Plot

This is a secondary plot or second story in a story that is complete and interesting in its own right introduced into a play or prose. It is also an arrangement of incidents that do not involve the protagonist but someone less important.

Example: Comic reliefs in some plays are sub-plots. See *Falstaff* in *Henry IV*.

32. Exposition

This is the opening portion of a plot, drama, or narrative in which the writer introduces the characters, the setting and the problems and discloses other background information about the characters necessary to allow the readers to understand and relate to the events that are to follow.

It is also a representative incident related to and closely preceding the event which precipitates or gives rise to the central situation or conflict in the story. In another aspect, exposition is one of the four major forms of discourse in non-fiction.

33. Climax

This is the moment of greatest intensity and interest in a story, which inevitably occurs towards the end of the story. It often involves an important event, decision, or discovery that affects the outcome of the story. It often takes the form of a decisive confrontation between the protagonist and the antagonist.

In another aspect, climax is the opposite of both bathos and anti-climax. Here, we have the arrangement of items or expressions in order of importance, where a writer moves from the deep up to the cliff, from "Nothingness" to "Somethingness." The effect is to arouse suspense in the listener, reader or audience.

Example: Mezie came to school, took his lessons, wrote his exams and obtained his school certificate.

34. Anti-climax

This refers to an unsatisfying and trivial turn of events in a literary work that occurs in place of a genuine climax involving a surprising shift in tone from the serious to the petty or ridiculous. Sometimes, the writers deliberately drop from the serious and elevated to the trivial and lowly to achieve a comic or satiric effect. It is also an arrangement of ideas in such a way that an unimpressive item is put at the end, following some items which are more significant. When done deliberately, it usually has a satirical or humorous effect. In most cases, it is used to deflate what is ordinarily gallantry or highly placed.

Example:

Love your country; tell the truth; and don't dawdle.
A better cavalier ne'er mounted a horse,
Or, being mounted, e'er got down again.

It can also be an arrangement of ideas, items or events in descending order.

She lost her husband, her daughter, and her wallet.
"Tis for the sake of the future of Nigeria, for our children and grandchildren, that I feel it is important to tell Nigeria's story, Biafra's story, our story, my story."

– *There Was A Country*, Chinua Achebe

35. Bathos

In literature, bathos refers to a sudden and unintentional descent or change (in speech or writing) while trying to be pathetic, passionate, or elevated. The writer overshoots the mark and drops from a serious subject into the trivial, the ridiculous, silly or unimportant.

Example: *Gods! Annihilate both space and time and make two lovers happy.*

Note: Anti-climax is sometimes employed as the equivalent of bathos. However, it is non-derogatory, while bathos is derogatory.

36. Dark Romantics

This is a group of 19th-century writers who explored the conflict between good and evil by delving into the dark side of human nature. They include Edgar Allan Poe, Nathaniel Hawthorne and Herman Melville. In contrast with the optimistic nature of the Transcendentalist writers, the Dark Romantics explored the potentially evil side of humanity, hinging on the psychological effects of guilt, sin and madness in the human psyche.

37. Anti-Hero

A protagonist who is lacking in one or more of the conventional qualities attributed to a hero. Instead of being dignified, brave, idealistic or purposeful, for instance, the anti-hero may be cowardly, self-centred or weak.

38. Empathy

This signifies the identification of oneself totally with an observed person or object that is so close that one seems to participate in the posture, motion and sensations that one observes. It is an involuntary projection of oneself into another person or object and sharing all that happens to them with them.

Example:

The snail, whose tender horns being hit,
Shrinks backward in his shelly cave with pain.

–   Venus and Adonis, Shakespeare

39. Sympathy

This denotes fellow feeling. It deals with the mental state and emotions of another.

Note that there is a difference between empathy and sympathy. While empathy involves feeling or projecting oneself into the physical state and sensation of another person or thing, sympathy involves feeling along with the mental state of another human being or non-human being to which we attribute human emotions.

40. Anti-thesis

Anti-thesis is a contrast or opposition in the meaning of words, clauses or phrases lying beside or next to each other that manifest parallelism. It balances opposing ideas, tones, or structures, usually to heighten the effect of a statement. In anti-thesis, there are always two statements, one of which is always in contrast with the other.

Examples:

- Resolved to win, he meditates the way.
- By force to ravish, or by fraud betray.
- Marriage has many pains, but celibacy has no pleasures.
- Man proposes, but God disposes.
- To err is human, but to forgive is divine.

Note that anti-thesis and oxymoron may look similar in that they place opposites or contrasts together, but their difference lies in the fact that in anti-thesis, words or thoughts are balanced in contrast, while in oxymoron, words are combined to form expressive phrases or epithets. Again, oxymoron is more or less a phrase and not a complete sentence like an anti-thesis.

41. Aphorism

This is a brief, cleverly worded statement that makes a wise observation about life. It involves humour, wit and wordplay. It suggests ways to overcome obstacles, solve problems, inspire, and often provide a kind of moral uplift.

Examples:

- *Art is long, life is short*
- *Love your neighbour; yet don't pull down your hedge.*
- *If a man empties his purse into his head, no man can take it away from him. An investment in knowledge always pays the best interest.*
- *Three may keep a secret only if two of them are dead.*
- *If you know the value of money, go and try to borrow some; he that goes a-borrowing goes a-sorrowing.*
- *A ploughman on his legs is higher than a gentleman on his knees.*

- *Keep your eyes wide open before marriage, half shut afterwards.*

42. Archaism

This is the literary use of words and expressions that have become obsolete in the common speech of the current era.

Example: Overwrought, methink, morn, steed, thou, mayest, thine, etc.

43. Aside

This is a device in which a character expresses their thoughts or intentions to the audience in a short speech, which, by convention, is inaudible to the other characters on stage.

Example:

In the play *Macbeth,* the protagonist, Macbeth, stated in the presence of Banquo: *"The Prince of Cumberland: that is a step on which I must fall..."* Banquo did not hear Macbeth make the statement and did not respond to it. It was made to reveal to the audience or readers what was going on in the speaker's mind.

44. Soliloquy

In drama, this denotes the convention by which a character, alone on stage, utters their thoughts aloud. This gives the audience insight into the character's inner life, private motivations and uncertainties.

Example:

"Pardon me, thou piece of earth,
That I am meek and gentle with these butchers!
Thou art the ruins of the noblest man
That ever lived in the tide of times."

– Mark Anthony, in Julius Caesar

45. Author

An author is an individual who, based on their experience and reading, purposefully creates a literary work that is distinctively their own through their intellectual and imaginative powers.

46. Biography

This connotes a written account of a particular person's life and experience.

Example:

Parallel Lives by Greek writer Plutarch documented the lives and times of notable Greek and Roman citizens. This was the source of Shakespeare's plays on Roman subjects. For instance, *Julius Caesar*.

See also *Lives of the English Poets* (1779-81) by Samuel Johnson.

47. Author Biography

This is a biography written by the subject about themselves.

48. Memoir

This is a record of people and events that the author has known or witnessed. It is a type of autobiography often focusing on a specific time period or historical event and telling the story from the author's point of view.

49. Diary

A record of day-to-day events in one's life written for personal use and satisfaction with little or no thought of publication.

50. Blank Verse

This is a poem consisting of unrhymed lines of iambic pentameter (that is, five-stress iambic verse). It is blank because there is no rhyme scheme.

51. Iambic

The adjective 'iambic' relates to rhythm in poetry. It is derived from the noun 'iamb,' which means an unstressed, short or weak syllable followed by a stressed, long or stressed syllable.

Example: *The cur/few tolls /the knell/of par/ting day*

52. Bombast

This denotes a wordy and inflated diction that is patently dispassionate to the matter that it signifies. The words used sound high and important but have little meaning and are only meant to impress people.

Example: *Now by kingdoms infernal rule of styx, Acheron, and the fiery lake of ever-burning Phlegethon, I swear that I do long to see the monuments and situation of bright-spendent Rome.*

Here, Christopher Marlowe succeeded only in saying, "By Hades, I'd like to see Rome."

53. Bibliography

It refers to studies devoted to the identification of the authorship, dates of issue, and editions and physical properties of books.

54. Bowdlerize

To delete from an edition of a literary work the passages that are considered indecent for a target audience or readers.

Example: Removing materials from a book is likely to trigger immoral thoughts to make it suitable for children to read without the risk of corrupting their young and innocent minds.

55. Burlesque

This is an imitation of a serious work of literature in terms of form and style, or the subject matter of a serious literary work or genre, in verse or prose, by making the imitation amusing in terms of a ridiculous disparity between the form or style and the subject matter. The imitator does this by treating the high and exalted form, style, subject matter, etc., in a trivial way or by discussing the trivial in exalted terms or mock dignity. This imitation is done for the sheer fun of it. It is a form of satire.

56. Parody

This is an imitation of the serious manner and characteristic features of a particular literary work or the distinctive style of a particular author, or the style and other features of a serious literary genre and deflates the original by applying the imitation to a lowly or comically inappropriate subject. A parody typically exaggerates distinctive features of the original work for humor or comic effect.

57. Mock Epic or Mock-Heroic

This is a parody in verse that sustainably imitates both the elaborate form and the ceremonious style of the epic genre but applies them to narrate a commonplace or trivial subject matter.
Example: Alexander Pope's *The Rape of the Lock (1714)*

58. Travesty

This is a form of burlesque that mocks a particular work by treating its lofty subject in an undignified manner and style.

59. Lampoon

This is a short satirical work or a passage in a longer work that describes the appearance and character of a particular person in a way that makes that person look ridiculous. It makes use of caricature.

60. Caricature

This is a verbal description that exaggerates or distorts, for comic effect, a person's distinctive physical features or personality traits.
Example:
In John Dryden's *Absalom and Achitohel (1681):*
"In the first rank of these, did Zimri stand?
A man so various that he seemed to be
Not one, but all mankind's epitome:
Stiff in opinions, always in the wrong;
Was everything by starts, and nothing long..."

61. Euphony

This refers to language that is smooth, pleasant and musical to the ear.

Example:
In John Keats' *The Eve of St. Agnes (1820):*
"And lucent strops, tinct with cinnamon;
Manna and dates, in argosy, transferred
From fez and spiced dainties, everyone,
From silken Samarcand to cedar'd Lebanon."

62. Cacophony or Dissonance

This refers to language (or a group of words) that is perceived to be harsh, rough, unmusical, or discordant to the ear. Discordance is not only of the sound but also of its significance.

Example:
In Robert Browning's *Pied Piper (1842):*
"Rats!
They fought the dogs and killed the cats…
Split open the kegs of salted sprats,
Made nest inside men's Sunday hats;"

63. Catastrophe

This usually applies to tragedy only. It denotes the outcome that is decided by the death of the hero.

64. Denouement

This term applies to both tragedy and comedy. It means the unknotting of the plot, where the conflicts are settled, the mystery is resolved, and the action or intrigue ends in success or failure for the protagonist. At this point, all the questions raised by the plot are answered.

65. Resolution

This is the final part of a narrative, the concluding action or actions that follow the climax, where the conflicts are settled, the mystery is resolved, or the misunderstanding is cleared away. It is a frequently used alternative term for the outcome of a plot.

66. Characters

These are the persons represented in a dramatic or narrative work who are interpreted by the readers as possessing particular moral, intellectual and emotional qualities by inferences from what they say and their distinctive way of saying them. Characters are agents of action in a work of art. They perform the actions in the work. A writer tells us about a character by telling us directly about the character, that is, whether they are generous, mean, sneaky, easy-going, etc., by describing how the character looks or dresses, by letting us hear the character speak, by revealing the character's effect or influence on other characters – showing how other characters feel or behave toward them, and by showing the character in action.

67. Characterization

This is the technique or method a writer uses to create, reveal, develop, or present fictional individuals in a narrative or work. This is also the examination of the different angles through which a writer presents the character traits of the individuals inhabiting the world of their story. There are four main methods that writers use in this regard:

- The appearance of the character or looks – which conveys something about what kind of persona the character is.
- The character's thoughts, speech and actions – What a character thinks, says, and does tell a lot about the kind of person they are.
- What other characters say about the character throws light on their personality.
- Direct statement made by the author about the character also reveals their personality.

68. Dialogue

This is what characters say on stage to one another. It has three major functions: it advances the plot, establishes the setting (time and space of action) and reveals character. It is one major narrative technique shared by both novels and dramas.

69. Flat Character

This is also known as a type or two-dimensional character. They are built around a single idea or quality, presented without much individualizing detail, and can be described adequately in a single phrase or sentence.

70. Round Character

This character is complex in temperament and motivation and is represented with subtle particularity. It is difficult to adequately describe them as a person in real life. Because of their unpredictable character, they are capable of surprising us.

71. Stereotyped Character

This character has more than one personality trait and is presented in a predictable way. They are usually used for comic effect and are not capable of surprising the audience or the readers.

72. Stock Characters

They are common or stereotypical characters that occur repeatedly in a particular literary genre. They are recognized as part of the conventions of the form.

Example: In the old comedy of the Greeks, we have the *alazon* (Impostor), *eiron* (self-derogatory and understating character), and the *bomolochos* (comic character).

Further examples are the mad scientist, the battle-scared veteran, or the strong but silent cowboy.

73. Choral Character

This is a character within a play which stands apart from the action and, through their comments, provides the audience with a special perspective on the other characters and events.

74. Refrain

This is a word, phrase, line or stanza repeated at intervals in a song or poem. This repetition not only affects the sound of a poem but also emphasizes important ideas and builds up certain feelings and expectations. If the refrain occurs in a song, it is called a chorus.

Example: *'there I lie'* in Lenri Peters' *The Fence.*

75. Chorus

This is a refrain in songs or poems. It can also refer to a group of people who stand on one side of the action of a drama and comment on the events as they unfold without participating in it.

Example:

In *Othello,* the sinister Iago speaks and comments on the events.

In Ola Rotimi's *Ovonramwen Nogbaisi,* the choral character delivers a song-like rendition which contains information that gives the readers a clue as to the mood or situations in the play, especially as it relates to the protagonist, Ovonramwen Nogbais. See the following passages as illustrations from the play:

1. "If I survive this one.
If indeed I survive this one,
I will lavish thanks upon
My maker;
For many a suffering have I
Known, but this one is the father of them all!"

2. "How could I know?
How could I know that
This would ever be
My fate?
Prayer of the orphan:
Without a father, without a
mother–
Gods,
May my next coming be
Different!"

3. "His health fails him:

Isiemwoenro,
Brother of the King himself.
His health fails him,
They say,
And the times are no more
His own:
For even the health-givers of Utekon
Can render no help now;
And the royal ones
Of Okhumwun stay their coming. It is well.
Let fate laugh on. It is well."

In modern usage, movie makers introduce in their movies works of musical artists or customized songs which are played in the background of the movie with lyrics that comment on or suggest the mood portrayed in the drama or the events as they unfold. A popular example is found in the movie *Titanic*, which made use of the lyrics and soundtrack of Celine Dion's *My Heart Will Go On*.

76. Classic

This applies to any literary work that is widely agreed to have achieved excellence and set a standard of its kind.

77. Closet Drama

This is a written work in dramatic form, with dialogue, indicated settings, and stage directions, but it is intended by the author to be read rather than to be performed on stage.

78. Comedy

This is a fictional work in which the materials are selected and managed primarily to interest and amuse. Usually, the action turns out happily for the chief characters; that is, it ends with a happy resolution of the conflicts faced by the main character or characters. One major characteristic feature of comedy is the use of humor. However, in literature, the word 'comedy' is not synonymous with humor. While some comedies are humorous, others are not. Other features of comedy include mimicry, parody and lampoon.

79. Comedy of Manners

It deals with the relations and intrigues of men and women living in a sophisticated upper-class society and relies, for comic effect, in large part on the wit and sparkle of dialogue, a witty conversation, give and take, constituting a kind of verbal fencing match as well as a violation of social standard and decorum.

Examples: Oliver Goldsmith's *She Stoops To Conquer*, Richard Sheridan's *The Rival* and *The School for Scandal*, Shakespeare's *Love's Labour Lost* and *Much Ado about Nothing*.

80. Comedy of Humors

This is a type of comedy based on the ancient physiological theory of the "four humours." The four primary fluids include blood, phlegm, choler (or yellow bile) and melancholy (or black bile), whose temperament was held to determine both a person's physical condition and type of character.

81. Comic Relief

A comic relief is the introduction of comic characters, speeches, or scenes in a serious or tragic work, especially a drama. It introduces a sharp contrast in mood to ease tension and add variety.

Example: The scene of the clownish Porter after Macbeth murdered King Duncan *in* Shakespeare's *Macbeth*.

82. Conceit

This is the term for figures of speech which establish striking parallels between or compare two unrelated or dissimilar things or situations.

Example: *I find no peace, and all my war is done; I fear and hope; I burn and freeze in ice.*

83. Concrete

A sentence is concrete when it makes an assertion about a particular subject. CONCRETE LANGUAGE is a term for a language that uses specific words and details to describe a particular subject. It makes use of words that engage the senses of hearing, touch, sight, smell and taste.

Example: *A fuzzy puppy with a round belly, Hilary is nice.*

84. Abstract Language

This is a term used to describe a language that deals with generalities and intangible concepts. Words such as happiness, despair, hope, beauty, and evil are examples of the abstract. Abstract language is useful in dealing with philosophical ideas.

Example: *Hope springs eternal in the human breast.*

85. Confidant (Confidante)

This is a minor character in a drama who serves the protagonist as a trusted friend or to whom the protagonist confesses intimate thoughts, problems and feelings. They provide the playwright with a plausible device for communicating to the audience the character's knowledge, thoughts and state of mind without the use of stage devices such as the soliloquy or aside.

86. Denotation

This refers to a word's primary signification or reference. It is the ordinary and natural meaning of a word.

87. Connotation

This refers to a word's secondary or associated signification. It is a secondary meaning which it commonly suggests or implies. We are dealing with connotation, where a word or a text implies or suggests a meaning beyond the literal. Consider these instances:

- *The building was very tall.*
- *The building was monstrous.*
- *The building was towering.*

These three sentences mean the same thing, literally. However, the word 'monstrous' connotes that the building is scary and imposing, and the word' towering' may connote that the building is impressive in its size and height.

Further, the word 'home' denotes a place or a house where one lives but connotes privacy, intimacy and cosiness.

88. Irony

This is a literary device in which a discrepancy of meaning is masked beneath the surface of what is said. It is an act of hiding what is actually intended to be said and saying the opposite. Irony highlights the discrepancy between appearance and reality in what is expected and what actually happens. Irony is not, however, intended to deceive but to achieve special rhetorical or artistic effects.

Dramatic Irony – When the reader knows what a character does not know.

Examples: Parrots FC is such a strong football Club that it lost all its home games this season. Gogo is such a bright student that he passed one out of nine exam subjects.

89. Verbal Irony

Here, the discrepancy is contained in spoken words. The meaning that a speaker implies differs sharply from what is ostensibly expressed.

Example: *"It is a truth universally acknowledged that a single man in possession of a good fortune must be in want of a wife."*

90. Situational Irony

The discrepancy here is in events or occurrences. It occurs when what actually happens differs from what one expects will happen.

Example: Suppose a heroic soldier is wounded as he battles through a war-torn terrain to rescue a fallen comrade, only to find out that the comrade is quite safe and never needed help. The irony of the situation shocks both the hero and the readers.

91. Irony of Fate

This is a situational irony. It is also known as Cosmic Irony, whereby a deity, or fate, is represented in literary work to deliberately manipulate events to lead the protagonist to false hopes, only to frustrate and mock them at the end. It hinges on the discrepancy between actions and their results, between what characters deserve and what they get, between appearance and reality. As a situational irony, it can be used for either tragic or comic purposes.

92. Dramatic Irony

This is a situation in a play or narrative in which the audience or readers share with the author knowledge of present or future circumstances which the character is ignorant of.

Examples: Sophocles' *Oedipus Rex*, Wole Soyinka's *The Gods Are Not To Blame.*

In Shakespeare's *Twelfth Night*, Malvolio believes in good fortune coming to him while the audience knows the truth that his hope is based on a fake letter.

93. Cyclorama

A theatrical device adopted by stage directors on stage to give an illusion or impression of distance.

94. Literary Criticism

This is a term for studies concerned with defining, analyzing, interpreting, and evaluating works of literature. It also implies a critique and an evaluation of a piece of literature, and, in some cases, it is used to improve a work in progress or a classical piece.

95. Décor

This denotes both scenery and properties or movable pieces of furniture on stage.

96. Decorum

This designates the view that there should be propriety, or fitness, in the way a literary genre, its subject matter, characters and actions, and the style of its narration and dialogue are matched to one another. For example, the level of style in the work should be appropriate to the social class of the speaker, to the occasion on which it is spoken, and to the dignity of its literary genre. For instance, the hero in a serious, tragic work should not be made to speak like a clown.

97. Diction

This signifies the kind or choice of words, phrases, sentence structures and, sometimes, figurative language used by a writer. A writer's diction can be analyzed under categories such as the degree to which the vocabulary and phrasing is abstract or concrete, Latin or Anglo-Saxon, informal (colloquial) or formal, technical or common, full of slang, poetic, ornate, plain, etc. Diction may depend on the writer's subject, purpose and audience. It has a powerful effect on the tone of a piece of writing.

98. Poetic Diction

This refers to the elevated language intended for poetry rather than for common use. It deviates markedly from common or normal speech. It also applies to poets who deliberately employ a diction that deviates not only from common speech or usage but also from the writings of other poets of their era. To them, the language of poetry is never the language of the age. Diction is manifest in the use of archaism. For example, the use of the following expression: "the finny tribe" refers to fish, and "the bleating kind" refers to sheep.

99. Poetic Licence

This refers to the liberty assumed by poets justifying their departure from normal rules of standard spoken or written language in matters such as syntax, word order, the use of archaic or newly coined words to achieve a particular effect, etc.

100. Didactic Literature

This applies to works of literature designed to expound a branch of knowledge or that embody, in imaginative or fictional form, a moral, religious, or philosophical doctrine or theme. In fact, such works were specifically designed or structured to instruct, educate and influence the minds and attitudes of the readers. They direct them to a desired path and enjoin them to go there. Writers devoted to didactic literature focus on the contents of their works.

Examples: In the dedication of the work *Random Reflections Vol. 1*, the author, a radio presenter, Ikechukwu Nwanze, enjoined his son, Chidera Udobata William Gideon Ikechukwu.

Son:
Transcend the threshold
Rise above the follies
Reach for the skies, for glory
Build on the strength.
Sure, your coast is clear
The price is paid
That yours be smooth.
Hope: joy, faith, love
Your path defined
Ride the storm if it dares!
May my weakness never hinder you
May my strength propel you
In mind, heart, body, soul and spirit
No gulf can breach the bond.
Go with Faulkner.
Don't merely endure,
Prevail!...

2. In the poem, *Good and Bad Children*, the poet had this to say:
Children, you are very little,
And your bones are very brittle;
If you would grow great and stately,
You must try to walk sedately.
You must still be bright and quiet,
And content with a simple diet;
And remain, through all bewild'ring,

Innocent and honest children,
Happy hearts and happy faces,
Happy play in grassy places–
That was how, in ancient ages,
Children grew into kings and sages.
But the unkind and the unruly,
And the sort who eat unduly,
They must never hope for glory–
Theirs is quite a different story!
Cruel children, crying babies,
All grow up as geese and gabies,
Hated, as their age increases,
By their nephews and their nieces.

– Child's Garden of Verses, Robert Louis Stevenson

3. 'My son, try to do another's will rather than your own. Always choose to have less rather than more. Always choose the lowest place and be less than everyone else. Always long and pray that the Will of God be fully realized in your life. You will find that the man who does all these walks in the land of peace and quietness.'

– Thomas a'Kempis, *The Imitation of Christ*

101. Elegy

This is a formal and sustained lament in verse for the death of a particular person. It usually ends in a consolation. Most elegies are written to mark a particular person's death, but others extend their subject to reflect on life, death and the fleeting nature of beauty.

Examples: Alfred Lord Tennyson's *In Memoriam* (1850). Sometimes, it refers to solemn meditations on mortality, Thomas Gray's *Elegy Written in a Country Church Yard (1757)*, W. H. Auden's *In Memory of W.B. Yeats (1940)*

102. Dirge

This is a short, less formal poem based on the expression of grief on a particular person's death. Dirge differs from elegy as it is short, less formal and usually meant to be sung.

Example: Shakespeare's *Full Fathom Five Thy Father Lies*

103. Threnody

This is a short poem mourning the death of a person. It is now used as an equivalent of dirge.

104. Monody

This is used as an equivalent of elegy or dirge and is presented as the utterance of a single person.

105. Pastoral Elegy

This is an elegy that represents both the poet and the one they mourn, who is usually also a poet or shepherd.

106. Drama

This is the form of literary composition designed for performance on stage or in the theatre, in which actors take the roles of characters, perform the indicated actions, and utter the written dialogue. It is also commonly called a play. We have three types of drama: tragedy, comedy and tragic-comedy.

107. Poetic Drama

This is a drama written in verse.

108. Dramatic Monologue

This is a type of lyric poem in which a single person, not the poet, utters the speech that makes up the whole poem and addresses and interacts with one or other persons. From what they say, their temperament and character, and the setting, the situation and the identity of the other characters are revealed to the readers.

Examples: Robert Browning's *My Last Duchess*, *The Bishop Orders His Tomb* and T.S. Eliot's *The Love Song of J. Alfred Prufrock*

109. Dramatis Personae

This is a list of characters that play roles in a drama. It is also known as cast.

110. Persona

This is the person or speaker who tells the story in a narrative poem or novel or whose voice we hear in a lyrical poem. They are a creation of the authors or poets to tell the story. They are personalities different from real authors or poets.

111. Tone

This is the expression of a writer's attitude towards the subject or their audience or readers. The tone of their utterance reflects how they stand towards those they are addressing. The way we speak reveals, by subtle clues, our conception of and attitude towards the things we are talking about. It is derived from a complex interplay of diction and style. Tone can be described in one word, for example, playful, sarcastic, etc.

112. Voice

This is the person behind all the dramatis personae and even behind the first-person narrator. Voice is an implied author.

113. Pantomime

This refers to acting on the stage without speech, using only posture, gesture, body movement and exaggerated facial expressions to mimic a character's action or express their feelings.

114. Dumb Show

This is an episode of pantomime introduced into a spoken play.

115. Utopia

This is a class of fictional writing that represents an ideal, non-existent political and social way of life.

Examples: Plato's *Republic* sets forth in dialogue the eternal idea of a perfect commonwealth, which, as we know, is an idea non-existent.

116. Dystopia

This means a bad place. It applies to works of fiction that represent a very unpleasant imaginary world in which ominous tendencies of our present social, political and technological order are projected into a disastrous future culmination. When everything goes wrong in an attempt to create a perfect society, instead of a paradise, a dystopia is created.

Examples: Aldous Huxley's *Brave New World (1932)*, George Orwell's *Nineteen Eighty-Four (1949)*

117. Epic

This is a long narrative verse on a serious subject, told in a formal and elevated style, which recounts the heroic deeds of a quasi-divine figure whose actions depend on the fate of a tribe, a nation or a human race. Its subject tends to be larger than life and embodies the values of their society.

The characteristics of Epic are:

- It is written in a grand style
- It is elaborate
- The hero has an imposing figure and stature
- The hero has a historical significance
- The subject matter is serious with philosophical significance
- It has a wide coverage of settings, usually extending into kingdoms
- It has a narrative objection
- It usually contains an initial invocation of muses requesting that they attend to the poet in their composition
- There is always the intervention of supernatural forces

Examples: Homer's *Iliad,* Dante's *Divine Comedy and* John Milton's *Paradise Lost.*

118. Epigram

This is a statement, whether in verse or prose, that is terse (concise), pointed and witty. It often contains proverbial wisdom and embodies apparent contradiction and a bit of satire.

Examples:

1. Swans sing before they die— 'twere no bad thing should certain people die before they sing!

2. More haste, less speed.

Speech was given to us to conceal our thought.

Every poet is a fool, agreed,

But not every fool is a poet;

The more you look, the less you see.

He who must save his life must first lose it.

Epigram is a short poem ending in a witty or ingenious turn of thought, to which the rest of the composition is intended to lead. It is often a malicious gibe with an unexpected stinger in the final line, perhaps in the very last word.

Examples:

I am his Highness' dog at Kew;

Pray tell me, Sir, whose dog are you?

— *Epigram Engraved on the Collar of a Dog Which I Gave To His Royal Highness,* Alexander Pope

In all things, a moderation keep,

Kings ought to shear, not skin, their sheep.

— Robert Herrick

119. Apothegm

This is the name for a prose epigram. It is a neat and witty statement in prose. Note: An apothegm is distinct from an aphorism, which is a pithy and pointed statement of a serious maxim, opinion, or general truth.

Example: *Art is long, life is short*

120. Epiphany

This is the standard term for the description, recurrent in modern poetry and prose fiction, of sudden flare into the revelation of an ordinary object or scene. It is also a heightened moment of secular revelation, insight, discovery or revelation by which a character's life is greatly altered.

121. Novel

This is an extended fictional work in prose. It is distinguished from a short story as its magnitude permits a greater variety of characters, a greater complication of plot and ample development of the setting.

Examples: Chinua Achebe's *Things Fall Apart*, Chukwuemeka Ike's *Bottled Leopard*, William Golden's *Lord of The Flies*, Leo Tolstoy's *War and Peace*, etc.

122. Novelette

This is a prose work of middle length.

123. Novella

This is a prose fiction longer than a short story but shorter than a novel. It is presently used as an equivalent of novelette. It contains between 30,000 and 50,000 words. Unlike a short story, a novella is long enough to be published independently as a brief book.

Examples: Joseph Conrad's *Heart of Darkness*, Thomas Mann's *Death in Venice*

124. Picaresque Novel

This is an episodic, often autobiographical novel about a rogue or picaro (a person of low social status) wandering about and living off their wits. A picaresque novel tends to be satiric and filled with petty details.

Examples: *Miguel de Cerventes, Don Quixote,* Henry Fielding's *Jonathan Wild*

125. Epistolary Novel

This is a novel in which the story is told through letters written by one or more of the characters.

Example: Mariama Ba's *So Long a Letter.*
Note: Another author replied to Mariama Ba's *So Long a Letter*. It was also done in the epistolary genre.

126. Prose Romance

This deploys characters that are sharply discriminated against or distinguished as heroes or villains, masters or victims. Its protagonist is often solitary and relatively isolated from a social context.

127. Epithalamion

This is a poem written to celebrate a marriage. It was originally written to be sung outside the bedroom (bed chamber) of a newly married couple.

128. Epithet

This denotes an adjective or phrase used to describe a distinctive quality of a person or thing. It is also a descriptive word or phrase frequently used to characterize a person or a thing.
Example:
The expression – *father of our country,* often used by American writers to characterize George Washington, is an epithet.
Silver snarling trumpets is also an epithet.

129. Essay

This is a short composition in prose that undertakes to discuss a matter, express a point of view, persuade us to accept a thesis on any subject, or simply entertain. It consists of a discussion of a topic from the author's point of view or perspective.

130. Euphemism

This is a mild and deliberate way of saying something serious. It is also an offensive expression used in place of a blunt one that is felt to be disagreeable or embarrassing. It substitutes an indirect statement for a direct one to avoid bluntness.

Example:
'Asibe passed on last month' – he died.
'The girl was put in the family way' — she is pregnant.
The basic psychology behind using euphemism is the desire to put something considered bad or embarrassing in a positive or at least neutral light.

131. Fantastic Literature
This refers to a writer's deliberate design to leave the readers in a state of uncertainty whether the events are to be explained by reference to natural or supernatural causes.

132. Fiction
This is a literary work that might contain factual information but is not bound by factual accuracy. It is based on or made up by the author's imagination. This term now more specifically refers to prose narratives and novels whose characters, settings and events are invented by the writer. The truth of a work of fiction depends not on facts but on how convincingly the writer creates the world of the story.

133. Figurative Language
This is a language that conspicuously departs from its standard meanings of words and expressions. Here, writers depart from what competent language users see as standard meanings of words or standard order of words to achieve some special meanings or effects.
Examples: Statements like *Juliet is a tower of strength, Jack is a pain in the neck* are cast figuratively. They describe one thing in terms of another and are not meant to be taken literally.

134. Figures of Speech
This is also known as rhetorical figures. They are words, phrases, or expressions used in a way different from their usual meaning to create a particular mental image or effect. Instead of relying on

their literal or standard meanings, they depart from them for a special effect.

Example: To say that someone is dumber than dirt is not literally but figuratively true.

135. Simile

This is a comparison between two distinctly different things indicated by the use of the words 'like' and 'as.'

Examples: My love's like a red, red rose.

And ice, mast–high, came floating by, as green as emerald.

136. Metaphor

This is a figure of speech that makes an implicit and imaginative comparison between two distinct things. It is a statement that one thing is something else, which, in a literal sense, it is not. It creates a close association between two distinctly different entities and usually underscores some important similarity between them.

The Greek philosopher Aristotle sees it as an intuitive perception of the similarity in dissimilarities. Here, instead of a thing being like or as another, it becomes that other thing. The comparison is made without the use of the specific words of comparison such as 'as,' 'like,' 'than,' etc. What points at metaphor is often the presence of the 'to be' words – 'is' and 'was' in the line.

Examples: Richard is a pig. Emeka is a lion.

137. Dead Metaphor

This is a metaphor that has become so common as a result of long and overuse that we have ceased to be aware of the discrepancy between the two compared objects (that is, the vehicle and the tenor).

Examples: The leg of a table, The heart of the matter.

138. Metonymy

Here, the literal term for one thing is applied to another thing that is closely associated with it. Thus, the crown or the scepter now stands for a king.

Example: *Doublet and hose ought to show itself courageous to petticoat.*

Here, 'doublet' and 'hose' refer to male clothes, while 'petticoat' refers to clothing for the female. With time, 'doublet' and 'hose' came to signify the male, while 'petticoat' came to signify the female.

"The pulpit and the pew ought to understand that both are in the same boat."

139. Synecdoche

This is a figure of speech whereby a part of something is used to signify the whole or a whole for a part.

Examples: All hands must be on deck.

The levy is for all heads in the village.

Abuja and Washington are meeting over small arms limitation.

140. Personification

Personification means giving human attributes to things that are nonhuman, inanimate, or abstract. The entities are treated or spoken of as if they are endowed with life or human attributes or feelings. Writers often use personification to achieve humorous or satirical effects. It also allows readers to imagine what the animals or nonhuman entities think, feel, and say about one another. Personification is also known as ANTHROMORPHISM.

Examples:

In *Paradise Lost*, John Milton wrote:

'Sky lowered and muttering thunder, some sad drops
Wept at completing of the mortal sin.'

2. Death made war upon that family.

3. Numo's time has come.

4. The sky will smile today.

The sun journeyed unceasingly from east to west.

'...Danger knows full well that Caesar is more dangerous than he.'

Note the difference between personification and apostrophe. In apostrophe, there is a direct address that is more striking and has deeper and clearer emotional effects, while in personification, there is no direct address.

141. Point of View

This is the way, angle, or mode in which a story is told. It is the means by which the readers are presented with the characters, actions, dialogue, setting and events constituting the narrative in a work of fiction.

142. Third Person Narrative

Here, the narrator is someone outside the story who refers to the characters in the story by name or as he, she, or they. The third-person narrative technique is highly objective. It creates a literary distance between the writer and the readers. It enhances the good development of characters and gives room for authoritative comments.

143. Third-Person Point of View

In this point of view, the narrator knows everything that needs to be known about the characters, their actions and events and has privileged access to their thoughts, feelings and motives.

144. Intrusive Narrator

This narrator not only reports but also comments on and evaluates the actions and motives of the characters and sometimes expresses personal views about human life.

145. Unintrusive Narrator

This narrator is impersonal and objective in their narrations, and he neither passes any personal judgment nor introduces their personal comments. They do not enter into the minds or thoughts of the characters but describe events as they unfold from the outside. They tell us what the characters say and what their faces look like, leaving us to infer their thoughts and feelings. It has been said by critics that under this point of view, the narrator disappears altogether.

Note: A narrator is the speaker in a work. For example, in Mark Twain's *Adventures of Huckleberry Finn*, the narrator is Huck Finn, a character in the story and the one from whose perspective the story is told. He is not the real-life author.

- **Innocent or Naïve Narrator:** A narrator who fails to understand all the implications of the story. Example: Huckleberry Finn in Mark Twain's *Adventures of Huckleberry Finn.*
- **Unreliable Narrator:** A narrator whom we perceive as deceptive, deluded, or deranged.

146. Limited Point of View

The narrator tells the story in the third person and does not go beyond what is perceived, thought, remembered and felt by a single or few characters within the story.

147. First-Person Point of View

This point of view limits the narrative to what the first-person narrator knows. The narrator is usually a participant in the story.

148. Second-Person Point of View

This is the mode of telling a story whereby the narrator addresses someone they call by the second person pronoun 'you,' who is represented as experiencing that which is narrated.

149. Self-Conscious Narrator

The narrator reveals to the readers that the narration is a fictional art and that what they are telling actually never happened.

150. Sentimentality

This is a failure of writers, who seem to feel a great deal of emotion about their subject and to give readers sufficient grounds for sharing their emotions. It may have arisen out of anger that tended to be greater than its object seems to call for or an enthusiasm quite unwarranted by its subject. They allow themselves to be clouded by the emotion they attach to the subjects they present and thus fail to give reasons supporting the emotional attachment.

151. Structure

Literary structure may be used interchangeably with form to designate the order, emphasis and rendering of a work's component subject matter and parts into a beautiful and effective whole of a determinate kind. It is also the arrangement of incidents in a novel. In prose and drama, the structure is made up of exposition, rising action, climax, falling action and denouement.

152. Free Verse

This is poetry that does not adhere to a formal poetic structure. It is printed in short lines instead of in continuous lines of prose. Its rhythmic pattern is not organized into a regular metrical form. Poets who write free verse try to reproduce the natural rhythms of spoken language without conforming to a regular meter or rhyme scheme.

Blank verse differs from free verse as it is metrically regular, while free verse is not.

153. Hudibrastic Poem

This name was derived from the book *Hudibras* by Samuel Butler, which satirizes rigid or excessive Puritanism where rather than experiencing dignified circumstances, the hero is faced with a humiliating misadventure described in doggerel verses and a ludicrously colloquial idiom. This poem satirizes rigid Puritanism, or an attitude tending towards the 'holier than thou' disposition among people. The subject matter is usually highly placed in the social cadre.

154. Doggerel

This is a term applied to rough versification full of Irregularities due to a poet's incompetence or deliberately employed for satiric or comic effect.

Example:

In *Colin Clout*, John Shelton wrote:

For though my rhyme be ragged,

Tattered and jagged,

Rudely rain beaten,

Rusty and moth-eaten,

If ye take well therewith,

It hath in it some pith.

155. Hyperbole

This is a figure of speech that uses bold, extravagant and incredible exaggeration or overstatement for the sake of emphasis or ironic or comic effect.

Examples:

- My wife is my all and all in this world.
- The crowd greeted Ekwelem, the successful wrestler, with a million cheers.
- We shall have a night of a thousand laughters at Martha's Mall this weekend.
- She ate a mountain of food in just a few minutes.
- When J.P. (Clark) arrived at the meeting, his voice rang out from several hundred feet away.
- Achebe, there was a country.

156. Understatement

This is also known as meiosis. Meiosis is a term that signifies a deliberate and euphemistic attempt at lessening the magnitude or importance a thing or situation ordinarily possesses. It implies that something is lesser in significance or size than it really is. In Greek, it means 'to make smaller, or to diminish'. The purpose of understatement is often ironic or comic.

Example: To refer to River Niger as a pond is an understatement or meiosis.

'...the great, much-dreaded ocean is just a puddle.'

– Galileo, Bertolt Brecht

157. Litotes

This is a special form of understatement used for the purpose of emphasis, involving the assertion of an affirmative by negating its contrary. It is the opposite of hyperbole. It is employed for rhetorical effect, principally via double negatives. In most cases, it employs words like 'no' or 'not'.

Example:

- That idea is not unattractive – This means that the idea is attractive.
- That is not the most unpleasant place – This means that the place is pleasant or good.
  Further instances include:
- Cypo is not the most intelligent man in the world – This means that he is dull or stupid.
- The house is not the most pleasant place – This means that the house is not good.
- I am a citizen of no mean nation – This means I am from a great nation.
- The man is not mean – This means that the man is liberal.

158. Idyll

This is often used synonymously with pastoral. It is a deliberate conventional poem expressing an urban poet's nostalgic image of the supposed peace and simplicity of the rural life of shepherds and other rural folk in an idealized natural setting.

159. Imagery

This is a collective set of images in a poem or other literary works. It is also the use of language to evoke a picture or a concrete sensation of a person, a thing, a place, or an experience. As a descriptive language, it appeals to the senses – sight, sound, smell, touch and taste. Images help readers share the experience of a writer and add immediacy to literary language. Imagery has also been described as one of the languages of art and a means by which experience in its richness and emotional complexity is communicated.

According to C. Day Lewis, an image is a picture made out of words.

160. Invocation

This is an address by a poet to a god or muse or any supernatural being to assist them in their composition.

Example: John Milton, in *Paradise Lost,* said: *And chiefly thou, O Spirit, that dost prefer before all temples its upright heart and pure, instruct me…*

161. Poetasters

These are referred to as untalented pretenders to the poetic art. By this, we mean those charlatans who are not really versed in the art of poetry but engage in it for economic reasons.

162. Deus Ex Machina

This is a Latin expression for "a god from a machine." Dramatists sometimes make use of this to resolve the entanglements of a play. It is a supernatural intervention. Greek playwrights sometimes end a drama with the introduction of a god in a mechanical device, which resolves the dilemmas of the human characters by his judgment and command. Currently, it can refer to any device by means of which a hard-pressed author resolves a plot.

163. Confessional School

This is a group of poets, including Robert Lowell, Sylvia Plath, Anne Sexton and John Berryman, who, in the 1950s, wrote frank and sometimes brutal poems about their personal or private lives. This group considers the poet as one and the same person whose voice is heard in the poems they compose. This being so, their composition should, of necessity, reflect personal experiences that can be attributed directly to them. These poems deal with personal or private experiences that modernist poets avoided dealing with directly, thus helping to reunite "the man who suffers and the mind that creates." Issues relating to emotional distress, alcoholism, illness, depression, etc., feature prominently in their compositions.

164. Cadence

The natural rhythmic rise and fall is noticed in language as it is normally spoken. It is different from the meter, in which stressed and unstressed syllables of a poetic line are carefully counted to conform to a regular pattern.

165. Interior Monologue

This is that species of stream of consciousness which undertakes to present to the readers the course and rhythm of consciousness (that is, internal flow of thoughts, memories and associations) precisely as it occurs in the mind of a character. It is an extended presentation of a character's thoughts in a narrative. It reads as if the character is speaking aloud for the readers or audience to hear.

166. Myth

This is a story of ancient origin, passed from one generation to another. Once believed to be true by a particular cultural group, it serves to explain why the world is as it is and why things happen as they do, providing a rationale for social customs, observances, etc.

It is also a traditional narrative of anonymous authorship that arose out of a culture's oral tradition. The characters are usually gods or heroic figures.

167. Legend

A legend is a traditional narrative handed down through popular oral tradition to illustrate and celebrate a remarkable character or an important event and explain the unexplainable. Unlike folktales, legends take place in real locations and often with genuine historical figures.

168. Motif

This is also known as leitmotif. It is an element or phrase that recurs significantly throughout a narrative work. It can be an image, idea, theme, situation, or action.

169. Lay

This is a short narrative poem meant to be sung.

170. Cyclorama

A theatrical device adopted by stage directors on stage to give an illusion or impression of distance.

171. Limerick

This is a short and usually comic verse of five anapestic lines, usually rhyming aabba.

172. Literary Canon

This designates in the world of literature those authors who, by a cumulative consensus of critics, scholars and teachers, have come to be widely recognized as major and to have written works hailed as literary classics.

173. Lyric

This is a fairly short poem, rendered by a single speaker, who expresses a state of mind or a process of perception, thought and feeling. Lyrical poems are often written in the first person and traditionally have a song-like immediacy and emotional force.
Example: William Wordsworth's *Tintern Abbey* and John Donne's *Canonization*.
In original Greek form, lyric signifies a song rendered to the accompaniment of a lyre.

174. Solecism

This is a conspicuous and unintentional violation of standard diction or grammar.

175. Malapropism

This is a type of solecism whereby a person mistakenly uses a word in place of another that resembles it. The effect is usually comic.

Example: It is malapropism to say the following:

- A progeny of learning instead of saying a prodigy of learning.
- A pineapple of politeness, instead of saying a pinnacle.
- He ran around like a chicken with its hat off, instead of heart.

176. Sonnet

This is a lyric poem consisting of a single stanza of iambic pentameter lines linked by an intricate rhyme scheme.

177. Petrarchan Sonnet

This is named after the poet Patriarch of the 14th Century Italy. It falls into two main parts: an octave (eight lines) rhyming aabbaaba and a sestet (six lines) rhyming cdecde or other variants such as cdccdc.

178. English or Shakespearean Sonnet

This has three quatrains and a concluding couplet, rhyming: abab, cdcd, efef, gg.

179. Spenserian Sonnet

This is like the English sonnet, but Spencer linked each quatrain to the next by a continuing rhyme: ababbcbccdcdee.

180. Stanza

This is a division or unit of a poem made up of verse lines often set off by a space in the printed text. Stanzas are of a similar form with similar or identical patterns of rhyme and meter. Some un-rhymed poems are also arranged in stanzas.

181. Couplet

This occurs when we have two consecutive rhyming lines of poetry that are of equal length.

Example:

The grave's a fine and private place,
But none, I think, doth ere embrace.

> — *To His Coy Mistress,* Andrew Marvell

If the two rhyming lines express a complete thought, they are called a "closed couplet."

Example:

If ever a wife was happy with a man,
Compare with me, ye women, if you can.

> — *To My Dear and Loving Husband,* Anne Bradstreet

182. Tercet or Triplet

This is a stanza of three lines, usually ending in the same rhyme.

Example:

Who e'er she be
That not impossible she
That shall command my heart and me.

183. Quatrain

This is a four-line stanza with various meters and rhyme schemes.

Example:

The great book o'ver the border went
And good folk, that was the end
But we hope you'll keep in mind
You and I were left behind.

184. Octavarima

This is a stanza of eight lines rhyming ababcc.

185. Style

These are all the distinctive ways or characteristic modes in which a writer uses language to convey their message in a literary work. A writer's style depends on their characteristic use of diction, imagery, tone, syntax and figurative language. Style is usually classified into three main levels: high (or grand), middle (or mean) and low (or plain). It is also the verbal identity of a writer that conveys their unique way of seeing the world. It is determined by sentence structure, word choice, use of figurative language and imagery.

186. Chronicle Plays

These are dramatic works based on historical materials or events.

187. Suspense

This is an enjoyable anxiety created in the minds of the readers by the author's handling of the plot. When the outcome of the events is unclear, the author's suspension of resolution intensifies the readers' interest, particularly if the plot involves a character to whom the readers or audience are sympathetic. Suspense is also created when the fate of a character is clear to the audience but not to the character. Suspense results from the audience's anticipation of how and when the character will meet their inevitable fate.

188. Surprise

This occurs when something beyond the expectations of the audience happens to a character.

189. Symbol

This is an object or action in a literary work that means more than itself and stands for something beyond itself. It is also applied to a word or phrase that signifies something or suggests a range of references beyond what it actually is.

Examples of symbols include: The cross, the green and white flag of Nigeria, etc. We have conventional or public symbols as well as private symbols.

190. Symbolism

This is the use of symbols to convey messages in literary works. It is also a coherent system composed of a number of symbolic elements. The purpose is to give meaning that transcends the physical representation. For example, the Cross symbolizes Christianity, while the Crescent and the moon placed inside its hollow centre symbolize Islam.

191. Synesthesia

This applies to descriptions of one mode of sensation in terms of another. Colour is attributed to sounds, odour to colours, sound to odour, etc. It is also called sense transference or sense analogy.

Examples: Saying loud colours, bright sounds and sweet music.

In Shelly's *The Sensitive Plant*, we have: *And the hyacinth purple, and white, and blue, which flung from its bells a sweet peal a new of music so delicate, soft and intense.* It felt like an odour within the sense.

Also, in John Keats' *Ode to a Nightingale,* he calls for a drink tasting of Flora and the country green, Dance, Provencal song and sunburnt mirth.

192. Tragedy

This applies to the dramatic representations of actions that eventuate or end in a disastrous conclusion for the protagonist (hero). The tragic action from the beginning to the end brings a morally good but imperfect tragic hero from happiness to unhappiness because of a mistaken act to which they are led by an error of judgment.

The protagonists of tragic works are often people of high or elevated class in their social milieu. It has also been described as a drama in which high-profile characters experience reversals of fortune, usually for the worse. It involves incidents arousing pity and fear. Tragedy is characterized by suspense, irony, conflict, supernatural elements (though not a regular feature), pathos, comic relief (though not a regular feature also), fatalism, etc.

Examples:

Shakespeare's *Macbeth* and *Julius Caesar*

Sophocles' *Oedipal the King*

In prose fiction, we have Chinua Achebe's *Things Fall Apart*.

193. Catharsis

Catharsis is the purgation or purification of emotion or the emotional release or calm the audience feels at the end of a tragic drama. At this stage, the feeling of pity and fear that, according to Aristotle, occurs in the audience is purged.

194. Tragic Flaw

It is a mistake or error of judgment by the hero or heroine in a drama or a novel. It is an offence committed in ignorance of some material fact, without deliberate criminal intent, and therefore free from blameworthiness. It eventually leads to the downfall of the hero or heroine.

Examples of tragic flaws include:

- Jealousy, as is the case with Othello in Shakespeare's *Othello*.
- Miscalculation, as is the case with Romeo in Shakespeare's *Romeo and Juliet*.
- Hot temper and fear, as is the case with Okonkwo in Chinua Achebe's *Things Fall Apart*.
- Over-ambition, as is the case with Macbeth in Shakespeare's *Macbeth*.
- Stubbornness and pride as is the case with Ezeulu in Achebe's *Arrow of God*.
- Pride and obstinacy, as is the case with Caesar in Shakespeare's *Julius Caesar*.

195. Hubris

This is overweening pride, outrageous behaviour, or insolence that leads a protagonist to disregard a divine warning or to violate an important moral law to their ruin, peril or detriment. It is also called HAMARTIA or PERIPETEIA.

196. Tragicomedy

This is a type of drama that combines or contains the elements of both tragedy and comedy. In tragicomedy, the standard characters and subject matter and typical plot forms of tragedy and comedy involve people of both high and low degrees.

Example: *The Merchants of Venice* by Shakespeare

197. Wit

This denotes a kind of verbal expression that is brief, deft, and intentionally contrived to produce a shock or comic surprise. As a designated species of the comic, wit may be an element in a work of literature – a character, event, or utterance designed to amuse the readers or audience.

Examples:

Epigram is a typical example of wit.

History repeats itself. Historians repeat each other.

198. Repartee

These are clever and amusing comments and replies made quickly by a person who seeks to outwit the other. It is a contest of wit, in which each person tries to check the remarks of the other or to turn them to their own advantage. Each tries to beat the other by being funnier.

199. Humor

This may denote the quality of a work that makes it funny or amusing. It can be ascribed to a comic utterance, appearance or mode of behaviour.

200. Masque

This is also spelt Mask. It is an elaborate form of entertainment combining poetic drama, music, song, dance, splendid costuming and stage spectacle. In this entertainment, the characters wear masks.

201. Melodrama

This is originally a play, featuring background music and sometimes songs to underscore the emotional mood of each scene. Melodramas are weak in characterization and motivation but strong in action, suspense and passion. It may also be a play produced with musical accompaniment, and its plot revolves around malevolent intrigues and violent action. Melodramatic characters are stereotyped villains, heroes and young lovers.

202. Meter

This is a fixed and recurring rhythm in a poem. It can also be described as the recurrence in regular units of a prominent feature in the sequence of speech sounds of a language. Meter depends on syllables and rhythms of speech.

SCANING is the analysis of a poem to determine its meter.

203. Rhythm

The patterns of stresses and pauses in a poem are cognizable, though varying patterns, in the beat of the stresses. In other words, it is the rise and fall of the voice, produced by alternating stressed and unstressed syllables in a line of prose or poetry. It is also the arrangement or organization of words with a view to producing a special kind of beat.

204. Accent

It refers to the stressed syllable of a polysyllabic word or a monosyllabic word that receives stress because it belongs to an "open class" of words (noun, verb, adjective, adverb) or because of "contrastive" or "rhetorical" stress.

205. Verse

This is a composition written in meter. It is the nature and form in which poems exist.

206. Morality Plays

These are dramatized allegories of a representative Christian life in the plot form of a quest for salvation, in which the crucial events are temptations, sinning and the climactic confrontation with death. The usual protagonist represents man or everyman. Other characters are personifications of vices, virtues, death and angels.
Examples: Everyman, Castle of Perseverance and Mankind.

207. Occasional Poems

These are written to celebrate or memorialize a particular occasion. Examples of such occasions include birthdays, marriages, funerals, etc.

208. Ode

This denotes a long lyric poem that is serious in subject and treatment, elevated in style and elaborate in its stanzaic structure.

209. Onomatopoeia

This is sometimes called Echoism. It designates a word or combination of words whose sound seems to closely resemble the noise they describe or a word imitating a sound.
Examples: Hiss, buzz, rattle, bang, boom, meow

210. Oral Poetry

This is also known as formulaic poetry. It is composed and transmitted by singers or people who engage in recitation. There is no fixed version of oral poetry since each performer tends to render it differently.

211. Oral Tradition

This is the tradition within a culture that transmits narratives by word of mouth from one generation to another. Fables, folktales, ballads and songs are examples of oral tradition.

212. Oxymoron

This is the juxtaposition (placing side by side) of two words or terms that, in ordinary usage, are contraries or opposites. The intention is to create a sharp contrast with the effect of creating surprise and shock and arousing the interest of the readers. It is also referred to as condensed antithesis. Emphasis is placed on contradicting words or phrases rather than the whole statement.
Examples:

O death in life, the days that are no more.
Pleasing pain; burn and freeze; loving hate.
Cold fire, Painful pleasure, sweet sorrow;
Deafening silence; and living death

Note that oxymoron and antithesis may look similar as they both place opposites or contrasts together, but their difference lies in the fact that in antithesis, words or thoughts are balanced in contrast, while in oxymoron, words are combined to form an expressive phrase or epithet. Again, oxymoron is more or less a phrase and not a complete sentence as in antithesis. Examiners usually exploit this difference, and a casual reader under exam conditions may miss it.

213. Palinode

This is a poem or poetic passage in which the poet renounces or retracts an earlier poem or an earlier type of subject matter.
Example: Geoffrey Chaucer's *Prologue to the Legend of Good Women* was written after he was charged by the god of love with having slandered women lovers in Troilus and Criseyde.

214. Paradox

This is a statement that at first strikes one as self-contradictory, untrue, or absurd but, on reflection, reveals a clever or deeper sense. It is used to capture attention and for emphasis. It is often achieved by a play on words. It expresses the complexity of life by showing how opposing ideas can be contradictory and true at the same time.

Examples: "Much madness is divinest sense" (Emily Dickson)
Parting is such sweet sorrow" (Shakespeare)
In *Death, Be Not Proud,* John Donne stated:
"One short sleep past, we wake eternally, and death shall be no more;
Death, thou shalt die."
"The ripest fruit is the saddest."
"The child is the father of the man."
"Heard music is sweet, but unheard ones are sweeter."
"Looking around, one could see a proud, devastated people."
– There Was a Country, Chinua Achebe

NOTE: The soul of paradox is the contrast between appearance and reality which the writer exploits for the sake of emphasis.

215. Paralipsis

Here, someone says they need not, or will not, say or do something yet proceeds to do so. Here, the speaker focuses their attention on a subject by pretending to neglect it.

Example: In *Julius Caesar,* Mark Anthony, in his funeral oration shortly after Caesar's murder, said: "I came to bury Caesar not to praise him." Anthony then proceeds to eulogize Caesar and incites the crowd against Brutus and his fellow conspirators.

216. Parallelism

This is an arrangement of words, phrases, clauses, or sentences side by side in identical grammatical or structural ways. Ideas are organized in a way that demonstrates their coordination to the readers.

Example: "The devil is waiting for them; hell is gaping for them; the flames gather and flash about them."

217. Pun

This is a figure of speech in which a word is used in such a way that it tends to suggest a double meaning. It is a play on words in which one word is substituted for another word that is similar or identical in sound but of very different meaning. It is mainly for comic effect.

Example:

"Thou art Peter (Petros), and upon this rock (Petra) I will build my Church."

— Mathew16:18

It is better to be late than to be late.
Your money is safe in the safe.

218. Equivoque

This is a special type of pun in which a single word or phrase has two disparate meanings in a context that makes both meanings equally relevant.

Examples:

Golden lads and girls all must,
As chimney sweepers, come to dust.

Shakespeare, *Cymbeline*:

When I am done, I hope it can be said:
His sins were scarlet, but his books were read.

219. Pathetic Fallacy

This signifies the representation of inanimate natural objects as if they have humane motions, sensations and capabilities. Here, nature is credited with human qualities.

Example:

"The spendthrift crocus, bursting through the mould
Naked and shivering, with his cup of gold,
The one red leaf, the last of its clan,
That dances as often as dance it can."

Pathetic fallacy is a procedure in which human traits are ascribed to natural objects in a less formal and more direct way than in the figure of speech, known as personification.

> *"The interment of Awolowo was a mystery*
> *The rainbow gloomily sliced across the sky*
> *The friendly sun refused to shine on earth*
> *It was like the world was coming to an end*
> *As followers proceeded towards the mausoleum."*

In the above poem, the rainbow and the sun are ascribed to the human attributes of gloom, friendliness and refusal to act as if they sympathize with the mourners.

220. Pathos

This is a quality in a play that stimulates pity for a character. It applies to a scene or passage designed to evoke feelings of tenderness, pity, or sympathetic sorrow from the audience.
Example: "Pray, do not mock me. I am a very foolish, fond old man."

221. Frame Story

This is a literary device or technique in which a story is enclosed in another story or a tale within another tale.

222. Dramatic Persona

This is the list of characters who take part in a drama.

223. Plot

In a dramatic or narrative work, the plot designates the sequence of events, situations and actions as rendered towards achieving particular artistic and emotional effects. It is the action element in prose. It is the arrangement of events that make up a story.

The plot consists of exposition representing the background information necessary for the development of the plot; the rising action representing the conflicts and crises; the climax representing the most decisive crisis; and the falling action – a follow-up that moves towards the resolution or denouement. To be effective, it must include a sequence of incidents that bear a significant or casual relationship with one another.

224. Inversion

This is the reversal of the normal word order in a sentence or phrase. English sentences are normally built on the order of subject–verb-complement. An inverted sentence reverses one or more of those elements. Poets often invert sentences to have words conform to the meter or to create rhymes.

Example:

The expression 'In silent night when I took rest' was inverted by a poet thus: "In silent night when rest I took." The inversion occurred in the order in which the words rest, and I and took appeared in the original sentence.

225. Poetic Justice

This is a term coined by Thomas Rymer, signifying the distribution, at the end of a literary work, of earthly rewards and punishments in proportion to the virtue or vice of the various characters.

226. Motivation

This refers to the underlying reason for a character's behaviour, temperament, desires and the moral nature of their speech and actions. A writer can reveal motivation directly by telling us what made a character the way they are. They can also reveal this through speeches and actions without telling us exactly why they behave as they do. Readers can still sift through the details and infer a character's motivation.

227. Prose

This consists of writing that does not adhere to any particular formal structures other than simple grammar. It is a discourse, spoken or written, which is not patterned into lines of either metric verse or free verse.

228. Prose Poems

These are compact, rhythmic and usually sonorous compositions that exploit the poetic resources of language for poetic ends. They are written as a continuous sequence without line breaks.
Example: Charles Bandelaire's *Little Poems in Prose*.

229. Prosody

This signifies the systematic study of versification in poetry – the principles and practice of meter, rhyme and stanza form.

230. Premiere

This is the first public performance or showing of a play or a cinema.

231. Problem Play

This is a type of drama popularized by Henrik Ibsen, where the situation faced by the protagonist is put forward by the author as a representative instance of a contemporary social problem and through a character who speaks for the author or by the evolution of the plot, or both, proposing a solution to the problem which is at odds with prevailing opinion.

232. Propagandist Literature

This is a didactic work organized and rendered to induce the readers to assume a specific attitude towards or take direct action on a pressing social, political, or religious issue of the time the work is written.
Example: Harriet Beecher Stowe's *Uncle Tom's Cabin*

233. Novel of Manners

This is a realistic novel that focuses on and describes in detail the social customs and habits, conversation, and ways of thinking of a particular social group.
Examples: Jane Austen's *Pride and Prejudice,* William Makepeace Thackeray's *Vanity Fair*

234. Realistic Novel

This is a fictional attempt to give effect to realism by presenting complex characters with mixed motives which are rooted in a social class.

235. Realism

This designates the representation of characters, events and settings in ways the spectator will consider plausible, based on consistency and likeness to type. It is an attempt to faithfully reproduce the surface appearance of life, especially that of ordinary people in everyday situations.

236. Romance

This is an extended fictional prose narrative about improbable events involving characters who are quite different from ordinary people. It presents life as we want it to be — more picturesque, fantastic, adventurous, or heroic than actuality.

Note: The distinction between realism and romance is that realism represents life as it really is, while romance is essentially made up to suit our fantasies.

Examples: Miguel de Cerventes' *Don Quixote*, Sir Philip Sidney's *The Arcadia*

237. Romantic Novel

This is a novel with a happy ending. It presents readers with characters engaged in adventure, filled with courageous acts, daring chases and exciting escapes.

238. Rhetorical Figures

These are figures of speech that depart from the literal use of language or what is experienced by competent users of standard language, mainly by arranging their words to achieve special effects.

239. Apostrophe

This is a direct and explicit address either to an absent person, an abstract or non-human entity. The person or object being addressed is incapable of listening.

Example: In grief, talking to a dead man as though he is still alive.

Apostrophe provides the speaker with the means to articulate thoughts aloud. It is usually recognized by the use of exclamation marks (!) or the use of expressions like "ah" or "oh", followed by the name of the object or person. Odes are constituted throughout in the mode of such an address.

Example: John Keats begins his *Ode on a Grecian Urn* apostrophizing the Urn thus: "Thou still un-ravished bride of quietness."

Note that there is a difference between Personification and Apostrophe. In apostrophes, there is a direct address that is more striking and has deeper and clearer emotional effects, while in personification, there is no direct address.

240. Chiasmus

This is a rhetorical figure in which a contrast is achieved by the reversal of clauses. It is a sequence of two phrases or clauses that are parallel in syntax but reverse the order of the corresponding words in the sentence. It achieves contrast by reversal of the clauses or phrases. It is also called Apotheosis.

Examples:

1. The years to come seemed a waste of breath, A waste of breath the years behind.
2. Do not fear to negotiate, and do not negotiate out of fear.
3. "Fair is foul, and foul is fair."
4. Do not live to eat, but eat to live.

241. Rhetorical Question

This is also known as EROTEMA. It is a question to which an overt answer is not expected. It is used to set up an explanation or to trigger a reader's mental response. Such a question presumes the audience agrees with the speaker on the answer.

Examples:

1. In Alexander Pope's *The Rape of the Lock*, Belinda asked:

> *Gods! Shall the ravisher display your hair,*
> *While the fops envy, and the ladies stare?"*

2.

> *"O, wind,*
> *If winter comes, can spring be far behind?"*
>
> *– Ode to the West Wind*, Shelley

3.

> *"These men doubt everything.*
> *Can society stand in doubt*
> *And not on faith?"*
>
> *– Galileo*, Bertolt Brecht

4. *"What will a man ever do when he is called to show his manhood fighting in alien lands and leaving his women behind with the demented and the old and the children and the other children?"*

> *– The Beautyful Ones Are Not Yet Born*, Ayi Kwei Armah

242. Zeugma

This is applied to expressions in which a single word has the same grammatical relations to two or more other words but an obvious shift in its significance. It is sometimes called a SYLLEPSIS.

Examples:

1. *Or stain her honour, or her new brocade.*
Obliged by hunger, and request of friends
2. *And the waves oozing through the port hole made*
His berth a little damp, and him afraid
3. *He fired the gun and his gardener.*
4. *The pretty girl stole my heart and my purse.*

243. Rhyme

This consists of the repetition of similar sounds in two or more words or the matching of final vowel or consonant sounds in two or more words. Examples of words that rhyme include: *Fate–late, follow-hollow, queue–stew.*

> *"May you now guard science' light.*
> *Kindle it and use it right,*
> *Lest it be aflame to fall*
> *Downwards to consume us all."*
>
> *– Galileo,* Bertolt Brecht

244. End Rhymes

They occur at the end of a verse line.

Example:

He stumbled through the gate
When I was having my date.

245. Internal Rhymes

They occur within a verse line.

Example: *Sister, my sister, o fleet sweet swallows.*

246. Masculine Rhyme

This consists of the rhyme of a single stressed syllable.

Example:

> *I listened, motionless and Still*
> *And as I mounted up the Hill*

247. Feminine Rhyme

It consists of a two-syllable rhyme (a stressed syllable followed by an unstressed syllable).

Example:

> *As if her song would have no ending*
> *And o'ver the sickle bending*

Feminine rhyme is also known as DOUBLE RHYME.

A rhyme involving three syllables is called TRIPLE RHYME.

248. Eye-Rhymes

This involves words whose spellings would lead one to think that they rhymed or whose endings were spelt alike and, in most instances, were pronounced alike but have, over time, acquired different meanings.

249. Rhyme Scheme

This is a recurrent pattern of rhyme within an individual poem. This is shown by using small letters to represent each end rhyme – a for the first rhyme, b for the second rhyme, and so on.
 The following lines rhyme abab.

> *Tell me not, in mournful numbers – a*
> *Life is but an empty dream! – b*
> *For the soul is dead that slumbers – a*
> *And things are not what they seem – b*
> – *A Psalm of Life,* Henry Wadsworth Longfellow

250. Caesura

This is a light but definite pause within a line of a poem. It usually occurs at a mark of punctuation but can still occur even if there is no punctuation. We often indicate caesura by double slanting lines: //.
 In the examples below, caesuras are marked by double vertical lines. The pauses are indicated by punctuation.
i. *Announced by all the trumpets of the sky,*
Arrives the snow, //and,// driving o'ver the fields,
Seems nowhere to alight; // the whited air Hills and wood
> – Ralph Waldo Emerson, *The Snow-Storm*
ii. *And priests in black gowns // were walking their rounds.*
And binding with briars // my joys and desires.
iii. *Cover her face: // mine eyes dazzle: // she died young*

251. End-Stopped

This is where a line ends in a full pause – usually indicated by some mark of punctuation.
Example:

> *"Was this the face that launch'd a thousand ship,*
> *And burnt the topless towers of Ilium?"*

252. Satire

This is a literary mode based on criticism of people and society through ridicule. It is the art of diminishing or derogating a subject matter by making it ridiculous and adding towards it attitudes of amusement, contempt, scorn or indignation. The satirist aims to reduce the practices attacked by laughing scornfully at them and being witty enough to allow the readers to laugh. They make profuse use of ridicule, exaggeration, irony and devices of comparison and contrast to achieve their purpose. Satire ridicules the shortcomings of people and institutions in an attempt to bring about change. It uses humour to critique people or institutions with the intention of improving them.

The following statements from Bertolt Brecht's *Galileo* are satiric:

- *'And there by a wind has arisen which blows up the gold-brocaded cloaks of Princes and Prelates so that fat or skinny legs are seen beneath, legs like our legs.'* – This suggests that certain events bring to light that our highly placed noble men and women can still look ordinary or vulnerable like you and me.
- *'For where Belief had sat for a thousand years, there today sits Doubt.'*
  In the work *The Lowest Animal*, Mark Twain satirizes the moral infirmity of the entire human race by ironically comparing the behaviour of humans with that of animals and finding the latter (that of animals) morally superior.

Other examples are: Jonathan Swift's *Gulliver's Travels*, Earl of Rochester's *A Satyr Against Man*.

253. Satiric Comedy

This is comedy in which human weakness or folly is ridiculed. It may be coolly malicious and gently biting, but it tends to be critical of people, their manners and their morals. It ridicules political institutions, policies, and philosophical or religious doctrines. It attacks disorders in a society or deviations from accepted social order by ridiculing the violators of its standards of morals or manners, showing the level to which human behaviour can sink. The aim of satiric comedy is to correct the ills ridiculed by humour.

Example: We have this in *Lysistrata*, where women of two warring cities quickly halted a war by agreeing to deny themselves to their husbands. The target is men who are so proud that they go to war rather than make the slightest concession. See: *Literature: An Introduction to Fiction, Poetry, and Drama* by X. J Kennedy & Dana Gioia, 2005 (9th Edition) p.1332 and Wole Soyinka's *Trials of Brother Jero.*

254. Science-Fiction and Fantasy

This encompasses novels and short stories that represent and imagine a reality that is radically different in nature, functioning from the world of ordinary experience. The stories are usually set on another planet or earth, projected into the future or an imagined parallel universe.

255. Prologue

This is the formal introduction to a play written in prose or verse form, previewing the events to come in the book.

256. Epilogue

This is the closing comment in a play which justifies an earlier course of action or fills an untreated gap in a play. It is not part of the story but still complements it.

257. Setting

This is the total environment for the action of a fictional work. It is also the general locale or place, historical time and social circumstance in which the action in a work occurs.

258. Décor

In theatrical production, décor denotes the properties or movable pieces of furniture on stage used in the production of the drama.

259. Short Story

This is a brief work of prose fiction consisting of between 1000 and 20,000 words. It is too brief to be published in a separate volume as a novella. Most of the terms for analyzing the component elements, types and narrative techniques of the novel are applicable to short stories as well.

260. Novella

This is a slightly elaborated anecdote of perhaps five hundred words.

Example: Joseph Conrad's *Heart of Darkness*.

261. Slapstick Comedy

This is a kind of farce featuring pratfall, pie throwing, fist cuff and other violent actions.

262. Prose Fiction

This includes allegories, parables, romances, novels, and short stories.

263. Fantasy Novel

This is a narrative that depicts events, characters, or places that do not exist in the real world. It explores the possibilities of the imagination and includes elements of magic and/or the supernatural. Such novels are set in non-existent worlds, such as under the earth, in a fairyland, on the moon, etc. The characters are often something other than humans or human-like characters with exaggerated or extraordinary capabilities.

Example: J. R. R. Tolkien's *The Hobbit*.

264. Fable

This is also known as apologue. It is a brief and often humorous narrative or a story in prose or poetry told to illustrate a moral. Some fables teach practical lessons on how to succeed in life. The characters in a fable are traditionally animals whose personality traits symbolize human traits. Particular animals conventionally represent particular human qualities or values. The ant represents industry, the fox represents craftiness, the tortoise represents wisdom, and the lion represents nobility.

Example: George Orwell's *Animal Farm* (1945) is also a satire of Russian totalitarianism under Joseph Stalin in the mid-20th century.

265. Farce

This is a kind of comedy designed to provoke the audience into simple and hearty (belly) laughter. It employs highly exaggerated or caricatured or stereo-typed characters put into improbable and ludicrous situations. It involves indecorous, silly and farfetched situations, including sexual mix-ups, crude verbal jokes, pratfalls and knockabout horseplay. The humour in a farce is often physical and slapstick, with characters being hit in the face with pies or running into closed doors.

Example: Wole Soyinka's *The Lion and the Jewel*

266. Verisimilitude

This is the achievement of an illusion of reality in a literary work. It is a quality that makes a literary work appear true to life or conform to our sense of reality. It requires that the action represented by a play approximate the actual conditions of the staging of the play. Realistic detail is used in characterization, description and dialogue.

267. The Unities

These are the three formal qualities recommended by Italian Renaissance critics to unify a plot and give it cohesive and complete integrity. The unities are action, time, and space (place). This requires that a play present a single series of interrelated actions that take place within 24 hours, and the setting must be a single and unchanging locale. In other words, the play tells a single story, has one setting, and takes place within a specified period of time of one day.

268. Rising Action

This is a part of a play or narrative following the exposition, in which events start moving towards a climax.

269. Falling Action

These are the subsequent events in a narrative that follow the climax and bring the story to its conclusion. In a tragedy, falling action is seen in a protagonist's dwindling fortunes, which progress to the inexorable end. It is also known as denouement.

270. History Play

This is also known as chronicle play. It is a play which draws its material from historical records. Shakespeare's *Julius Caesar* and *Macbeth* are historical plays.

271. Concrete Poetry

These are also known as pattern poems. They are visual poems composed exclusively for the eye on pages in which a picture or image is made of printed letters and words. It was intended to blur the lines between language and visual art.

272. Conflict

This is the central struggle between two or more opposing forces or characters in a story (usually the protagonist and the antagonist), whereby some persons, things, or forces prevent the protagonist from achieving their intended goal. Internal conflict involves opposing forces within a character's mind, while external conflict involves a character and another character, a natural or artificial force, or society.

273. Contrast

A contrast between the two literary works is achieved by placing them side by side to point out their differences.

274. Comparison

This focuses on the likeness or otherwise of two literary works.

275. Convention

This is an established feature or technique in literature that is commonly understood and followed by authors and readers.

Example: It is a convention that a fairy tale commences with the: "Once upon a time."

276. Cosmic Irony

This is also called Irony of fate. It is the irony that exists in a character's aspiration and the treatment they receive at the hands of fate.

277. Crisis

This is the point in drama when a crucial action or decision is made, marking the turning point or reversal of the protagonist's fortunes.

278. Dramatic Point of View

This is a point of view in which the narrator merely reports dialogue and action with minimal interpretation or access to the characters' minds.

279. Dramatic Question

This is the primary unresolved issue in a drama as it unfolds. This question raises suspense and expectation in a play's action as it moves towards its outcome.

Example: Will the Prince in Hamlet achieve what he intends or has been instructed to do?

280. Dramatic Situation

This is the basic conflict that initiates or forms the basis or background of a work or establishes a scene. This usually describes both a protagonist's motivation and the forces that oppose its realization.

281. Editing

This is an act of proofreading a draft write-up to correct mistakes, eliminate excess words, and improve it.

282. Epigraph

This is a brief quotation preceding a story or other literary works, usually suggesting the subject, theme, or atmosphere the story will explore.

283. Elision

This is the omission of an unstressed vowel or syllable to preserve the meter of a line of poetry.

284. Playwright

This is the writer or author of a dramatic work.

285. Flashback

This is a scene relived in a character's memory and presented to the audience or readers. It allows the author to include or recreate events that occurred before the opening of the story, which may show the readers something significant that happened in the character's past or give an indication of what sort of a person the character used to be.

It is also an interruption of a work's chronology to describe at present an incident that occurred prior to the main time frame of the action or the current narration of events in a fiction or drama. Flashbacks are useful for exposition, filling the gap between a character or place or the background of a conflict. Flashback techniques include memories, dreams and stories of the past told by characters.

286. Foreshadowing

This is the use of hints and clues to suggest what will happen later in a plot. In other words, it is a technique of arranging events and situations in a plot in such a way that later events are prepared for or shadowed beforehand. The author introduces specific words, images, or actions to suggest significant later events in the work. It is used by writers to create suspense or to prefigure later events by giving hints as to the direction the story is going.

287. Folklore

This is the body of traditional wisdom and customs, including songs, stories, myths and proverbs of a people, collected and transmitted through or contained in oral tradition.

288. Foot

This is the unit of measurement in metrical poetry. Different meters are identified by the pattern and order of stressed and unstressed syllables in their foot, usually containing two or more syllables, with one syllable accented.

289. Form

This designates the genre or literary type that determines how a work is ordered and organized. It is a mode or means by which a literary work conveys its meaning. It includes the totality of ways in which it unfolds and coheres as a structure of meaning and expression.

290. Genres

These denote the classes or types into which literary works have been grouped over the years. Literary works have been grouped under numerous genres. The most enduring classification comprises three large classes: lyric, epic and drama. Similar classifications are poetry, prose fiction and drama. We also have tragedy, comedy, satire, biography, essay and novel as literary genres.

291. Gothic Fiction

This is a genre that creates supernatural horrors and an atmosphere of unknown terror and suspense. It is usually set in an isolated castle, mansion or monastery populated by mysterious or threatening individuals, where ghosts and sinister humans roam menacingly.

Example: Horace Walpole's *Castle of Otranto*

292. High Comedy

This is a comic genre evoking intellectual or thoughtful laughter from an audience that remains emotionally detached from the play's depiction of the folly, pretence and incongruity of human behaviour.

293. Low Comedy

This is a comic genre or style that arouses laughter through jokes, slapstick, humor, sight gags and boisterous clowning. Unlike high comedy, it has little intellectual appeal.

294. Locale

This is the location where a story takes place.

295. Microcosm

This is a small world created by a poem, play, or story that reflects the tensions of the larger world beyond.

296. Peripeteia

This is also pronounced as peripety. It signifies a sudden and irredeemable change or reversal of fortune or the circumstances of the protagonist. It occurs in a plot when a sudden change of circumstance affecting the protagonist occurs rather than what is expected. What usually happens is the opposite of what is expected. It can also include a change in the intent of the protagonist.

Example: In the work, *The Gods Are Not To Blame*, the protagonist expects to discover the identity of the murderer of the former King. However, when a messenger informs him that he is the one, the protagonist's intent changes to include the search for his true parentage.

297. Pulp Fiction

This is a type of fictional work quickly written and produced for cheap, mass-circulating magazines. Works of this nature have been popular but critically sneered at for having sub-literary quality (little value).

298. Run on Line

This is a line of verse that does not end in punctuation but carries on grammatically on the next line. The idea in one line runs into another and may not complete the message until the next line. It is also called an enjambment.

An example is found in Robert Browning's *My Last Duchess*:

1. *Sir, 'twas not*

> *Her husband's presence only, called that spot*
> *Of joy into the Duchess' cheek: perhaps*
> *Fra Pandolf chanced to say, 'Her mantle*
> *Must never hope to reproduce the faint*
> *Half-flushed that dies along* her throat'
> *Was courtesy, thought…*

2. *When the world rises*

> *In the early hours*
> *Both animate and inanimate objects*
> *Give glory to the Lord.*

299. Sarcasm

This is a conspicuously bitter form of irony in which the ironic statement is designed to hurt or mock its target. It is also a sneering criticism in which disapproval is often expressed as ironic praise.

Example: 'Verily, ye are the people and wisdom shall die with you.' This means that they are senseless.

300. Satiric Poetry

This is poetry that blends criticism with humor to convey a message. Its tone is usually one of detached amusement, contempt and implied superiority, using irony to drive its point home.

301. Static Character

This is another term for a flat character.

302. Tall Tale

This is a short narrative that provides a wildly exaggerated version of events. Usually, in oral form, a tall tale assumes that its audience knows that the narrator is distorting the facts of the events.

303. Tone

This is the attitude of a writer towards their readers and the subject conveyed in a literary work. It is the net result of the various elements used by an author in creating the work, reflecting their mood, manner and moral view. It may be formal, informal, playful, sarcastic, ironic, sad, solemn, optimistic, pessimistic, or any other possible attitude.

304. Troubadours

These were minstrels (lyric poets) of the Middle Ages who sang to aristocratic audiences in Southern France and Northern Italy, mostly about chivalry and love.

305. Stage

This is a raised area or platform, usually in a theatre, where actors and dancers perform before an audience.

306. Stage Direction

This is a playwright's descriptive or interpretative comments that provide readers (and actors and producers) with information about the dialogues, setting and action of a play. It describes the appearances and actions of characters as well as the settings, costumes, props, sound and light effects of the drama.

307. Archetype

This is an old imaginative pattern that has appeared in literature throughout the ages. Archetypes can be plotted, for example, the death of the hero, the boy winning the girl, etc. They can be characters, for example, the trickster, the saviour, the rescued maiden, etc. They can also be images, for example, a place where people never die, a golden cup, hoarded treasure, etc.

308. Plot

This is the central organizing idea that unites character, action, language, and style in a work of fiction. It is also the bare outline of the story arranged in logical order. To be good, the plot must possess intrigue.

309. Naturalism

This is a 19th-century literary movement that claimed to portray life exactly as it is, with detachment and objectivity.

310. Stream of Consciousness

This is a style of writing that conveys the inner and sometimes chaotic workings of a character's mind. According to X. J. Kennedy and Dana Gioia, it is the procession of thoughts moving through the mind, a kind of selective omniscience that involves the presentation of thoughts and sense impressions in a lifelike fashion, not in a sequence arranged by logic but mingled randomly.

311. Ambiguity

In literature, this is the technique by which a writer deliberately suggests two or more different, and sometimes conflicting, interpretations or meanings in their writings or work. In poetry, a poem may present two mind-sets, and it is unclear which of the two is being endorsed by the poet.
Example: Robert Frost's *Mending Wall*

312. Repetition

This is the recurrence of certain sounds, words, phrases, or lines in a poem to achieve rhythmic or emotional effect. See our earlier discussion on this.

313. Analogy

This is a comparison between two things to show how they are alike. It is a process of comparing one thing with another with similar features to explain it.

Example: In *Crisis, No.1,* Thomas Paine draws an analogy between a thief breaking into a house and the king of England interfering in the affairs of the American Colonies.

314. Atmosphere

This is the mood or feeling created in a piece of writing. It might be peaceful, festive, menacing, melancholic, etc. Let the students know the meanings of these adjectives and look out for the multiple-choice questions.

315. Amphiboly

This is a statement that conveys double meanings designed to mislead or deceive the person to whom it is directed. The statement is always true in one interpretation and false in another.

Example: *'If Croesus went to war with Persia, a mighty Kingdom will be destroyed.'*

The person to whom this statement was directed, King Croesus, was deceived into believing that he would destroy the great Kingdom of Persia if he went to war with it when, in actual fact, it was their own kingdom that was destroyed.

316. Negritude

This depicts a literary ideology or movement whose primary aim is to revive, through literature, the cultural values, identity and authenticity of Africans and to uplift the ancestral glories and beauty of Africa.

Leopold Senghor is reputed to have been the greatest exponent of this ideology.

317. Adaptation

This is the transformation of a literary work from its original form or medium to another. It involves, for instance, rewriting a drama into prose form or a prose work into drama form.
Examples: *Lamb Tales from Shakespeare* and *More Lamb Tales from Shakespeare* by Charles and Mary Lamb.

318. Cliché

This is a word or phrase, often a figure of speech, which has become lifeless because of overuse. It also signifies an expression that deviates from ordinary usage to call attention to itself and has been used so often that it is felt to be hackneyed or stereotyped.
Examples: "Green with envy", "as quiet as a mouse", "pretty as a picture", "I beg your pardon", or "sincerely yours."

319. Audience Participation

This is a technique in stage production whereby both the stage and the auditorium are involved in a play's production. The audience takes an active part in the realization of the drama at the point where the dividing line between it and the stage varnishes as the ongoing action spills over into the audience, which then transforms itself and plays the role of either a crowd, an assembly, or a congregation, etc., as may be required by the plot of the drama.

320. Dejavu

This is a system of plot development which creates the future through anticipation and the past through memory. The creation of the future through anticipation is done by weaving the story of a literary work around what is expected or hoped for or what should be the case based on certain facts on the ground, available, or a conviction about a situation. The creation of the past through memory involves drawing from past events and painting a picture of the past in a literary work.

321. Literati

This is a body of imaginative men and women of letters or a group of educated and intelligent people who enjoy literature.

322. Lineation

This is the arrangement of lines in verse form. Poems are written and arranged in lines that are metrically measured.

323. Literary Techniques

These are techniques used by authors to enhance the written framework of a piece of literature and to produce specific effects. It encompasses a wide range of approaches to crafting a work. They indicate to a reader that there is a familiar structure and presentation to a work. For example, the epistolary technique comes in the form of letters.

324. Literary Devices

These are specific constructions within a narrative that make it effective.

Examples: Metaphor, simile, ellipsis, narrative motif, allegory, wordplay, stream of consciousness, etc.

325. Suspension of Disbelief

This is a temporary willingness to see things through the spectacle of a writer. This term, coined by Samuel Taylor Coleridge, often applies to fictional works of action, comedy, fantasy and horror genres whereby a writer infuses a human interest and a semblance of truth into a fantastic tale, which makes the readers or audience suspend judgment concerning the implausibility of the narrative. Here, the readers or audience willingly overlook the limitations of a medium in such a way that they do not interfere with the acceptance of what has been presented. It can also be said to be the willingness to believe the unbelievable as reason or logic is jettisoned or cast aside for implausibility. It enables the readers or audience to better appreciate the drama or have a true imaginative experience of it without obvious limits.

Example: In certain fantastic movies, viewers are made to accept or believe, and not to doubt, natural man's capacity to transform into ferocious animals or beings or exhibit attributes normally beyond man's capacity.

326. Hendiadys

This is a rhetorical figure in which a sole or single idea is represented by two words connected by a conjunction.

Example: Football is a game and a religion in Brazil.

Please note the close resemblance of hendiadys and zeugma. While Hendiadys focuses on a sole idea being represented by two words that are connected by a conjunction, zeugma focuses on a single word that stands in the same grammatical relations to two or more other words but with an obvious shift in its significance.

Example: He fired the gun and his gardener.

327. Metaphrase

This is changing a literary work from its particular or original form to another. For example, turning prose into verse, or drama; or verse into prose or drama, or rendering a work cast in a particular form into a different style or form. For example, some of the Shakespearian plays were re-cast into prose by Charles and Mary Lamb. In the film industry, works like *Time to Kill* by John Grisham, *Mayor of Casterbridge* by Thomas Hardy, and *Lord of the Flies* by William Golden, which were prose fiction, have been re-cast into drama. See also Adaptation.

328. Portmenteau Word

This is an artificial word that combines parts of other words to express some combination of their qualities. It is a fusion of two meanings packed into one artificial word.

Examples: "Smog" from "smoke" and "fog"

"Brunch" from "breakfast" and "lunch"

329. Poetic Drama

This is a play wholly written in verse, which can be performed or simply read as in Cheset drama.

Examples: Milton's *Samson Agonistes* (ib71),
Bigron's *Manfred* (1817), T. S. Eliot's *Murder in the Cathedral*

330. Projection

This is a technique opposite of flashback. Here, the playwright goes into the future to show the readers the consequences of current or present actions.

Projection differs from foreshadowing as projection shows the full record of an event to come later while foreshadowing hints at what is to come.

331. Prompter

This is an actor off stage with the role of assisting the actual actors in carrying out their assigned performance roles.

332. Audition

This is theatre practice whereby actors of a play are selected to play specific assigned roles in the performance.

333. Bildungsroman

This is also called an apprenticeship novel. It refers to a novel of growth and development. It centres on the development of the mind and character of a protagonist as they pass from childhood through varied experiences and spiritual crises to maturity.

Examples: Charles Dickens's *David Copperfield*
James Joyce's *Portrait of the Artist as A Young Man*

334. Monodrama/Monologue

This is an extended speech by a single actor. It is a solo speech that has listeners. Being an unbroken speech by one character to another silent character or characters, it is different from soliloquy, where the character speaks only to himself/herself.

335. Domestic Tragedy

This is a form of tragedy that retains all the basic elements of tragedy but differs in its setting and characterization. Here, the main characters are middle-class people, and their downfall takes place within a family relationship. This differs from classical tragedies, where characters are great personalities like kings, generals, princes, etc.

Chapter 10

Selected Essay and Objective Test Questions

It is essential to take practice or mock tests before the actual exam. This helps the students or candidates determine the level of their preparation for the exam. It also helps them identify any particular weakness they have in any section of the subject despite having prepared well for the exam.

The essence of including sample questions in this book is to show the candidates how the exam questions are. At the end of the book, a provision has been made for sample answers for both the objective and essay test questions. For the essay questions, the answers are rather in sketch format (for lack of space). It is meant to show the candidates how to present or structure their answers. It will help them understand the best way to approach the questions. The answers have been supplied by experienced teachers and examiners in the subject. Candidates may choose to pattern their answers in the form given. However, they are free to vary the pattern as the ones provided here are mere illustrations and are not particularly detailed enough to satisfy the demands of the questions. What is important here is to present a kind of format to show what the answers should look like and contain in line with what the examiner demands in the questions beautifully and logically presented.

For multiple-choice questions, it is also essential that candidates make adequate use of past exam questions on the subject for the exam bodies and different years. This is because new questions are rarely asked by the examiners, except perhaps the ones on set texts. What we usually have are the same or recycled questions showing up from time to time, slightly rephrased or modified to make them appear different from the earlier ones.

Exercise A (Essay Questions)

Prose

1. Examine the character of Aku.
2. Comment on the effectiveness of Okpewho's narrative technique in the novel.
3. Compare village and city life as portrayed in the novel.
4. Examine any two of the following traditions in the novel:
   A. Marriage
   B. Childbearing
   C. Superstition
5. Discuss the relationship between Richard and his family.
6. How are the blacks treated at the orphanage in the novel?
7. How is village life portrayed in the novel?
8. Assess the contribution of Eppie to the development of the plot.

Poetry

1. Comment on the thematic pre-occupation of the poet in *The Dash Between.*
2. How did the poet present the issue of death in the poem?
3. Comment on the tone of the poet in Sola Owoniyi's *Homeless Not Hopeless.*
4. Comment on the use of symbolism in the poem.

Drama

1. Discuss the theme of racial discrimination in the play.
2. Comment on the use of comedy in the play.
3. Discuss the use of irony in the play.
4. Examine the relationship between James and his two children, Maanan and Aaron.
5. How is corruption exposed in the play?
6. Examine the use of mistaken identity in the play.
7. How does Thomas More demonstrate moral uprightness in the play?
8. Examine the role of the common man in the play.

Exercise B (Objective Test Questions)

1. *A: Aha, confession…Now? (Pause) Well, it's not a good time to hear confessions…I hear confessions in the church from 4 to 6 p.m…*
B: What shall I advise?
A: Putting some money into the box before she does a confession. An offering is also a sign to repent wholeheartedly; you know better than me, Sister.

–   Jesus of Gold Crown, Dong-Jin Lee

From the excerpt, it can be inferred that Speaker A is a:

    A. Doctor
    B. Priest
    C. Psychologist
    D. teacher

2. Speaker B is a:

    A. Lay reader
    B. Nurse
    C. Reverend Sister
    D. Catechist

3. The excerpt can best be described as a/an:

    A. Eulogy
    B. Alliteration
    C. Satire
    D. Tragedy

4. Essentially, plays are meant to:

    A. Excite pleasure
    B. Instill fear
    C. Be presented on stage
    D. To best studied

5.

"You cannot know
And should not bother
Tide and market come and go
And so shall your mother."

In this verse, the poet uses:
    A. Alternate rhymes
    B. Mono-rhyme
    C. Couplets
    D. Blank verse

6. *The Comstocks belonged to the most dismal of all classes, the middle–middleclass, the landless gentry. In their miserable poverty they had not even the snobbish consolation of regarding themselves as an 'old' family fallen on evil days.*
        The writer's tone is:
    A. Melancholic
    B. Matter-of-fact
    C. Bitterly humorous
    D. Sympathetic
    E. Sad

7. Which of the following is odd?
    A. Raisin in the Sun
    B. Twelfth Night
    C. Ozidi
    D. The Concubine
    E. Romeo and Juliet

8. Point out the odd item:
    A. Plot
    B. Metaphor
    C. Zeugma
    D. Hyperbole

9. An image in poetry usually gives a clue to one of the following:
    A. Rhyme
    B. Assonance
    C. Paradox
    D. Refrain
    E. Theme

10. *That year the harvest was sad, like a funeral, and many farmers wept as they dug up the miserable yam. One man tied his cloth to a tree branch and hanged himself.*

The mood conveyed in this passage is one of:
A. Excitement
B. Sadness
C. Joy
D. Elation
E. Triumph

11. A good poem must:
A. Have regular rhyme
B. Be about love
C. Be about sweet events
D. Be difficult to understand
E. None of the above

12. One of the following is a narrative technique in the novel:
A. Flashback
B. Character
C. Interesting story
D. Social relevance
E. Logical conclusion

13. Which of these is true of a novel?
A. It deals with human experience
B. It is a copy of historical events
C. It is a story about the author's life
D. It does not make use of imagery

14.

"And your laughter like a flame
Piercing the shadows
Has revealed Africa to me.
Beyond the snows of yesterday
'Shadows' in the above signifies
Lazy figures appearing before the poet."

Experiences which have hidden Africa from the poet's life are:

A. A period of suffering in the poet's life
B. Unclear ideas which the poet has
C. The ghosts of the dead

15. One of the following is better known as a playwright than as a novelist:

A. Wole Soyinka
B. Chinua Achebe
C. J. P. Clerk
D. C. Ekwensi
E. Gabriel Okara

16. The plot of a novel is best described as:

A. The bare outline of the story arranged in logical order
B. The story in all its details
C. The story grossly
D. Summary of the story
E. The beginning, middle and end of the story

17. A narrative poem must:

A. Tell a story
B. Preach a sermon
C. Describe natural scenery
D. Argue a question
E. Propound a philosophy

18. Literature is studied in school because:

A. It exposes students to the realities of life
B. It provides entertainment
C. It gives additional work to students
D. It teaches the use of words
E. It provides a pastime

19. Exposition in a play means:
    A. The initial unfolding of the necessary background for the play
    B. Its climax
    C. The marriage of the hero and the heroine
    D. The untangling of the plot
    E. The private speech of a character

20. A good plot must possess:
    A. Many exciting events
    B. Good and interesting characters
    C. A pleasant setting
    D. Intrigue
    E. A single, complete and ordered action

21. A novel can be described as:
    A. A story
    B. A narration of facts
    C. A brief description of a concept or point of view
    D. An extended prose narrative covering a wide range of characters and experience
    E. A narration of an accident

22. Pick out the odd item.
    A. Metaphor
    B. Characterization
    C. Personification
    D. Rhythm
    E. Simile

23. A play is drama because:
    A. It contains characters
    B. It does not contain any story
    C. It cannot be read silently
    D. It can be acted
    E. It is written in verse

24. Which one of the following is a mark of good poetry:
    A. An interesting story
    B. Imaginative use of language
    C. Realistic characterization
    D. Flashback
    E. Audience

25.

> *"At mankind's feast, I take my place*
> *In solemn, sanctimonious state*
> *And have the air of saying grace*
> *While I defile the dinner plate."*

The tone of this passage may be described as:
    A. Solemn
    B. Self-mocking
    C. Dead earnest
    D. Serious
    E. Angry

26.

> *"The woods decay, the woods decay and fall.*
> *The vapors weep their burthen to the ground.*
> *Man comes and fills the field*
> *And lies beneath,*
> *And after many a summer dies*
> *The swan"*

The theme of these lines is:
    A. The falling of leaves
    B. The ground on which leaves fall
    C. Man as a farmer
    D. The power of death over every life
    E. The flight of birds in certain seasons

27. *A woman cried out. The policeman was edging nearer carefully and slowly. But it was not that that had made the woman cry out. She had seen one of the man's hands slip. He was now holding on by one hand*

only. The crowd was tense. This was the kill. Automatically, they moved forward in a body. The doctor was in the lead.

The author of this passage creates in the reader:
- A. Disbelief
- B. A feeling of nostalgia
- C. A feeling of light-hearted relaxation
- D. Suspense
- E. A feeling of uncertainty

28. The main purpose of drama is to:
- A. Tell the story of dead people
- B. Teach us how to write
- C. Educate us
- D. Entertain us
- E. Both educate and entertain us

29.

"Stars, hide your fires;
Let no light see my black
And deep desires.
The eye wink at the hand
Yet let that be
Which the eye fears, when
It is done to see."

In these lines, the author uses:
- A. Hyperbole
- B. Metonymy
- C. Onomatopoeia
- D. Simile
- E. Apostrophe

30. Poetry deals with one of the following:
- A. Emotion only
- B. Death only
- C. Ideas only
- D. Emotion and idea
- E. Beauty only

31.

> *"Comes this season of cassia flower,*
> *And pent passion peers through the bower,*
> *Comes this season and all labour is fallen*
> *All earthen pitchers as china broken"*

The rhyme scheme in this passage is:
- A. Alternate
- B. Triplets
- C. Couplets
- D. Free verse
- E. Blank verse

32. Drama is essentially different from poetry because:
- A. It always involves many characters
- B. It exists mainly in action
- C. It uses elevated language
- D. It uses localized imagery
- E. It deals with tragic experience

33. Which of the following best describes comedy?
- A. A play in which nobody dies
- B. A play which evokes slaughter
- C. A play in which the hero is a clean character
- D. A play which ends happily
- E. A play which is not boring

34. *"Such drizzling can go on for many days,"* she said in dull voice. *They both relapsed into silence, making a picture of bereaved children from whom life has suddenly lost warmth, colour, and excitement. There was no fire in the hearth.*

The mood captured in this passage is one of:
- A. Excitement
- B. Warmth
- C. Hopefulness
- D. High spirits
- E. Sadness

35.

> *"Had I the heavens' embroidered cloths:*
> *Enwrought with golden and silver light.*
> *The blue and the dim and the dark cloths*
> *Of night and light, and the half-light,*
> *I would spread the cloths under your feet.*
> *But I, being poor, have only my dreams:*
> *I have spread my dreams under your feet.*
> *Tread softly because you tread on my dreams."*

The poet of these lines:

- A. Shows cheap love
- B. Is incapable of seriousness
- C. Considers heaven's cloths worthless
- D. Is a sensitive, serious lover
- E. Is a non-realistic, wishful man

36.

> *"The celebration is now ended*
> *But the echoes are all around,*
> *Whirling-wind throwing dust around*
> *And hands cover faces and feet grope."*

The last line suggests that the occasion celebrated:

- F. Brought peace to the land
- G. Did not lead to joyful times
- H. Did not receive general approval
- I. Produced more merriment
- J. Affected climatic conditions

37.

> *"The clouds were thickening in the red sky*
> *And night had charmed*
> *A black power into the pounding waves."*

The figure of speech used in these lines is:

- A. Personification
- B. Metaphor
- C. Simile
- D. Synecdoche

    E. Oxymoron

38. An interlude is a brief:
    A. Presentation in the interval of a dramatic performance
    B. Play before the main dramatic performance
    C. Presentation after the main dramatic performance
    D. Dialogue between two persons

39. An epic is a heroic story which includes:
    A. Ballad
    B. Lyric
    C. Myth
    D. Dialogue

40. Farce can be described as a dramatic piece marked by:
    A. Movement from a serious to a light-hearted mood
    B. Comic and exaggerated actions
    C. Actions devoid of meaning
    D. Gloomy actions with momentary relief

41. A long story narrating a series of complicated events is called a:
    A. Saga
    B. Discourse
    C. Monologue
    D. D. Harangue

42. Oxymoron is the use of two contrasting words that are:
    A. Placed far apart
    B. Different in meaning
    C. Placed side by side
    D. Similar in meaning

43. A line or a group of lines repeated in the course of a poem is called:
    A. Chorus

   B.   Refrain
   C.   Repetition
   D.   Prologue

44. Limerick is a light verse which consists of five lines that are:
   A.   Anapestic
   B.   Trochaic
   C.   Dactylic
   D.   Spondaic

45. A short narrative or lyric poem intended to be sung is a:
   A.   Leich
   B.   Lay
   C.   Lauda
   D.   Lectrilla

46. A figurative device in which a statement is made and then withdrawn is referred to as:
   A.   Metaphysical
   B.   Metanoia
   C.   Metalanguage
   D.   Metalepsis

47. A literary work which imitates another in a distorted form is called:
   A.   Exordium
   B.   Isocohen
   C.   Metonymy
   D.   Burlesque

48. *You do not have to be brutal to be a soldier, or rather you are brutal not because you are a soldier, but because there is a sadist, a rapist, a fascist, and a murderer in you who is waiting for war and army uniforms to give them expression.*

—Heroes, Festus Iyayi

The speaker contends that:
   A.   Soldiers are generally wicked

B. Human nature has to do with a profession
C. Soldiers are characteristically gentle
D. The latent brutality in man finds expression in war

49. *But the towering earth was tired of sitting in one position. She moved, suddenly, and the houses crumbled, the mountains heaved horrible, and the work of million years was lost.*
The subject matter of the passage is likely to be:
  A. Earthquake
  B. Demolition
  C. Flood
  D. Storm

50. The image depicted is one of:
  A. Destruction
  B. Dejection
  C. Happiness
  D. Admiration

51.

"She even thinks that up in heaven
Her class lies late and shores
While poor black cherubs rise at seven
To do celestial chores"

The tone of the poem above is:
  A. Satiric
  B. Affectionate
  C. Indifferent
  D. Sympathetic

52.

My heart leaps up when I behold
A rain in the sky:
So was it when my life began;
So be it when I grow old
Or, let me die!

The child is the father of the man;
And I could wish my days to be
Bound each to each by natural piety

-William Wordsworth

The expression 'the child is the father of the man' is an example of:

A. Paradox
B. Metaphor
C. Simile
D. Ellipsis

53. A character that heavily relies on cultural types for their manner of speech, their personality, and other distinguished characteristics is:

A. A fictional character
B. A stock character
C. A round character
D. An antagonist

54. Monometer is a:

A. Single meter of Coleridge's poem Christabel
B. Single foot used in John Milton's sonnets
C. Line repeated in the first syllable of a word
D. Line of a verse consisting of a metrical foot

55. Zeugma is a figurative device in which a:

A. Noun refers to two parts of an expression
B. Conjunction governs two parts of an expression
C. Verb refers to two parts of an expression
D. Pronoun governs two parts of an expression

56. Black theatre is drama concerned with:

A. Mourners dressed in black
B. Actors of black origin
C. The identity of black Americans
D. Africans of West Indian origin

57. The quality in a literary work that evokes tenderness, pity or sorrow is:
- A. Pathos
- B. Patois
- C. Pataphysics
- D. Pathopoeia

58. The moment of recognition of truth, when ignorance gives way to knowledge in a character, is known as:
- A. A. Hamartia
- B. B. Anagnorisis
- C. C. Hubris
- D. D. Amnesia

59.

> *"The hunter dies*
> *And leaves*
> *His poverty to his gun.*
> *The blacksmith dies*
> *And leaves his poverty to his anvil."*

The above extract is an example of:
- A. Elegy
- B. Ballad
- C. Epic
- D. Eulogy

60.

> *"O fleeting gleam of noon dream,*
> *You incensed my clothed cream."*

The literary device used in the lines above is:
- A. Repetition
- B. Refrain
- C. Consonance
- D. Assonance

61. The physical setting within which the action of a narrative takes place is the:
    A. Stage
    B. Scene
    C. Locale
    D. Location

62. An anti-social action taken by the tragic hero which results in a catastrophe is called:
    A. Anagnorisis
    B. Premonition
    C. Hamartia
    D. Empathy

63. A work which takes place in a non-existent world or which concerns an incredible character is:
    A. Romance
    B. Fantasy
    C. Parody
    D. Superstition

64. A humorous scene, incident or speech in the course of a serious fiction or drama is:
    A. Play-within-play
    B. Comic scene
    C. Comic relief
    D. Tragic-comedy

65. A travelogue is:
    A. The account of the travails of a character in a novel
    B. A record of the writer's experiences during a journey
    C. A variation of a novel written in freestyle on a writer's journey
    D. The account of the experiences of an individual during their lifetime

66. Flashback in literary work helps:
    A. To fill in the missing link
    B. To reveal the characters' mindset
    C. To place the story in proper perspective
    D. To relate events that are extraneous to the story

67. An address to a metaphysical source of inspiration by a poet
is called:
    A. Clairvoyance
    B. Inspiration
    C. Invocation
    D. Nemesis

68. The sides of a stage are called:
    A. The ways
    B. Both sides
    C. The pits
    D. The wings

69. A metrical pause occurring in the middle of a line in a poem is
called:
    A. Rhythm
    B. Tetrameter
    C. Assonance
    D. Caesura

70. *"The ripest seed is the saddest encounter"* – The expression is a:
    A. Metaphor
    B. Euphemism
    C. Paradox
    D. Hyperbole

71.

> *"And the promised pleasure*
> *Will never ever be found*
> *In the face of vanished treasure,*
> *In the face of plundered pound*
> *Hidden beneath roots of greener grasses,*
> *In a land far from the masses."*

The tone of the poem above is:

    A. Interrogative
    B. Persuasive
    C. Optimistic
    D. Pessimistic

72.

> *"My heart is a quiet drum,*
> *Sometimes, it flares like a*
> *Parched thunder*
> *Cracking through a damask sky.*
> *It lifts me in its fired spectacle."*

The imagery in the excerpt above is:

    A. Auditory and visual
    B. Tactile
    C. Olfactory and visual
    D. Olfactory and tactile

73.

> *"Where has my love blown his horn?*
> *The tune of his horn is well-known.*
> *Young men of my clan,*
> *Have you heard the horn of my love?"*

The overall feeling of the persona in this extract is:

    A. Frustration
    B. Joy
    C. Certainty
    D. Anxiety

74.

"It is a beauteous evening, calm and free.
The holy time is quiet as a nun,
Breathless with adoration; the broad sun
Is sinking down in its tranquility;
The gentleness of heaven broads o'er the sea.
Listen, the mighty being is awake
And doth with his eternal motion make
A sound like thunder everlastingly."

The rhyme scheme of the stanza above is:
A. Abbcadde
B. Ddccbbca
C. Bbacddac
D. Cbbacdda

75. When an object is invested with a meaning beyond its immediate reference, it becomes:
A. A symbol
B. A subject
C. An epigram
D. An irony

76. A poem without a regular rhyme scheme is a:
A. Lyrical poem
B. Traditional poem
C. Blank verse
D. Ballad

77. A short, carefully phrased expression meant to elicit amusement and surprise is:
A. Wit
B. Tercet
C. Hyperbole
D. Limerick

78. Cast in a play refers to:
    A.   Three of the actors
    B.   An exclusive social class in the play
    C.   All the actors
    D.   A few of the actors

79. Aesthetics in literature has to do with the creation of:
    A.   Lines
    B.   Theme
    C.   Imagery
    D.   Beauty

80. Unity of time in a tragedy implies that all action should take place:
    A.   Within the same locale
    B.   In a single revolution of the sun
    C.   Intermittently
    D.   Simultaneously

81. A careful choice of words dictated by a particular mood or an event refers to:
    A.   Tone
    B.   Register
    C.   Cadence
    D.   Rhyme

82. A deliberate imitation of a literary style to ridicule is:
    A.   Paradox
    B.   Parody
    C.   Prosody
    D.   Pun

83.

"The gloom will give way to light
And the thorny path cleared of pain.
The storms will bow to the prompting of peace.
Moments of glory will be restored

> *And strangled opportunities reborn:*
> *We shall yet regain the dawn."*

The suggestion that runs through the short poem above is that of:
- A. Fear of change
- B. Anxiety and worry
- C. Sorrow and dejection
- D. Anticipation of positive change

84.

> *"To see the world in a grain of sand*
> *And a heaven in a wild flower,*
> *Hold infinity in the palm of your hand*
> *And eternity in an hour."*

>   – *William Blake*

The predominant figure of speech used in the lines above is:
- A. Hyperbole
- B. Metaphor
- C. Simile
- D. Paradox

85. *If God is the sole author of man's life and all that befall him on earth, does it not stand to reason that all evils that befall man are God sanctioned? If man generally turns to God to bail him out of evil or bad occurrences, is one wrong then to conclude that He allows evils to befall man to bring him back to Him?*

The literary style used in the passage above is:
- A. Interrogative
- B. Discursive
- C. Accusative
- D. Rhetorical

86. Periphrasis in poetic diction is marked by:
- A. Irony
- B. Parable
- C. Circumlocution

    D. Proverb

87. In a narration, the first person is:
    A. The author
    B. The publisher
    C. Participant
    D. An observer

88. The poetic device that forcefully brings together two seemingly unrelated ideas or concepts is:
    A. Couplet
    B. Diatribe
    C. Conceit
    D. Contrast

89. For a play to be successful on stage, it must not be short of:
    A. Speeches
    B. Actions
    C. Characters
    D. Audience

90. The exclusive right given to authors to protect their works from unlawful production is:
    A. An authority to write
    B. An author's right
    C. Legal writ
    D. A copyright

91. Denouncement in a literary work is:
    A. The point of disagreement in a narrative
    B. The point of the resolution of the puzzling issues in the work
    C. Cathartic point in a tragedy
    D. The point at which the major character is shown in their true colours

92.

> *"Since you left here,*
> *My mind longs after there.*
> *Now, in the dark, I grope*
> *Keenly striving to cope."*

—   *Gbemisola Adeoti*

The dominant technique used in the lines above is:

A. Metaphor
B. Irony
C. Alliteration
D. Rhyme

93.

> *"The guilty are too well-fed*
> *To pass through the needle's*
> *Eye of our scorn.*
> *The noose of public contempt*
> *Hangs idle at the market place."*

—   *Odia Ofeimun*

The allusion in the excerpt above is:

A. Biblical
B. Mythical
C. Classical
D. Historic

94.

> *"Everywhere now, freedom is on the loose*
> *And in its name, men and women slaughter*
> *One another with terrible abandon:*
> *Carnage has become the means of*
> *Settling simple scores with our friends."*

—   *Okinba Launko*

The dominant rhetorical device in the poem above is:

A. Limerick
B. Oxymoron
C. Assonance

    D. Innuendo

95. *"This thing you are doing is too heavy for you," he said. "I went to school only a little, but I have killed many many more years in this world than you have."*

– Gabriel Okara: The Voice

What can be inferred from the passage is:
    A. The speaker is a porter
    B. The speaker is more experienced
    C. The listener is wise
    D. The speaker is a murderer

96. The form of poetry that celebrates with nostalgia the ideal world of the countryside is referred to as:
    A. A ballad
    B. An ode
    C. A pastoral
    D. An elegy

97. In literary convention, 'aside' is used:
    A. To distinguish between events
    B. To emphasize scenes as different from acts
    C. To gossip about other characters
    D. To make a pointed remark

98. The tragic character is the person whose experiences arouse:
    A. Pity and sympathy
    B. Pity and terror
    C. Laughter and horror
    D. Laughter and frustration

99. Allegory is used to describe a work in which:
    A. Both animals and humans swap roles
    B. Humans are transposed into animals
    C. Abstract ideas are personified
    D. Animals are given human characters

100. The writing convention in which the events in a narrative are scrambled as they come to the writer's mind without any attempt to arrange them in orderly sequence is called:
 A. Psycho-consciousness style
 B. Narrator's mind style
 C. Stream of consciousness
 D. Shifting style

101. Farce thrives on:
 A. Big events
 B. Incidents
 C. Premonition
 D. Absurdity

102. The author of a novel sustains the reader's interest through the use of:
 A. Suspense
 B. Ambiguity
 C. Prologue
 D. Absurdity

103. 'Theatre in the round' is employed to achieve a:
 A. Quick resolution of conflicts
 B. Contrast between the hero and the villain
 C. Close rapport between players and spectators
 D. Hilarious ending

104.

"And the hyacinth purple, and white, and blue,
Which flung from its bells a
Sweet peal a new
Of music so delicate, soft and intense.
It was felt like odor within the sense."

– *Shelly*

The dominant literary device used in the above poem is:
 A. Assonance

    B. Caesura
    C. Synesthesia
    D. Parallelism

105. The device synesthesia relates to:
    A. Play on words
    B. Sense transference
    C. Metrical analysis
    D. Diction

106. Which of the following is true of convention in literature?
    A. A tacit agreement between the author and audience on devices used in an artistic medium
    B. Laid down rules and regulations used in literary discourse and criticism
    C. International agreements as they relate to literary discourse
    D. An assemblage of literary men

107. 'Aside' is different from 'soliloquy' because:
    A. It is inaudible to the other characters
    B. It is audible to the other characters
    C. It is audible only to a few characters close by
    D. It conveys information about a character's mood and state of mind

108. In its classic form, the short story is distinguished by its:
    A. Prosaic conception
    B. Narrative form
    C. Resolution
    D. Compact plot

109. *I am not going to be drawn into that old trap of an argument and be picked up by the trail like some wet rat out of a sewer.* – The speaker in the statement is:
    A. Symbolical
    B. Analogical

C. Metaphorical
D. Parabolical

110. A body of imaginative men and women of letters is generally referred to as:
    A. Litterateur
    B. Laureates
    C. Literaria
    D. Literati

111. A poem written to celebrate one's wedding is:
    A. Pastoral
    B. An epithalamium
    C. A prothalamium
    D. A terza rima

112. An iambic metrical foot consists of:
    A. A nun stressed syllable following a stressed syllable
    B. A stressed syllable following another stressed syllable
    C. A nun stressed syllable
    D. A stressed syllable following an unstressed syllable

113. Empathy is achieved when the audience:
    A. Feels betrayed by the director
    B. Denounces and humiliates the protagonist
    C. Vicariously participates in the stage experience
    D. Attacks the character foil

114. An irredeemable reversal of the hero's fortune in a tragedy is called:
    A. Anagnorisis
    B. Peripety (periteteia)
    C. Purgation
    D. Hubrils

115.

"Ibadan,
Running splash of rust
And gold—flung and scattered
Among seven hills like broken
China in the sun."

– *J.P. Clark*

The poem is largely built around the device of:
  A. Visual imagery
  B. Auditory imagery
  C. Tactile imagery
  D. Olfactory imagery

116. The term 'running splash of rust/and gold' as used in the poem is:
  A. Personifying
  B. Onomatopoeic
  C. Metaphorical
  D. Hyperbolic

117. 'Like broken/china in the sun' is a(n):
  A. Simile
  B. Exaggeration
  C. Euphemism
  D. Metaphor

118. The most important concepts in poetry are:
  A. Story and action
  B. Plot and rhythm
  C. Rhythm and imagery
  D. Plot and character

119. The literary device that anticipates that an event will take place is best described as:
  A. Foreshadowing
  B. Rising action
  C. Flashback

    D. Parody

120. The overwhelming or overweening pride that destroys the tragic hero is called:
    A. Tragedy
    B. Nemesis
    C. Catharsis
    D. Hubris

121. A farce refers to a drama that has the elements of the:
    A. Serious
    B. Satiric
    C. Comic
    D. Tragic

122. Catharsis is experienced:
    A. After a play is written
    B. When a play is being staged
    C. Before watching a play
    D. After watching a play

123. An extended fictional narrative which is realistic is known as a
    A. Diary
    B. Novel
    C. Novella
    D. Short story

124. The technique in which both the stage and auditorium are involved in a play production is called:
    A. Theatre of the absurd
    B. Role playing
    C. Audience participation
    D. Total theatre

125. A character who does not develop or experience change in the course of their existence in a novel is a:
    A. Round character
    B. Flat character
    C. Protagonist
    D. Major character

126. A panegyric poem is composed to:
    A. Elaborate
    B. Abuse
    C. Condemn
    D. Praise

127. The narrator in a prose work who is also a character is a/an:
    A. Objective narrator
    B. Omniscient narrator
    C. Subjective narrator
    D. Participatory narrator

128. A primary ballad is associated with:
    A. Educated people
    B. Urban folk
    C. The nomads
    D. Rural folk

129. A trio-logy is the:
    A. Sequence of three plays written by the same author
    B. Set of three one-act dramas written by related authors
    C. Collection of three poems of equal length
    D. Series of related stories divided into three equal parts

130. A figure of speech in which the poet attributes some characteristics of a thing to another thing closely associated with it is:
    A. Transferred epiphany
    B. Transferred metaphor
    C. Transferred epithet

D. Transferred comparison

131. A trimester is:
   A. A verse consisting of three metrical feet or three primary stresses per line
   B. A verse of three lines
   C. A verse of three lines, two of which are a couplet
   D. All of the above

132. A novel which focuses on the adventures of a rogue who does not change much in the course of the story is:
   A. Romanesque
   B. Grotesque
   C. Picaresque
   D. Burlesque

133. The term given to a type of incident or device which recurs frequently in literature is:
   A. Motif
   B. Ritual
   C. Refrain
   D. Concept

134. Using the name of one thing for something else with which it is closely associated is:
   A. Transferred epithet
   B. Parallelism
   C. Metonymy
   D. Paradox

135. Mock-heroic poetry elevates:
   A. The beauty in human relationships, as exemplified in Homer
   B. Trivial subject matter by using the style of the classical epic
   C. The stripping off of appearance in a witty manner

D.   The important tales of a hero's past

136.

"Those who have nothing but guns for the hungry
And think of nothing but death and dying,
Let them spend our earth's fortune
Harvesting blood from the fields of war.
The last banquet shall be their children's children's blood.
– *Blood Harvest*, Kofi Anyidoho

The above stanza succinctly presents the:
A.   Problem of war
B.   Problem of hunger
C.   Folly of soldiers
D.   Repercussion of violence

137.

"Nightfall! Nightfall!!
You are my mortal enemy."

The dominant figure of speech used in the above lines is:
A.   Ode
B.   Allusion
C.   Apostrophe
D.   Dramatic monologue

138. The line "Under snakeskin shoes and Mercedes tyres" is a good example of:
A.   Alliteration
B.   Metonymy
C.   Contrast
D.   Similitude

139. A denouement in a play:
A.   Causes conflicts
B.   Creates conflicts
C.   Resolves conflicts
D.   Creates catastrophe

140. A couplet refers to:
    A.   Two successive lines of rhyming verse
    B.   Two stanzas that cannot stand alone
    C.   Four irregular verses in stanzas
    D.   Poetry that is presented on stage

141. In drama, the term 'climax' is used:
    A.   As a figure of speech connoting beauty
    B.   For the point of highest dramatic tension
    C.   When the crisis in a play is resolved
    D.   When the hero's tragic flaw is revealed

142. A foil in drama is also known as:
    A.   Flat character
    B.   Protagonist
    C.   Round character
    D.   Antagonist

143.

"Whereat; with the blade, with bloody blameful blade,
He bravely broached his boiling blood best."

The dominant figure of speech used in the above lines is:
    A.   Simile
    B.   Alliteration
    C.   Assonance
    D.   Repetition

144. A humorous play based on an unrealistic situation is considered in drama as a:
    A.   Comedy
    B.   Tragedy
    C.   Farce
    D.   Burlesque

145. The device used by writers to give truths by indirection is called:

   A. Satire
   B. Hyperbole
   C. Paradox
   D. Irony

146.

"You amble on;
We can no longer
Wait for nature's course;
We must deliver
You with force."

The mood in the above lines is one of:
   A. Fear
   B. Sorrow
   C. Joy
   D. Indignation

147. The main unities in drama are those of:
   A. Action, time and place
   B. Time, space and action
   C. Place, time and action
   D. Space, action and time

148. Poems not written in meter or regular length are called:
   A. Short verses
   B. Rhythmic verses
   C. Free verses
   D. Irregular verses

149. An elegy is a poem that mourns the:
   A. Deceased
   B. Bereaved
   C. Accused
   D. King

150. When a statement is self-contradictory, we have an example of:

A. Irony
B. Paradox
C. Contrast
D. Parallelism

151.

'If winter comes, can spring be far behind?'

–Ode to the West Wind, Shelly

The literary device used here is:
A. Apostrophe
B. Allegory
C. Poetic license
D. Rhetoric

152. A melodrama is based on:
A. A melodious manipulation of events
B. Ingredients that mellow down events
C. Sensational plot and characters
D. The playwright's didactic overtones

153. Romantic poetry emphasizes:
A. The beauty of nature
B. Intimate relationships
C. The love in human nature
D. The romance in human aspiration

154. In drama, a conspicuous weakness in the character of the protagonist contributing to their downfall is referred to as:
A. Anagnorisis
B. A tragic flaw
C. Catharsis
D. A catastrophe

155.

"The woman whose breast I sucked is gone to the worms."

–Orphan, Oaili

The line illustrates:
    A. Sadism
    B. Sophism
    C. Satire
    D. Euphemism

156.

"Like as the waves make towards the pebbled shore
So do our minutes hasten to their end."

–*William Shakespeare*

In the above lines, the writer is thinking of the:
    A. Passing of time and shortness of life
    B. Swift passing of waves from sea to shore
    C. Passing of time from hours to minutes and seconds
    D. Movement of pebbles to the shore

157. *"And why must we be sad when the messiahs are with us to hound*
us and butt-gun us into greater tomorrow?"

– *The Messiahs*, Odia Ofeimun

The tone of the lines above is:
    A. Satiric
    B. Sarcastic
    C. Indicting
    D. Self-pitying

158. Which of the following are literary genres?
    A. Poetry, farce and fiction
    B. Fiction, poetry and drama
    C. Drama, fiction and biography
    D. Poetry, orthography and fiction

159. An epic is:
    A. A story that exalts a historical character
    B. An epoch-making event
    C. A description of a character
    D. A narrative prose describing a character

160. Point of view is a technique commonly associated with:
   A.   The narrative structure
   B.   Characterization
   C.   Plot
   D.   Atmosphere

161. *From Debbies' room comes the sound of the typewriter.*
It is an old mechanical typewriter; its noises are metallic and clicking. It chitters on to the end of a line, then there is the clash of the return, and the musical, oral most musical 'cling' of the little bell.

—Artwork, A. S Byatt

   A striking figure of speech used in the passage above is:
   A.   Zeugma
   B.   Onomatopoeia
   C.   Assonance
   D.   Paradox

162.

   "When to the seasons of sweet silent thought,
   I summon up remembrance of things past."

—Sonnet XXX, Shakespeare

The lines above contain the predominant use of:
   A.   Motif
   B.   Irony
   C.   Sarcasm
   D.   Alliteration

163. Hyperbole refers specifically to:
   A.   Exaggeration for adornment
   B.   Exaggeration for emphasis
   C.   Understatement of ideas
   D.   Restatement of ideas

164. The term 'assonance' refers to:
   A.   Repetition of alphabets in lines of a poem
   B.   Agreement of vowel sounds in a line

    C. Repetition of vowels in a line
    D. Agreement of consonance in a line

165. A story which explains the origin of a natural phenomenon is a:
    A. Fiction
    B. Legend
    C. Parable
    D. Myth

166. A legend is distinct from a myth because:
    A. It involves rituals
    B. The protagonist is usually a human being
    C. The protagonist is usually a supernatural being
    D. The story is usually invented

167. When a protagonist is purged of the dominant emotions of pity and fear at the end of a tragedy, it is called:
    A. Catharsis
    B. Dementia
    C. Purgation
    D. Redemption

168. When a statement is made on stage by a character to the hearing of only the audience, it is called:
    A. Prologue
    B. Soliloquy
    C. An aside
    D. A diatribe

169. To solve the dilemma of their characters by rescuing them from impossible circumstances using extra-human devices, a playwright will employ:
    A. Deus ex machina
    B. Contrived manipulation
    C. Dramatic reversals
    D. Magic

170.

> *"In the arena,*
> *They began to sing my song.*
> *We could hear it faintly*
> *Passing through the air."*
>
> – *Song of Lawino,* Okot P. Bitek

The figure of speech used in the lines above is:
- A. Metaphor
- B. Irony
- C. Personification
- D. Simile

171. An inherent quality of the lyric is that it is set:
- A. To be sung to a musical accompaniment
- B. To be sung by the poet who composes it
- C. To express the poet's subjective emotions
- D. To be simple and successful

172. The literary term that describes the angle at which a writer tells their story is:
- A. Story angle
- B. Storyline
- C. Aside
- D. Point of view

173. A character who remains unchanged in a work of art is called?
- A. A stereotypic character
- B. A usual character
- C. A flat character
- D. A round character
- E. An illusive character

174.

> *"O murderous slumber!*
> *Layest thou thy laden mace*

> *Upon my boy,*
> *That plays thee music."*

The above is an example of:
- A. Rhetorical question
- B. Personification
- C. Simile
- D. Apostrophe
- E. Allusion

175. The narrator who tells their story as if all actions in the story revolve around them is called:
- A. An omniscient narrator
- B. A first-person narrator
- C. A second-person narrator
- D. A third-person narrator

176. A satire employs:
- A. Comedy to amuse
- B. Farce to comment on societal conduct
- C. Irony to mock a situation
- D. Sarcasm and humour for social criticism

177. Poetic license refers to:
- A. The license to write poems
- B. The license to enjoy poems
- C. The writer's freedom to write what he/she pleases
- D. The writer's freedom to use words as he/she pleases

178. A poem is said to be good if it:
- A. Has elevated style
- B. Has rhyme and rhythm
- C. Is difficult to understand
- D. Has a regular rhythm

179. Dialogue is crucial in a piece of drama because:
- A. It makes the audience laugh
- B. It is like a discourse

C. It reveals the characters' minds

D. It makes the characters honest

180. A peculiar feature of drama in general is:
   A. Humor
   B. Satire
   C. Sarcasm
   D. Action

181. Which one of the following applies to both tragic and comic plays?
   A. Climax
   B. Happy ending
   C. Temper
   D. Sympathetic ending

182. In poetry, an image reveals one of the following:
   A. Refrain
   B. Theme
   C. Rhyme
   D. Intent

183. A deliberate use of understatement for humour or emphasis is also known as:
   A. Litotes
   B. Hyperbole
   C. Autonomy
   D. Metonymy

184. The expression – 'The pen is mightier than the sword' is a case of:
   A. Metonymy
   B. Synecdoche
   C. Antonomasia
   D. Synesthesia

185. The short story as a literary form is closest to:
   A. The play
   B. Poetry
   C. Short drama
   D. The novel

186.

"What time of night it is
I do not know
Except that, like some fish
Doped out of the deep
I have bobbed up belly-wise."

— *Night Rain*, J. P Clark

Which of the following figures of speech has been employed here?
   A. Alliteration
   B. Assonance
   C. Hyperbole
   D. Onomatopoeia

187. A figure of speech in which an absent person or an object is addressed as if present is referred to as:
   A. Assonance
   B. Apostrophe
   C. Elegy
   D. Personification

188. When a writer refers to past events to throw light on current ones, they are employing:
   A. Retrospection
   B. Flashback
   C. Historical drama
   D. Dramatic shift

189.

"I cannot blind myself
To putrefying carcasses in the

> *Marketplace, pulling*
> *Giant vultures*
> *From the sky."*
>
> – *How can I Sing? By* Odia Ofeimum

The tone of the lines above is:
- A. Defiance
- B. Anger
- C. Mourning
- D. Anxiety

190. The expression 'the sun kisses the earth' is a:
- A. Simile
- B. Metaphor
- C. Personification
- D. Paradox

191.

> *"O Julius Caesar, thou art mighty, yet thy spirit walks abroad."*
>
> –*Julius Caesar,* Shakespeare

This statement is:
- A. A ghost story
- B. A superstition
- C. An apostrophe
- D. An exaggeration

192. A didactic piece is one in which the writer:
- A. Teaches a human lesson
- B. Condemns human foibles
- C. Dictates to their readers
- D. Discusses dialectic themes

193. An over-used expression is:
- A. A cliché
- B. A cacophony
- C. An epigram
- D. An archetype

194. The literary device in which there is a difference between what is stated and what is actually the case is called:
    A. A metaphor
    B. A simile
    C. A personification
    D. An irony

195. A sub-plot is:
    A. A major turn or complication in the main story
    B. The second part of the main plot
    C. A secondary plot dealing with a different theme
    D. An aspect of the main plot recited by a different narrator

196. What basically distinguishes literature from other disciplines is its:
    A. Use of creative imagination
    B. Exposition of human experience
    C. Communication of ideas
    D. Portrayal of places

197. 'Stream of consciousness' is the name for:
    A. A narrative mode that produces a character's random thoughts and associations
    B. An Italian rhyme scheme that came into vogue in the sixteenth century
    C. A stage device in which the actor addresses the audience directly
    D. A cultural phenomenon of the eighteenth century

198. *"But everything does have a beginning, and so if I am to tell this story, I must begin. Yet I do not know the starting point of my tale."*
                    –The Circling Song, Nawal El Saadawi
The speaker in this statement is the:
    A. First-person narrator
    B. Protagonist
    C. Antagonist
    D. Omniscient narrator

199.

> *"The fair breeze blew, the white foam flew,*
> *The furrow followed free.*
> *We were the first that ever burst into that silent sea!!"*
>   *–The Rime of the Ancient Mariner,* Coleridge

The dominant figure of speech used in the above lines is:

    A. Repetition

    B. Free verse

    C. Sarcasm

    D. Alliteration

200.

> *"Here lies our Sovereign Lord the King,*
> *Whose word no man relies on,*
> *Who never said a foolish thing,*
> *Nor ever did a wise one."*
>   – *Epitaph on King Charles II,* John Wilmot Rochester

The form of the above stanza is an example of:

    A. A praise poem

    B. A lamentation

    C. An epigram

    D. A satiric poem

201.

> *"Full fathom five thy father lies*
> *Of his bones are corals made*
> *These are pearls that were his eyes*
> *Nothing of him that doth fade."*

The rhyme scheme of the above stanza is:

    A. baab

    B. abab

    C. abba

    D. aabb

202. An insincere literary work is known as:
   A. Parody
   B. Paradox
   C. Satire
   D. Pathos

203.

"Now I fear disturbance of the quiet season.
Winter shall come, bringing death from the sea,
Ruinous spring shall beat at our doors,
Root and shoot shall eat our eyes and our tears."

The dramatic technique employed in this passage is:
   A. Anti-climax
   B. Foreshadowing
   C. Flashback
   D. Irony

204. A creative process in which abstract entities, such as virtues and vices, are used with intended double meaning is called:
   A. Tragedy
   B. Allegory
   C. Farce
   D. Fallacy

205. In literature, a round character is associated with:
   A. Change and growth
   B. Stability and determination
   C. Simplicity and modesty
   D. Running down other characters

206. The technique used in bringing the plot of a play to an abrupt end is:
   A. Denouement
   B. Climax
   C. Endnote
   D. Deu ex machina

207. When words or phrases in either poetry or prose rise and fall measurably, it is said that they:
    A. Are accented and unaccented
    B. Have a regular rhythm
    C. Have a rhyme
    D. Are well-structured

208. The ode and the elegy are examples of:
    A. Sonnet
    B. Lyrical poetry
    C. Narrative poetry
    D. Blank verse

209. A play that tells a single story, has one setting, and takes place within a specified period is said to:
    A. Be heavily moralistic
    B. Be clearly cohesive
    C. Possess the unities
    D. Have straight forward storyline

210.

"With beaded bubbles winking at the brim
And purple-stained mouth."

The above is an example of:
    A. Tautology
    B. Comic relief
    C. Euphemism
    D. Consonance

211.

"Still stand stubborn
To stones that strangle the dawn.
Still stand stubborn
To stones that maim the morn.
Still stand stubborn
To stones that assail the sun."

–   *Sunset Sonata,* Atukwei Okai

The literary device employed in the above lines is:

- A. Onomatopoeia
- B. Repetition
- C. Metonymy
- D. Alliteration

212. When a story is told in a song and passed down by word of mouth, it is called:

- A. A sonnet
- B. An epic
- C. A ballad
- D. A singer's story

213. The purgation of the emotions of pity and fear in tragedy is called:

- A. Catharsis
- B. Tragi-comedy
- C. Dementia
- D. Cleansing

214. The use of humorous characters, speeches or scenes in a tragic work is known as:

- A. Catharsis
- B. Comic relief
- C. Wit
- D. Clowning

215. A quatrain is:

- A. The last line of a poem
- B. The fourth line of a sonnet
- C. A poem that ends with a question
- D. A stanza consisting of four lines

216. An exaggeration or overstatement in literature is a:

- A. Hexameter
- B. Hyperbole

   C. Metaphor
   D. Soliloquy

217. A form of symbolism in which ideas or abstract qualities are represented in a poem is an:
   A. Allegory
   B. Allusion
   C. Ambiguity
   D. Abstraction

218. The word 'image' is associated with:
   A. Altitude
   B. Mood
   C. Tone
   D. Abstraction

219. The stylistic device that uses the name of one thing to describe another thing is called a:
   A. Synonym
   B. Metonymy
   C. Metaphor
   D. Antonym

220.

> *"Whether the nymph shall break*
> *Diana's law, or*
> *Some frail china jar receive a*
> *Flaw or stain her honour,*
> *Or her new brocade."*
>
>   – *The Rape of the Lock,* Alexander Pope

The figure of speech used here is:
   A. Similitude
   B. Repetition
   C. Pathetic fallacy
   D. Zeugma

221. In which of the following genres is the term 'soliloquy' generally used?
    A. Novel
    B. Drama
    C. Epic
    D. Poetry

222. A burlesque is:
    A. An exaggerated mockery of a literary work
    B. A sentimental comedy
    C. An account of a famous person's life
    D. A rhetorical device used for effect in poetry

223. The 'dum, dum' of the drum is a good example of:
    A. Assonance
    B. Onomatopoeia
    C. Metaphor
    D. Simile

224. One major narrative technique novels share with drama is:
    A. Scenes
    B. Dialogue
    C. A dirge
    D. Soliloquy

225. A speech made at the end of a dramatic performance is generally called:
    A. A prologue
    B. An epilogue
    C. A dirge
    D. A monologue

226. A stanza of three lines linked by rhyme is generally called a:
    A. Couplet
    B. Ballad
    C. Tercet
    D. Quatrain

227.

> *"If it is true*
> *That the world talks too much,*
> *Then let's all keep quiet*
> *And hear the eloquence*
> *Of silence."*

One striking device used by the poet here is:
- A. Rhythm
- B. Contrast
- C. Alliteration
- D. End rhyme

228. The basic idea of any given work of art is its:
- A. Imagery
- B. Style
- C. Theme
- D. Tone

229. When a character in a literary work exists primarily to enhance, through contrast, the portrayal of the personal traits of another character, that first character is a:
- A. Protagonist
- B. Antagonist
- C. Mirror character
- D. Foil

230. A statement whose meaning is contrary to that openly expressed is an example of:
- A. Metaphor
- B. Oxymoron
- C. Irony
- D. Personification

231. Which of the following is central to narrative fiction?
- A. Sequence of events
- B. Dialogue

    C. Objectivity

    D. Subjectivity

232. Which of the following can be applicable to all genres?
    A. Symbolism
    B. Rhythm
    C. Action
    D. Narration

233. In literary criticism, a casual reference to a figure or an event is regarded as an:
    A. Alliteration
    B. Allegory
    C. Allusion
    D. Ambiguity

234. A paradox is:
    A. Applied to a word or combination of words whose sound resembles the sense it makes
    B. A statement which seems self-contradictory or absurd but turns out to have a valid meaning
    C. An episode of pantomime introduced through gesture and bodily movement in a play
    D. An elaborately conceived poem expressing an urban poet's nostalgia for life in the country

235. A necessary quality of every work of literature is that it:
    A. Shows a creative use of language
    B. Has to be publishable to gain wide acceptance
    C. Teaches a moral lesson
    D. Uses characters or actors

236.

> *"I die, yet depart not,*
> *I am bound, yet so free;*
> *Thou art and thou art not,*
> *And ever shall be!"*

–   *City of Dreams,* Robert Buchanan

The literary device consciously used in the above extract is:
- A. Metaphysical conceit
- B. Paradox
- C. Oxymoron
- D. Meiosis

237. In a work of literature, the plot is constructed on:
- A. The principles of conflict
- B. Exciting and memorable episodes
- C. The use of figurative language
- D. Recurring events

238. In literary work, setting refers to the:
- A. Starting point of the story
- B. Sum total of physical, social and historical circumstances
- C. Orderly arrangement of episodes
- D. Point at which the fortunes of the hero begin to decline

239. The prologue of any work is the:
- A. Conclusion
- B. Introduction
- C. Middle
- D. Turning point

240. A story, exemplifying a moral thesis in which animals talk and act like human beings, is called:
- A. An anecdote
- B. A fable
- C. An exemplum
- D. A parable

241. The main distinguishing feature of literature is that it:
- A. Tells stories
- B. Tells untrue stories
- C. Is relevant to life

D.   Presents fictional accounts of human experience

242. A poem written in honour and praise of someone else is:
   A.   An epic
   B.   A eulogy
   C.   An epigram
   D.   A lyric

243. In literary criticism, the vocabulary or language used by a writer is generally known as:
   A.   Diction
   B.   Figures of speech
   C.   Characterization
   D.   Rhythm

244.

> *"Hee, thou great Anna!*
> *Whom three realms obey,*
> *Dost sometimes counsel take -*
> *And sometimes tea."*

The literary device used in the lines above is:
   A.   Antithesis
   B.   Climax
   C.   Epigram
   D.   Anti-climax

245. The persons who take part in a play are sometimes referred to as:
   A.   Audience
   B.   Dramatists
   C.   Dramatis personae
   D.   Comedians

246. A form of writing in which the poet writes with nostalgia about simple village life is:
   A.   Pastoral
   B.   Ballad
   C.   Romance

D. Epic

247. An imitation, bordering on ridicule, of an author's style and ideas is known as:

    A. Mime

    B. Paradox

    C. Criticism

    D. Parody

248. A dirge is a:

    A. Romantic poem

    B. Poem on nature

    C. Poem of expedition

    D. Poem of lament

249. Criticism is a literary activity, which seeks to:

    A. Discover the beauty of a literary work

    B. Find faults in a literary work

    C. Analyse and evaluate a literary work

    D. Compare literary works of different authors

250. In poetry, 'run-on-line' can be found:

    A. In most kinds of poems

    B. Only in free verse

    C. Uniquely in blank verse

    D. Peculiarly in rhyming couplets

251.

> *"I find no peace, and all my war is done,*
> *If ear and hope, I burn and freeze like ice;*
> *I flee above the wind, yet I cannot arise;*
> *And naught I have and all the world in season."*

The predominant figure of speech used in this passage is:

    A. Oxymoron

    B. Alliteration

    C. Euphemism

    D. Hyperbole

252. Caricature is used to:
    A. Ridicule a person by distorting their most prominent features
    B. Censure an individual by emphasizing their weakness
    C. Expose the folly in literature
    D. Elicit the artistic potentials of dramatists

253. The substitution of a mild and pleasant expression for a harsh and blunt one is called:
    A. Climax
    B. Ambiguity
    C. Peripety
    D. Euphemism

254. The novel, the novella and the short story are the major sub-genres of:
    A. Non-fiction
    B. Prose fiction
    C. Poetry
    D. Drama

255. An antagonist is a character in a narrative who:
    A. Uses abusive language to antagonize other characters
    B. Works against the interests of the protagonist
    C. Works against the interests of other characters
    D. Champions the cause of the protagonist

256. A sonnet is a poem of:
    A. Ten lines
    B. Fourteen lines
    C. Seven stanzas
    D. Six stanzas

257. A couplet is a:
    A. Succession of three rhyming lines
    B. Succession of two rhyming lines
    C. Poem of two stanzas

D. Poem of three stanzas

258. An allegory is a story:
   A. In which people or things or events have another meaning
   B. Which aims at teaching a moral lesson
   C. In which allegations are made about the characters
   D. Which is told in verse

259. An ode is best described as a:
   A. Story told in poetic form
   B. Poetic composition of fourteen lines
   C. Narration about nature and natural objects
   D. Lyrical poem addressed to some person or thing

260. *"Have you got any hands today?"*
"No, I am working alone. My helpers are on strike."
"Would you like to engage me? My fees are reasonable.''
"No, thank you."
The first line of the above dialogue contains the device known as:
   A. Synecdoche
   B. Paradox
   C. Oxymoron
   D. Hyperbole

261. Which of the following is a permanent feature of a poem?
   A. Rhyme
   B. Repetition
   C. Rhythm
   D. Symbolism

262. Which of the following is exclusive to drama?
   A. Dialogue
   B. Plot
   C. Protagonist
   D. Soliloquy

263. The relationship between the protagonist and the antagonist is called:
   A. Antithesis
   B. Romance
   C. Conflict
   D. Cat and dog

264. An antagonist who is evil or capable of cruel and criminal action is the:
   A. Antihero
   B. Villain
   C. Boss
   D. Foil

265. An antihero is:
   A. A derailed protagonist
   B. An elevated foil
   C. A villain
   D. A protagonist lacking some qualities of a hero

266. The literary work which uses ridicule to correct social ills is known as:
   A. Epigram
   B. Satire
   C. Critique
   D. Hyperbole

267. A poem of mourning and dedication written on the death of an individual is called:
   A. An elegy
   B. A eulogy
   C. A Sonnet
   D. An Ode

268. One distinguishing factor between elegy and dirge is that of:
   A. Subject matter
   B. Length and formality

C. The poet's state of mind
D. The mindset of the subject matter

269. The type or form of elegy which represents both the poet and the one they mourn is:
   A. Romantic elegy
   B. Monody
   C. Pastoral elegy
   D. Threnody

270. A poem written on a grand or elevated theme, in an appropriate grand style, dealing with heroic figures is called:
   A. A tragedy
   B. An epigram
   C. An epic
   D. A ballad

271. Characterization in a novel means the:
   A. List of characters featured in it
   B. Mode of presenting fictional individuals
   C. Peculiar mannerisms of the narrator
   D. Resolution of the conflict between the characters

272. "...*In Soviet Union, everything is prohibited, including that which is permitted*" – This statement is an instance of:
   A. Innuendo
   B. Euphemism
   C. Paradox
   D. Allusion

273. In a work of literature, a hero is the one:
   A. Whose name is mentioned most in the work
   B. Who is antagonistic to everyone
   C. Whose experiences provide the central conflict in the work
   D. Who dies in course of the story

E.   Who performs brave and heroic deeds

274. As a literary form, the short story is closely associated to:
   A.   Poetry
   B.   The discourse
   C.   Tragedy
   D.   The novel
   E.   Drama

275. A short, emphatic, witty saying, often involving antithesis or paradox, is an:
   A.   Epithet
   B.   Epigram
   C.   Invective
   D.   Impression
   E.   Analogy

276. The plot of a story generally refers to the:
   A.   Intrigue made by a character against the hero
   B.   Intrigue hatched by the hero against their enemies
   C.   Way the writer begins and ends the story
   D.   Way the events of the story are organized

277. To be complete, a play must have:
   A.   A prologue and epilogue
   B.   A dramatic irony
   C.   A conflict
   D.   Several soliloquies

278. Which of the following was not written by Wole Soyinka?
   A.   The Interpreters
   B.   The Lion and the Jewel
   C.   The Trials of Brother Jero
   D.   Kongi's Harvest
   E.   The Strong Bread

279. *"To drag your father from his farm is as difficult as dragging a child away from his mother's breast"* – The dominant literary device used in the sentence is:
   A. Metaphor
   B. Personification
   C. Simile
   D. Amplification

280. When a poem has no regular rhyme scheme, it is called:
   A. A prose verse
   B. A dramatic verse
   C. A lyrical verse
   D. A blank verse

281. A poem without any regular beat and rhyme is referred to as:
   A. A blank verse
   B. A free verse
   C. A Solomon's verse
   D. A traditional verse

282. *"How can he compare our church outing with theirs? After all millions of people attended ours while very few people were seen at theirs."* – The speaker is likely to be accused of the use of:
   A. Paradox
   B. Oxymoron
   C. Hyperbole
   D. Comparison

283. When one work of art attempts to imitate the style of another work in a mocking manner, we describe the newer work as a(n):
   A. Parody
   B. Innuendo
   C. Pun
   D. Farce

284. A literary work whose mode of narration is the letter is a(n):
    A. Letter prose
    B. Letter narration
    C. Epistolary work
    D. Romantic work

285. The dominant idea in a literary work is called:
    A. Technique
    B. Content
    C. Theme
    D. Menu

286. When a word is used in a superficial manner, it is said to have been used in its:
    A. Figurative sense
    B. Connotative sense
    C. Literal sense
    D. Play players

287. The main antagonist in a play is referred to as the:
    A. Buffoon
    B. Villain
    C. Hero
    D. Protagonist

288. In a play, the list of actors and actresses is called the:
    A. Cast
    B. Dramatis
    C. Personages
    D. Play players

289. A term used in determining an effective choice of words in a literary work is:
    A. Diphthong
    B. Diction
    C. Denotation
    D. Dialogue

290. The moment of heightened tension in a play is called:
   A. Denouement
   B. Denotation
   C. Conflict
   D. Climax

291. The figure of speech in which a poet implicitly compares an object or idea with another object or idea totally different from that is called:
   A. Simile
   B. Denotation
   C. Connotation
   D. Metaphor

292. *"I listened as the car screeched and squelched its tires on the road, and mangy dogs roared and howled before I took another step."* – The dominant literary device used here is:
   A. Onomatopoeia
   B. Oxymoron
   C. Enjambment
   D. Metonymy

293. A figure of speech in which a part stands for a whole and a whole for a part is referred to as:
   A. Personification
   B. Partition
   C. Synecdoche
   D. Metonymy

294. Another term used for the denouement of a play or story is:
   A. Reference
   B. Interlude
   C. Inference
   D. Resolution

295. In a play or story, we refer to the character who contradicts the protagonist as the:
    A. Opponent
    B. Obstacle
    C. Villain
    D. Agroikos

296. *"A bashful smile of appreciation illuminated Nelly's pretty face."* – The figure of speech implied in the use of 'illuminated' is:
    A. Personification
    B. Metaphor
    C. Simile
    D. Meiosis

297. *'Hedwing, in spite of her misfortune, held her head high to high heavens.'* – The dominant literary device in the statement is:
    A. Alliteration
    B. Anagnorisis
    C. Personification
    D. Prolesis

298. .... determines the atmosphere of a poem.
    A. Tone
    B. Theme
    C. Structure
    D. Synopsis

299. A type of play which is funny and whose action is difficult to believe is called a:
    A. Melodrama
    B. Prosaic drama
    C. Farce
    D. Comedy

300. The principal aim of drama is to:
    A. Educate and entertain us
    B. Educate us

    C. Entertain us
    D. Strengthen and beautify us

301. Poetry is focused on one of the following:
    A. Emotion and ideas
    B. Beauty only
    C. Emotion only
    D. Ideas only

302. Drama differs from poetry because it:
    A. Involves many languages
    B. Deals with tragic experiences
    C. Uses elevated language
    D. Exists mainly in action

303. A novel is a:
    A. Prose writing about great people
    B. Prose writing about various people
    C. Long prose narrative fiction
    D. Long story involving human characters

304. The expression – 'All the world's a stage' is an illustration of the figure of speech referred to as:
    A. Simile
    B. Paradox
    C. Metaphor
    D. Parody

305. Identify the odd literary device from the list given below:
    A. Enjambment
    B. Plot
    C. Rhyme
    D. Alliteration

306. We study literature in school because it:
    A. Provides a means to kill time

    B. Exposes students to life realities
    C. Provides readers with entertainment
    D. Teaches readers the use of words

307. Dramatic irony entails:
    A. The praise of the audience
    B. A statement with a deeper significance
    C. A statement hilarious and sarcastic
    D. The praise tag of a great person

308. The echoing of the meaning of a word by its sound is called:
    A. Phonetics
    B. Oxymoron
    C. Personification
    D. Onomatopoeia

309. A comedy is a play in which:
    A. Nobody dies
    B. There is a happy ending
    C. There is real laughter
    D. The hero is a clown

310. A play is said to be tragic when:
    A. The author paints life as a hopeless venture or adventure
    B. The author presents life as absurd
    C. There is much bloodshed in the play
    D. A weakness in the principal character causes their downfall

311. The central organizing element which links characters, action, style and language in a work of art is referred to as:
    A. Theory
    B. Plot
    C. Theme
    D. Paradox

312. When a question is asked in a piece of work without an answer being sought, such a question is known as a:
    A. Rhetorical question
    B. Paradoxical question
    C. Leading question
    D. Pointed question

313. 'Assonance' in a poem results from the use of:
    A. Many consonants
    B. Similar-sounding vowels
    C. Similar-consonants
    D. Different-sounding vowels

314. A saying that is short, emphatic, witty, and bears antithesis or paradox is said to be an:
    A. Analogy
    B. Epiphany
    C. Apology
    D. Epigram

315. What we describe as 'tragic flaw' is the:
    A. Slip made by a character which results in their fall
    B. Unsuccessful play written by an otherwise wonderful dramatist
    C. Typographical error which recurs in a work of drama
    D. Element of plot which makes an artistic work faulty

316. To be total or complete, a play needs to have a(n):
    A. Soliloquy
    B. Conflict
    C. Prologue
    D. Epilogue

317. The plot of a novel is best described as:
    A. The outline of the story in a logical order
    B. The story with its beginning

C. The distinct summary of the story
D. The story in all its details

318. A writer of plays is known as a:
   A. Playwriter
   B. Playwrite
   C. Playwrighter
   D. Playwright

319. A narrative poem:
   A. Preaches a sermon
   B. Tells a tale or story
   C. Propounds a philosophy
   D. Argues in a narrative manner

320. A ballad is a:
   A. Poem bearing a thesis and an antithesis
   B. Love story told by a singing poet
   C. Poem that tells a folk story
   D. Poem bearing an interesting climactic episode

321.

"I am monarch of all I survey;
My right there is none to dispute;
From the center all round to the sea.
I am lord of the fowl and brute."

         – *William Cowper*

The poetic excerpt above is an example of:
   A. Melodrama
   B. Dramatic irony
   C. Dramatic monologue
   D. Metonymy

322. The above stanza can be said to be a:
   A. Couplet rhyming alternately
   B. Quatrain rhyming alternately
   C. Tercet with a single rhyme

    D. Ottava rima

323. The tone of the poet suggests:
    A. Conquest
    B. Mimicry
    C. Meiosis
    D. Obeisance

324. The rhyme scheme is:
    A. aabb
    B. abab
    C. aabc
    D. aacc

325. The last line is a case of the use of:
    A. Metaphor
    B. Personification
    C. Simile
    D. Pun

326.

"O serpent heart, hid with a flowering face!
Did ever dragon keep so fair a cave?
Beautiful tyrant: fiend angelical
Despised substance of divinest show!
A damned saint, an honourable villain!"

— *Shakespeare*

The poetic passage above is a case of:
    A. Invective
    B. Litotes
    C. Meiosis
    D. Conflict

327. Which One of the following was lavishly used in the poem?
    A. Hyperbole
    B. Onomatopoeia

C. Innuendo

D. Oxymoron

328. The tone of the poem is that of:

A. Anger

B. Wonder

C. Optimism

D. Pessimism

329. The dominant device deployed in the first line of the poem is:

A. Alliteration

B. Inversion

C. Innuendo

D. Synecdoche

330. The poem's structure is:

A. Epigrammatic

B. Parodic

C. Apostrophic

D. Dramatic

331.

> *"Old men wait at the stop*
> *Huddling from rain*
> *Under a tree*
> *As I pass*
> *Running to catch up*
> *With my reflection*
> *In a puddle*
> *They laugh*
> *And talk of death."*
>   – *Waiting for the Bus*, Amin Kassam

Which one of the following is not the type of contrast portrayed in the poem?

A. Old/young

B. Rain/sun

C. Waiting/running

D. Black/white

332. The term' bus' is a metaphor for:

    A. Life

    B. Death

    C. Help

    D. Love

333. Which one of the following is the theme of the poem?

    A. Even old men love

    B. Young men wait at the bus stop

    C. Youth is the period of exuberance

    D. Old men are patient and careful

334. The 'I' in the poem refers to a/an:

    A. Old man

    B. Young man

    C. Bus driver

    D. Bus conductor

335. In 'They laugh/And talk of death,' the poet uses the literary device called:

    A. Pun

    B. Oxymoron

    C. Metonymy

    D. Metaphor

336. The expression 'to catch up with one's reflection in a puddle' suggests:

    A. Uneasiness

    B. Going berserk

    C. Mirror gazing

    D. Friendliness

337.

> *"While round the herd the stallion wheels his flight,*
> *Engine of beauty rolled with delight*
> *To roll his mare among the trampled lilies."*
>
>   –   *Roy Campbell*

The poet describes the movement of a(n):

     A.   Female horse

     B.   Male horse

     C.   Electric current

     D.   Motor vehicle

338. The phrase 'engine of beauty' used in the poem is a(n):

     A.   Metaphor

     B.   Assonance

     C.   Simile

     D.   Synecdoche

339. A prominent literary device deployed by the poet in lines 1 & 3 is:

     A.   Onomatopoeia

     B.   Synesthesia

     C.   Irony

     D.   Personification

340. The rhyme scheme of the above poem is:

     A.   aab

     B.   aax

     C.   aba

     D.   abc

341.

> *"I saw his round mouth's crimson deepen as it fell*
> *Like a sun, in his last hour;*
> *Watched the magnificent recession of farewell*
> *Clouding, half gleam, half glower..."*
>
>   –   *Wilfred Owen*

In the lines of the poem above, Owen is talking about:

A. Farewell between friends
B. Those having sex in the dark
C. Farewell between spouses
D. The moment of death

342. The dominant image in the poem is that of the:
A. Approach of darkness
B. Approach of the sun
C. Dissolution of the clouds
D. The moment of the sun

343. The phrase 'his round mouth's crimson' is the metaphor for:
A. Redness
B. Life
C. Death
D. Blackness

344. The dominant literary device used by the poet in line 2 is:
A. Metaphor
B. Allusion
C. Simile
D. Prolepsis

345. The dominant literary device used by the poet in the last line is:
A. Symbolism
B. Irony
C. Alliteration
D. Enjambment

346.

"Some say the world will end in fire
Some say mice.
From what I've tasted of desire
I hold with those who favour fire
But if it had to perish twice,

> *I think I know enough of hate*
> *To say that for destruction, ice*
> *Is also great*
> *And would suffice."*
>
> – *Robert Frost*

The poem is built around:
    A. Innuendo
    B. Allusion
    C. Projection
    D. Supposition

347. What is the poet-speaker's choice of destruction in the end?
    A. Fire
    B. Desire
    C. Hatred
    D. Ice

348. The rhyme scheme of the poem is:
    A. abbccddcc
    B. abaaccdbc
    C. ababcbcb
    D. abbxccxdc

349. The expression – 'I hold with those who favour fire' means:
    A. I support those who want the world's destruction by fire
    B. I hold fire as those other people
    C. I support those who fire others
    D. Those who think the world will be destroyed by fire are correct

350. A limerick has:
    A. Ornate style, humour, irony and seven lines
    B. Humor, rhyme scheme and five lines
    C. Formal and elaborate style and humour
    D. A stinging climax, rhyme scheme and five lines

351.

> *"The curfew tolls the knell of parting day,*
> *The lowing herd winds lowly o'er the lea,*
> *The plowman homeward plods his weary way*
> *And leaves the world to darkness and to me."*
> — *Elegy Written In A Country Church Yard, Thomas*
> *Grey*

In the above, the imagery is:

    A. Of an approaching night in a rustic setting
    B. Of an approaching death in a village
    C. About a village under a curfew one night
    D. Of a man abandoned in his homeward journey

352. *Naomi: Shut up! Who taught you to speak like that? Now, go on with the sum you are doing. That woman whose mouth never closes is coming.*

Rebecca: I'll not shut up! (Enter Oyidia)

Naomi: I say shut up! You are never happy unless you are beaten up.

Oyidia: What has she been doing?

Naomi: What did she do before?

Oyidia: Oh, I am sorry. I heard she's always insulting you and evangelist.

Naomi: Who said? You are always hearing ugly things about people.

Oyidia: You can't drive a nail through my lips. I don't know how to hide things.

Naomi: The only things you can hide are your own domestic problems. Did I not hear that your new husband nearly beat you to death when he came home drunk as usual the other night? Have you heard me say it to anyone?

Oyidia: Who told you that after-supper fairy tale? Is there a worse drunk than your old evangelist husband?

Naomi: If you came to my house to quarrel with me, tell me. I'm ready to face you.

Oyidia: Why is your mouth so bitter? I came here just to greet you, and you began throwing your tongue about...

— *Sonny Oti: Evangelist Jeremiah*

The events of the extract are centered around:

    A. Tragic clash
    B. Denouement
    C. Dramatis personae
    D. Conflict

353. The physical setting of the extract is a:
    A. Village
    B. City
    C. Classroom
    D. Church

354. Naomi accuses Oyidia of:
    A. Husband snatching
    B. News-mongering
    C. Infidelity
    D. Dishonesty

355. When Naomi says, 'I am ready to face you,' she means *I am ready to*:
    A. *Quarrel with you*
    B. *Fight with you*
    C. *Compare height with you*
    D. *Look at your face*

356. 'You can't drive a nail through my lips' means you can't:
    A. Stop me from opening my mouth
    B. Stop me from talking
    C. Stop me from smiling or drinking
    D. Stop me from gossiping

357. The technique found in drama in which the audience knows what the actor does not know is called:
    A. Stage direction
    B. Dramatic irony
    C. Setting
    D. Improvisation

358. One peculiar feature of drama is:
    A. Humor
    B. Action
    C. Satire
    D. Sarcasm
    E. Exposition

359. Dialogue in drama:
    A. Excites the audience
    B. Sustains time
    C. Reveals the minds of characters
    D. Makes characters honest
    E. Ensures none is cheated

360. Which of the following was written by a Nigerian?
    A. The Beautyful Ones Are Not Yet Born
    B. Weep Not Child Mine Boy
    C. Man of the People
    D. Facing Mount Kenya

361. Point out the odd item from the following options:
    A. Eze Goes To School
    B. Beware Soul Brothers
    C. An African Night Entertainment
    D. One Week One Trouble
    E. Satanic Verses

362. Point out the odd item from the following options:
    A. Enjambment
    B. Rhyme
    C. Alliteration
    D. Assonance
    E. Plot

363. A novel is:
    A. A long narrative prose fiction

    B.   An interesting story about a hero

    C.   A prose writing that deals with various people

    D.   A prose writing about the lives of great or interesting people

    E.   A long story on new ideas and principles

364. Identify the odd item from the following options:

    A.   Prose

    B.   Poetry

    C.   Melodrama

    D.   Catastrophe

    E.   Drama

365. The 'setting' in a novel refers to:

    A.   The point in the story where we first encounter the main character

    B.   The overall social and physical background of the actions and events in the novel

    C.   The home country of the hero or heroine

    D.   The location where the main event in the novel takes place

    E.   All the various places mentioned in the novel

366.

> *"There is no frigate like a book*
> *To take us lands away,*
> *Nor any coursers like a page*
> *Of prancing poetry:*
> *This traverse may the poorest take*
> *Without oppress of toll;*
> *How frugal is the chariot*
> *That bears the human soul!"*
>
> *–   Emily Dickson*

    The poem praises:

    A.   The book

    B.   Poetry

    C.   Frugality

D. Traveling

367. The words 'coursers' and 'chariots' are united by the fact that:
    A. Both of them have to do with horses
    B. Both of them are drawn
    C. Both of them are carriers
    D. Both of them convey human souls to heaven

368. In the poem, the book is said to be:
    A. Transporter
    B. Free passageway
    C. Course
    D. Toll-taker

369. The term 'frigate' connotes:
    A. Free entrance
    B. Exploration
    C. Closed entry
    D. Agitation

370. The term 'book' may also mean:
    A. Paper
    B. Ticket
    C. Passport
    D. Knowledge

371. 'Frugal' means:
    A. Economical
    B. Intelligent
    C. Knowledgeable
    D. Free moving

372. Which one of the following applies to both tragedy and comedy?
    A. Happy ending

    B.   Tragic hero
    C.   Climax
    D.   Stanza
    E.   Alliteration

373. *Nowadays, anyone who wishes to combat lies and ignorance and to write the truth must overcome at least five difficulties. He must have the courage to write the truth when truth is everywhere opposed; the keenness to recognize it, although it is everywhere concealed; the skill to manipulate it as a weapon; the judgment to select those in whose hands it will be effective; and the cunning to spread the truth among such persons. These are formidable problems for writers living under Fascism, but they exist also for those writers who have fled or been exiled; they exist even for writers working in countries where civil liberty prevails.*

– *Writing the Truth: Five Difficulties*, Bertolt Brecht

The writer of the above passage implies that:
    A.   Truth is truth, whether told under fascist or liberal regimes
    B.   Telling the truth takes nothing
    C.   Writing about the truth is formidable
    D.   Lies are insuperable
    E.   Writing about the truth has challenges

374. From the passage, the skill to manipulate the truth suggests:
    A.   Ability to tell the truth with fraudulent intention
    B.   Cunning way of getting what you want
    C.   Ability to apply the truth to secure appropriate result
    D.   Ability to change the truth
    E.   None of the above

375. The theme of this passage is:
    A.   Truth
    B.   Shortcomings of telling the truth
    C.   Associated problems with telling the truth
    D.   Merits of telling the truth
    E.   Truth and Ignorance

376. The writer is convinced that:
    A. Truth is everywhere concealed
    B. Truth requires cunning to be told
    C. Aggression towards truth is everywhere
    D. Truth has five enemies
    E. It is difficult to recognize the truth

377. The dominant image in the passage is that of the:
    A. Triumph
    B. Oppression
    C. Melancholy
    D. Nostalgia

378. The tone of the writer of the passage is:
    A. Matter of fact
    B. Persuasive
    C. Interrogative
    D. Frustration

379.

"Would that you could live on the fragrance of the earth,
And like an air plant be sustained by the light.
But since you must kill to eat
And rob the newly born of its mother's milk to quench
Your taste,
Let it then be an act of worship..."
–The Prophet (On Eating And Drinking), Kahlil Gibran

The speaker in the above passage:
    A. Desires to end oppression
    B. Desires that the addressee should kill and drink
    C. Cares less of oppression
    D. Recommends the ritual of killing and drinking

380.

"Now, while the birds thus sing a joyous song,

And while the young lambs bound
As to the tabor's sound,
To me alone, there came a thought of grief:
A timely utterance gave that thought relief,
And I again am strong…."

— *William Wordsworth*

The rhyme scheme of the above extract is:
  A. abbacc
  B. abcdaa
  C. abbcca
  D. aabbcc

381.

"My life has been a joy to me
No matter where I go,
I've learnt to live in harmony
With kindly friend or foe."

— *Nnamdi Azikiwe*

The above piece is an example of:
  A. Quartet
  B. Perfect rhyme
  C. Sonnet
  D. Couplet

382.

"Thank the Lord for little mercies,
Forever glorify His name
Though you feel submerged in crisis
And your spirit is weak and lame,
He who cares is watching unseen
And sure His help will come between."

— *M. A. Begho*

In the above lines, the poet made noticeable use of:
  A. Allusion/rhythm
  B. Enjambment/rhyme
  C. Invocation/mime
  D. Chorus/prosody

383.

"It was the best of times; it was the worst of times:
It was the age of foolishness; it was the age of wisdom,
It was the epoch of belief; it was the epoch of incredulity,
It was the season of light; it was the season of darkness,
It was the spring of hope; it was the winter in despair..."

– *Charles Dickens*

The writer made profuse use of:

A. Similes
B. Tautology
C. Contrasts
D. Conceit

384.

"But when the days of golden dreams had perished,
And even Despair was powerless to destroy,
Then did I learn how existence could be cherished,
Strengthened, and fed without the aid of joy..."

–   *Emily Bronte*

The poet of the above piece sounds:

A. Jocular
B. Paradoxical
C. Cohesive
D. Confused

385.

"Endless is Thy greatness so pure the way,
Endless Thy creations o beautiful the day;
So many things to watch, so much to hear,
Yet the veil of darkness will not clear;
O, how many the creations and the world beyond,
Where was the beginning, O Nanak, where the end?"

– *G. T. S. Sidhu*

A striking device used in the above lines is:

A. Metonymy

B. Rhetorical question
C. Allusion
D. Conversation

386.

> *"The Rainbow comes and goes,*
> *And lovely is the Rose;*
> *The Moon doth with delight*
> *Look round her when the heavens are bare;*
> *Waters on a starry night*
> *Are beautiful and fair;*
> *The sunshine is a glorious birth;*
> *But yet, I know, where'er I go*
> *That there hath passed away a glory from the earth."*
>
> — *William Wordsworth*

Lines 1, 3, 4, 5 and 6 of the above poem are instances of:
A. Hyperbole
B. Pun
C. Metaphor
D. Personification

387.

> *"OH! There is never sorrow of heart*
> *That shall lack a timely end,*
> *If but to God we turn, and ask*
> *Of Him to be our friend!"*
>
> — *William Wordsworth*

The rhyme scheme of the above poem is:
A. Couplet
B. Petrachan
C. Alternate
D. Spenserian

388.

> *"If what I wish is good,*
> *And suits the will divine;*
> *By earth and hell in vain withstood,*
> *I know it shall be mine."*

— *Charles Wesley*

A subtle device used in line 3 of the above piece is:

    A. Irony

    B. Symbolism

    C. Chiasmus

    D. Metonymy

389.

> *"Hypocrisy, thou art wide awake,*
> *Thy holiness is but a fake;*
> *Stop wearing the motley hat*
> *And tell the world what thou art."*

— *M. A. Begho*

The above piece of verse is:

    A. An invocation

    B. An Apostrophe

    C. A sarcasm

    D. A transferred aggression

390.

> *"If Joy shall at thy bidding fly,*
> *And grief's dark day come on,*
> *We, in our turn, would meekly cry:*
> *Father, Thy will be done!*
> *Should friends misjudge, or foes defame,*
> *Or brethren faithless prove,*
> *Then, like thine own, be all our aim*
> *To conquer them by love."*

— *John Hampden Gurney*

The poet's attitude is that of:

    A. Defiance

    B. Submissive

    C. Gentility

    D. Despondency

391. *"On the first day of school, my teacher, Miss Mdingane, gave each of us an English name and said that from thenceforth, that was the name we would answer to in school. This was the custom among Africans in those days and was undoubtedly due to British education, in which British ideas, British culture, and British institutions were automatically assumed to be superior. There was no such thing as African culture."*

– Nelson Mandela, Long Walk to Freedom

The last sentence of the above extract suggests that African culture is:
   A. Inferior to British culture
   B. Is at per with British culture
   C. Superior to British culture
   D. Is non-existent

392. *"As a leader, I have always followed the principles I first saw demonstrated by the regent at the Great Place. I have always endeavoured to listen to what each and every person in a discussion had to say before venturing my opinion. Oftentimes, my own opinion will simply represent a consensus of what I heard in the discussion. I always remember the regent's axiom: a leader, he said, is like a shepherd. He stays behind the flock, letting the most nimble go out ahead, whereupon the others follow, not realizing that all along they were being directed from behind."*

The writer of the above extract suggests that:
   A. Leaders must lead from the rear
   B. It is good to listen to others
   C. Meetings should end in a consensus
   D. Followers need not know their actual leader

393. *"They had a hundred old photos of Joel Backman. They had studied every square centimeter of his face, every wrinkle, every vein in his eyes, and every strand of hair on his head. They had counted his teeth and his dental records. Their specialist across town at the headquarters of Israel's Central Institute for Intelligence and Special Duties, better known as Mossad, had prepared excellent computer images of what Backman would look like now, six years after the world last saw him.*

There was a series of digital projections of Backman's face at a hefty 240 pounds, his weight when he pled guilty. And another series of Backman at 180, his rumored weight now. They had worked with his hair, leaving it natural, predicting its color for a fifty-two-year-old man. They colored it black, and red and brown. They cut it and left it longer. They put a dozen different pairs of glasses on his face, then added a beard, first a dark one, then a gray one."

– The Broker, John Grisham

The language of the above extract is:
- A. Expressive
- B. Descriptive
- C. Threatening
- D. Blurred
- E. Expository

394. The above passage is:
- A. Ironic
- B. Hyperbolic
- C. Euphemistic
- D. Fantastic

WAEC Chief Examiners' Report on the Performance of Candidates of Literature-in-English Examination over the Years

Introduction

Teachers preparing students for any examination are always worried about the potential weaknesses in answers that their students will provide during examinations.

Fortunately, the main examining body, the West African Examination Council, has a culture of providing WASSCE candidates' strengths and weaknesses in previous Literature-in-English examinations.

The essence of incorporating these reports in this book is to draw the attention of students, candidates and teachers of the subject to the required standards and competencies expected of them in the study of literature in English and the examinations that follow. Due to the lack of space, this segment will dwell only on candidates' weaknesses in the written part of the examination.

The reviews leading up to these observations were carried out by the Chief Examiner of WAEC over the years. We shall paraphrase them.

In the first year of the years under review, the Chief Examiner observed that the section of the Literature-in-English exam on poetry was not adequately attempted by many of the candidates, and those who did performed poorly. According to the Chief Examiner, there was no indication that many of the candidates prepared for the examination as they depicted hazy knowledge of the recommended texts. As a remedy, he suggested:

- Efforts should be intensified to provide the prescribed textbooks in schools, and students and candidates should be encouraged to read them under the guidance of competent teachers.
- Qualified teachers should be employed to teach Literature-in-English.
- More teachers should be trained in the teaching of Literature through seminars and workshops.

In the second year, the Chief Examiner stated that candidates' weak performance in the exam was exhibited in their answers to questions on the application of literary skills such as style and criticism. The candidates indicated their inability to critically analyse and comment on issues from the texts according to the demands of the questions. They also portrayed shallow knowledge of the prescribed texts. To remedy this, the Chief Examiner suggested:

- Students should be encouraged to develop a good reading culture.
- Government and other stakeholders in education should train and retrain teachers of Literature by organising workshops and seminars.
- Teachers of Literature should endeavor to make the subject more appealing to students by introducing new teaching techniques and approaches, such as live performances of drama and poetry. Recorded videos on some of the texts in prose and drama can be used in teaching the subject in classrooms.

In the third year, the Chief Examiner's complaint was that many candidates portrayed a lack of in-depth knowledge of the texts. While some provided scanty answers to the questions they attempted, others wrote out of context, and their answers were too general and without close references to the texts. He never minced words when he suggested:

- Schools, the government and parents should endeavor to buy the prescribed texts for the students to use.

- More qualified graduate teachers of English Language should be employed to teach Literature-in-English in schools.
- Extra-curricular activities that can promote reading culture among the students should be encouraged.
- The government and other stakeholders in education should organise workshops and seminars to train and retrain Literature-in-English teachers.
- Teachers of Literature-in-English should endeavor to attend WAEC Marking Co-ordinations as a form of training programme or refresher courses. This will assist them in updating their knowledge of the examiners' expectations and in teaching the subject better in class.

As though the trend will not end, the exam body recorded poor performance in the subject in the fourth year under review. The Chief Examiner complained bitterly that some candidates' answers were pointless, while others exhibited shallow knowledge of the set texts and poor communication skills. According to him, there was clear evidence that most of the candidates had never read the original texts and thus were unable to present their ideas and responses with appropriate textual references. He, therefore, suggested:

- Stakeholders in education should encourage the candidates to read by providing the prescribed texts in school libraries.
- Candidates should learn to appreciate literature texts by acquiring adequate skills and techniques of literary appreciation through extensive reading.
- Candidates should desist from relying only on short notes and summaries on the subject or texts for study purposes.

In the fifth year, the situation was not different. According to him, candidates were weak in poetry and questions on style because they lacked the skills of adequate expression. The majority of candidates answered off context. He, therefore, suggested:

- The government and other stakeholders in education should organise periodic seminars to train and retrain literature teachers who will, in turn, have the same impact on the students.
- Students should be encouraged to study very well and cover the syllabus before exam time.
- Qualified English teachers should be employed to teach Literature, and students should be discouraged from relying only on abridged text summaries and handouts for study purposes.
- Efforts should be made to provide prescribed textbooks in schools, and candidates should be encouraged to read them under the guidance of competent teachers.

In the sixth year following, the Chief Examiner observed that questions were not answered as expected; candidates shunned techniques and merely narrated the storyline in the set texts. He, therefore, recommended:

- Candidates for the examination should be encouraged to read and prepare for the examination. They should be taught how to analyse the texts for the purpose of their examination. The prescribed books should be made available to school libraries by stakeholders in education, and they should ensure that the students make use of them.
- Attending tutorial classes/school by private candidates will boost their performance in the examination.
- Candidates must learn the skills of literary appreciation which is needed for answering questions in Literature-in-English exams.

It was all lamentations when, in the seventh year, the Chief Examiner noted that the standard of the paper was within the academic level of the candidates and of equivalent standard with those of previous years, the questions were unambiguous and straightforward, and the marking scheme was quite detailed. However, there was no significant improvement in candidates' performance compared to previous years. He also observed that candidates' performance showed that they lacked essential skills for literary appreciation and exhibited a poor understanding of the recommended texts. He suggested, among other things:

- Well-stocked libraries should be made available in schools, homes and public centres to help candidates develop a reading culture.
- Candidates should be discouraged from relying only on short notes and summaries for study purposes.
- Candidates should learn the basic facts and literary aspects of prescribed texts to achieve the educational objectives of Literature-in-English as a subject.

As though complaints will never end, the Chief Examiner observed in the eighth year that many of the candidates lacked the ability to interpret questions and gave answers out of context, while others merely narrated the content and the storyline of the texts. This shows that candidates failed to study the prescribed texts and lacked the basic skills of analysing and appreciating literature. Candidates' performance in poetry that year was generally poor, and therefore, he recommended:

- Stakeholders in education should encourage the candidates to read by providing the prescribed texts in the libraries.
- The private candidates should also endeavor to buy and study the prescribed texts. Qualified teachers should be employed to teach Literature-in-English.
- Teachers should attend training programmes such as seminars and workshops to improve their teaching skills.
- The reading culture is dwindling; therefore, parents and teachers should inculcate the habit of reading in their children from the early stage of life. There is no particular type of book to encourage them to read. However, in the words of Maya Angelou, "Any book that helps a child to form a habit of reading, to make reading one of his deep and continuing needs, is good for him."

The Chief Examiner complained that in the ninth year's exam the questions were not answered as expected. Many of the candidates generalised their answers; some wrote out of context, while others merely narrated the storylines of the texts. He, thus, suggested:

- Schools, governments and parents should encourage students to read by providing the prescribed texts in the library and at home.
- Training programmes, such as seminars and workshops, should be organised by stakeholders in education to train and retrain teachers of Literature-in-English.
- Extra-curricular activities that can promote reading culture among the students should be encouraged in schools.
- Teachers of Literature-in-English should attend WAEC marking coordination as a training programme. This will assist them in teaching the subject better in class.

In another year, the Chief Examiner complained that candidates failed to focus on the demands of each question. They derailed by reproducing the storylines of the texts. The candidates' responses indicated that they lacked in-depth knowledge of the set texts, as they paid attention to only the major characters in books. He, therefore, suggested:

- Parents, the government and school authorities should intensify their efforts to provide set texts for the candidates.
- More qualified teachers should be employed to prepare candidates.

In 2018, the Chief Examiner reported that candidates exhibited poor knowledge of literary appreciation, inability to write good English, poor and illegible handwriting, wrong interpretation of questions, writing irrelevancies, poor sentence construction, etc.

He, therefore, suggested the following remedies:

- The candidates should buy and read the set texts and not depend on summary notes on the texts.
- The candidates should make references to the set texts.

- The candidates should ensure their handwritings are legible and readable.
- The candidates should read the questions and ensure they understand what is required of them before attempting to answer them.
- Qualified teachers should be employed to teach the subject.
- The teachers should attend workshops and seminars occasionally to acquaint themselves with the demands of the subject.

The conditions were better in 2020 Paper 2. The Chief Examiner noted the candidates' strengths as follows:

- A number of candidates showed a good understanding of the questions and responded appropriately to them.
- Some candidates wrote good introductions devoid of biographies of authors and set out for the task ahead. Good answers were written point-by-point, and the analysis was clearly made.
- A good number of candidates displayed in-depth knowledge of the texts and supported their points with relevant references.

However, the paper also recorded some lows as some of the candidates' weaknesses manifested as follows:

- There were instances of very poor knowledge of the texts. In some cases, it was apparent that the candidates had not read the texts at all.
- A good number of candidates failed to either state the relevant themes or identify the characters or both.
- Some of the candidates only regurgitated notes, commentaries, etc., which were not the requirements of the questions.
- There were others who only presented sketchy answers; in some cases, their answers were only eight lines or less than half a page of their answer sheet.
- Many of the candidates demonstrated a lack of understanding of the questions as they presented

answers that did not actually address the questions they were supposed to be responding to.

- A few of the candidates misspelt names of some characters and places in the books.

To overcome the above weaknesses, the Chief Examiner suggested the following measures:

- The candidates should be made to understand that questions are set to elicit specific lines of reasoning and analysis, not mere narration of the entire plot.
- They should, therefore, be able to raise points and develop them for good marks.
- The students must be encouraged to buy and read set texts.
- A lot of assignments should be given, marked and discussed with students in class by the teachers.
- Teachers should read the yearly Chief Examiner's reports to know the weaknesses of students and correct them.
- Teachers should guide students in identifying the various themes of the set texts and relating such themes to some practice/past questions.
- Workshops for teachers of Literature-in-English should be organised from time to time.
- Students must be taught the techniques of answering questions.
- Teachers should encourage students to first read the prescribed text before reading any commentaries on them. For Paper 3 of 2020, the Chief Examiner observed that:
- Several candidates exhibited some familiarity with the text.
- Some candidates wrote good essays devoid of mere narrations.
- Good answers spelt out points and supported their points with relevant references from the texts.

However, candidates also displayed some weaknesses thus:

- They generally used poor English.

- They included irrelevant biographical details of authors in their answers.
- Relevant textual references were often ignored, and candidates preferred reading commentaries instead of reading the set texts.

Remedies

To overcome the weakness of candidates, the following suggestions are made:

- Teachers should ensure that students study the prescribed texts and are given essay type exercises in class.
- Students must be taught how to answer questions appropriately.
- Students should engage in intensive and extensive reading of relevant novels and other supplementary readers to broaden their knowledge and acquire adequate vocabulary.
- There should be effective teaching and learning to ensure that the syllabus is totally covered before the examination.
- Teachers should also read the Chief Examiner's Report to be able to guild the students aright in their preparations.
- Teachers should guide students to identify the various themes of the set texts and the relation of such themes to some practice/past questions.

For Paper 2 of 2021WAEC WASSCE, the Chief Examiner observed that:

- A few of the candidates seemed to have a good knowledge of the texts.
- Some candidates managed to quote important portions of the text to support their points.
- Remarkably, some candidates engaged more in the discussion of key points in the texts than mere narration.

However, some candidates displayed some weaknesses as:

- Poor grammatical and structural sentences abound in most of their responses.
- Most candidates showed little or no knowledge of the texts.
- Some candidates' over reliance on commentaries of the texts was evident in their responses as they wrote very similar introductions and conclusions.
- Ideas were presented haphazardly by some candidates and this marred their work.

Suggested Remedies

- Teachers must adequately involve candidates in class discussions of the novels to help candidates bring out their own ideas and interpretations of the novels.
- Teachers need to urge students to read the selected texts as required; give them reading assignments and have reading sessions in class.
- Each point/idea presented in their responses must be adequately supported with textual evidence.

For Paper 3 of 2021 WAEC WASSCE, the Chief Examiner observed that:

- A number of the candidates displayed some level of knowledge and understanding of the texts.
- The demands of the various questions appeared to have been generally understood.
- Attention was focused more on attempting to answer questions than on irrelevant introductions on writer's background and other published works.
- Candidates scoring higher marks also demonstrated a skillful use of the language, good knowledge of texts and clarity of thought.

However, some candidates displayed some weaknesses as a result of:

- Blind reliance on commentaries without significantly making contact with the texts.

- Churning out some wrong or inconsistent answers verbatim.
- Some candidates producing answers that were not related to the texts, or producing their own versions of the scene.
- Candidates indulged in over generalization where specific references to the texts were required.
- Some candidates being unable to identify the genres and referring to them in a mutually inclusive manner.
- General unpreparedness, leading to the presentation of answers that could have been memorized and written under loose supervision.

Suggested Remedies

- Candidates should be encouraged to reason and write independently of others in the examination halls.
- Candidates could avoid writing profiles of authors that have no bearing on the questions asked.
- Where texts have film or video versions, candidates should stay off extraneous scenes that are not found in the texts.
- For all texts studied, candidates should be able to identify themes, characters, and literary terms and briefly elaborate on them.
- Where questions on texts have contemporary relevance, candidates should not be over tempted to avoid specific references to the relevant parts of the texts.

Note:

The observations here are instructive and should be taken seriously by students and candidates. The recommendations are helpful as they prepare for the exams as it relates to the use of the recommended texts and other study materials.

On the other hand, teachers of the subject should see the observations and recommendations as pointers and guide for classroom work.

Finally, it is suggested as did the Chief Examiner that school authorities, parents, government and other stakeholders in educations should ensure that competent teachers who have passion for the subject are employed, adequately equipped and motivated for the task.

WAEC Literature-in-English Scheme of Examination

- There will be three Papers – Papers 1, 2 & 3.
- Papers 1 & 2 will be a composite Paper and will be taken at one sitting.
- Paper 1 will be a multiple choice objective test.
- It will contain fifty questions distributed as follows:
- Twenty questions on General Knowledge of Literature.
- Five questions on an unseen prose passage.
- Five questions on an unseen poem.
- Twenty context questions on the prescribed Shakespearean text. Candidates will be required to answer all the questions within 1 hour for 50 marks.

Paper 2 will be an essay test with two Sections, Sections A & B. Section A will be on African Prose and Section B on Non-African Prose.

Two essay questions will be set on each of the novels prescribed for study.

Candidates shall be required to answer one question only from each Section within 1 hour 15 minutes for 50marks.

Paper 3 will be on the Drama and Poetry Components of the syllabus. It will be put into four sections, Sections A, B, C & D as follows:

- Section A: African Drama
- Section B: Non-African Drama
- Section C: African Poetry
- Section D: Non-African Poetry

There shall be two questions on each of the prescribed drama texts for Sections A and B. There shall also be two questions for each of the poetry sections (Sections C & D). Candidates shall be required to answer one question from each of the sections, making a total of four questions. The Paper will take 2 hours 30 minutes to complete and will carry 100 marks.

Note:

The Unseen Prose passage for Paper 1 shall be about 120 – 150 words long. Only context questions shall be set on the Shakespearean text. The context questions will test such items as theme, characterization, style and setting in the Shakespearean text.

No essay questions shall be set on the Shakespearean text.

Chapter 12

Answers to Test Questions

Exercise A – Essay Questions

Note:
The written responses to the essay questions in this book were provided with the sole aim of demonstrating to students what examiners expect from their answers to questions. They serve only as examples and guidelines as to format. The answers are somewhat brief, and are intended only to provide guidance to the students on how to present their answers logically and clearly. Due to limited space, these responses may lack the necessary details as expected; however, candidates are expected to back up their own answers with essential details, references or examples (where appropriate) while utilizing their own unique style of presentation. It is crucial that they tailor their responses towards the examiner's line of thought as it pertains specifically to each question and to remain within its contextual boundaries. Candidates must also ensure that they use proper English language skills throughout their response, paying close attention not only to sentence structure and length but also to manner of presentation and tense usage where applicable.

1. Aku, the wife of Oshevire and mother of Oghenovo, finds herself victim to Toje's exploitation during a time of vulnerability. With her husband detained on false charges and ostracized by her neighbours, Aku is left to manage the home front alone. Overwhelmed by Toje's demands, she still has to keep the home front. At a point, she is unable to withstand the pressure of Toje's demand. She is disillusioned and gets into an affair with Odibo.

2. Okpe employs the episodic narrative technique, which entails presenting the story from a character's perspective in a confessional manner. This approach highlights the

characters' roles and prevents monotony. Oghenovo speaks like a child without punctuation marks, creating an authentic portrayal.

3. The novel's plot progresses from rural to urban settings, each with its unique values and differences. Ibuza represents the rural environment where people follow traditions, while Ebute-Metta depicts a diverse group of city dwellers who must adapt to their surroundings. Women maintain their domestic responsibilities and also earn income to support their families, whereas men now take up jobs previously considered feminine.

4. (i) Marriage: The society practices polygamy, with women expected to uphold the institution, manage domestic duties and bear children. Men, on the other hand, are at liberty to take multiple wives as they please. The payment of dowry is strictly observed.

    (ii) Childbearing: Married couples are obliged to procreate; infertility is regarded as a shortcoming. Bearing children is viewed as an investment that ultimately enhances family life while ensuring the continuity of their lineage.

    (iii) Superstition: Both rural and urban communities in the novel exhibit superstitious tendencies. The medicine man - believed to possess supernatural powers - holds a significant role within these societies. Sacrifices are made to Nnu Ego's chi in Ibuza and similarly in cities. Dibia consultation is sought for matters such as guitars that play themselves.

5. Richard was raised in a challenging environment by White individuals. His interactions with family members mirror those of his wider society: he purposefully provokes his father, displays aggression towards Aunt Addie, and remains indifferent towards his grandmother. The sole individual within his family whom he admires is Uncle Hoskins; tragically, this role model is killed by Whites.

6. Richard and his sibling were admitted to an orphanage overseen by a person of mixed race when their mother could no longer provide for them. The youngsters subsisted in conditions of almost famine-like proportions: the meagre rations they received were scanty at best. Furthermore, they endured frequent physical abuse and were deprived of any semblance of affection. The facility was anything but homely; instead, it represented suffering and a dearth of love and care. It was a place better left forgotten - an embodiment of deprivation where survival necessitated an indomitable willpower.

7. The novel portrays village life as fundamentally communal, exemplified in the diligent care provided to the ailing deacon by members of the assembly who take turns keeping watch over him in Lantern Lard. Similarly, in Raveloe, individuals take pride in their respective professional skills and are dedicated to looking out for one another. Furthermore, socializing through conversation and music is a cherished pastime in the community.

8. Eppie was conceived through an illicit love affair. She stumbled into Silas' life, drawn by the warmth emanating from his hearth on a chilly evening. Eppie provided immediate solace for Silas' bereavement over his stolen gold, and this comfort only grew with time. In order to ensure that Eppie lived a fulfilling life, Silas began participating in village affairs he had previously avoided.

Poetry

1. The thematic or poetic pre-occupation of the poet is the quality of our actions while alive on earth. The poet stresses the need for us to fill our days with good deeds that distinguish us and ensure that we are remembered even when we are long dead.

   The poet focuses on the dash between the two dates on the tomb of his late wife. The dash, as used in the poem, signifies the legacy or legacies of our time while alive. The legacies are what we leave behind and to be remembered when we are no more.

2. The theme of death is central to the poem. It focuses on the inevitability of death and compares the two major states of life and death. Houseman treats death as a transition from a transient world to one of permanence. Death is also viewed as a means of welcome escape from the travails of the world. The living beings are disillusioned because they are "Runners whom renown outran."

3. The poet articulates pain and anguish in response to the deplorable and debasing circumstances that afflict impoverished and marginalized individuals of the world. These individuals are bereft of both a domicile and basic amenities, subsisting solely on meagre remnants from the tables of the privileged few. The poet empathizes with their plight while censuring society for its indifference towards their suffering. Nonetheless, he retains optimism regarding a more promising future (the second phase). The poet's tone conveys despondency but ultimately evinces an underlying glimmer of hope.

4. The title is symbolic of a journey embarked upon, replete with both perilous risks and exhilarating thrills. The divergent paths serve as symbolic representations of the myriad obstacles and choices that beset human existence. This includes its allurements, diversions and possibilities - all inherent to the act of decision-making. The persona embodies mankind's earthly struggle against forces that either benevolently bless or malevolently oppress him.

Drama

1. The principal figures in the play serve to embody racial subjugation and bias. African Americans are prohibited from obtaining employment, rendering their mobility restricted and rights deprived by those of Caucasian

descent. The play's central theme is rooted in racism, reflecting the experiences of Black individuals through the character Outa Jacobs, who endures insufferable circumstances culminating in a miserable demise. The entirety of this work constitutes an appraisal of government-sanctioned discriminatory policies targeting a particular sector of society.

2. Comedy serves a dual purpose in the play, functioning as both a satirical instrument for denouncing the racist regime and an antidote to the oppressive system. Mimicry is extensively employed on both black and white characters to alleviate the tension wrought by racial discrimination. The language itself is laced with humorous overtones and biting invectives that effectively ridicule the discriminatory practices at hand.

3. The play is replete with irony. James' stance on career selection is ironic, as is the conduct of Bonu, a lawyer who should exemplify society's moral standards but instead does the opposite. It is ironic that Aunt Fosuwa encourages Maanan to pursue a relationship with Lawyer Bonu while assuming James would approve of the relationship. Furthermore, Awere, who is hitherto seen as a bad influence, later proves to be a source of inspiration to Aaron.

4. James is autocratic and very rigid when it comes to making decisions about his children's career choices. Unlike Hannah, James is very strict with the children, and so they hardly relate to him. He recommends flogging as the solution to Aaron's not changing his mind about painting. He later changes his views when he realizes that one can become famous through painting.

5. All the characters in the play are embodiments of corruption and societal rot. The man is the epitome of corruption, and all his officials are physically filthy and symbolically decadent. The presentation of the officials as physically filthy by the playwright is intentional. This

appearance is meant to point to their moral ineptitude. The merchants also exploit the system for their own selfish ends, just like Hlestakov.

6. The entire play revolves around the use of mistaken identity. The panic caused by the corrupt government officials upon the knowledge that a government inspector was on his way from St. Petersburg was utilized by smartly dressed Hlestakov.

   Hlestakov is mistaken for the inspector. He does not attempt to correct the mistake but milks the corrupt officials and leaves before the arrival of the real inspector. The mistaken identity also creates humour and satirizes the corrupt system.

7. Thomas More believes that a man's conscience should guide his actions as opposed to men like Cromwell and Norfolk, who believe that a man should not have any view contrary to the dictates of the state. More sees the King's views as a personal wish, which becomes immoral when it dabbles into the church. He, therefore, maintains his stance throughout his arrest, trial, imprisonment and execution without compromising.

8. The Common man plays several roles in the play. He represents that which is "common to all ages." He is used as a commentator and actor and also performs the dual role of being both inside and outside the play at various stages. He is a steward, boatman, inn-keeper, jailer, foreman of the jury and the headsman. The few instances of humour in the play are also a result of the witty statements of the Common man.

Exercise B

Objective Test Questions

1B	51A	101 D	151D	201B	251A	301 A	351 D
2C	52A	102A	152C	202A	252A	302D	352D
3C	53C	103C	153A	203B	253D	303C	353A
4C	54D	104C	154B	204B	254B	304C	354B
5A	55C	105B	155D	205A	255B	305B	355A
6E	56B	106A	156A	206D	256B	306B	356B
7D	57A	107A	157B	207B	257B	307B	357B
8A	58B	108D	158B	208B	258A	308D	358B
9E	59A	109B	159A	209C	259D	309B	359C
10B	60D	110D	160A	210D	260A	310D	360D
11E	61C	111B	161B	211D	261C	311B	361E
12A	62C	112A	162D	212C	262D	312A	362E
13A	63B	113C	163B	213A	263C	313B	363A
14B	64C	114B	164C	214B	264B	314D	364D
15A	65C	115A	165C	215D	265D	315A	365B
16A	66D	116B	166C	216B	266B	316B	366A
17A	67C	117A	167A	217A	267A	317A	367A
18A	68D	118C	168C	218D	268B	318D	368A
19A	69D	119A	169A	219B	269C	319B	369B
20E	70C	120D	170C	220D	270C	320C	370D
21D	71D	121C	171A	221B	271B	321C	371A
22B	72A	122D	172D	222A	272C	322B	372C
23D	73D	123B	173C	223B	273C	323A	373E

24B	74A	124C	174D	224B	274D	324B	374C
25B	75A	125B	175B	225B	275B	325A	375C
26D	76C	126D	176D	26C	276D	326A	376C
27D	77A	127D	177D	27D	277C	327D	377B
28E	78C	128D	178D	228C	278E	328A	378A
29E	79D	129A	179C	229D	279C	329A	379A
30D	80B	130C	180D	230C	280D	330C	380C
31C	81A	131A	181A	231A	281B	331D	381A
32B	82B	132C	182B	232A	282C	332B	382B
33B	83D	133A	183A	233C	283A	333C	383C
34E	84D	134C	184A	234B	284C	334B	384B
35D	85D	135B	185D	235A	285C	335B	385B
36B	86C	136D	186D	236C	286B	336A	386D
37A	87C	137C	187B	237D	287B	337B	387C
38A	88C	138A	188B	238B	288A	338A	388B
39C	89B	139C	189B	239B	289B	339D	389B
40B	90D	140A	190C	40B	290D	340A	390B
41A	91B	141B	191C	241C	291D	341D	391A
42C	92D	142D	192A	242B	292A	342A	392B
43B	93A	143B	193A	243A	293C	343B	393B
44A	94D	144C	194D	244D	294D	344C	
45B	95B	145D	195C	245C	295C	345C	
46D	96C	146D	196A	246A	296A	346B	
47D	97D	147A	197A	247D	297A	347D	
48D	98B	148C	198A	248D	298A	348C	
49A	99C	149A	199D	249C	299A	349D	
50A	100C	150B	200C	250A	300C	350B	

Bibliography

i.   Abrams, M. H., and Geoffrey Galt Harpham. *A Glossary of Literary Terms*. 9th ed. Wadsworth Cengage Learning, 2009.

ii.   Amaechi, Martins Izuchukwu. *Comprehensive Literature-in-English for Senior Secondary Schools*. Revised ed., 2010.

iii.   Bertolt Brecht. *Galileo*. English version by Charles Laughton. Ramsed Edition, 2004.

iv.   Dickson Spring, Erika. *Teaching Literature-in-English at High School Level*. 2015.

v.   Exam Ethics Project in Partnership with the Federal Republic of Nigeria. *How to Excel in Exams: Secondary Edition*. 2003.

vi.   Holt, Rinehart, and Winston. *Elements of Literature: 5th Course*. Austin, TX: Holt, Rinehart, and Winston, 2007.

vii.   Ilozue, R. O. C. *Authority on Literature-in-English*. 2008.

viii.   Joint Admission and Matriculation Board. *Syllabuses for the University Matriculation Examination 2022/2023*. Bwari: JAMB, 2007.

ix.   Kennedy, X. J., and Dana Gioia. *Literature: An Introduction to Fiction, Poetry, and Drama*. 9th ed., Interactive ed. New York: Pearson Longman, 2005.

x.   Littel, McDougal. *The Language of Literature*. Evanston, IL: McDougal Little Inc., 2001.

xi.   Nwachukuw-Agbada, J. O. J., et al. *Exam Focus Literature-in-English for WASSCE, 2006–2010*. Ibadan: University Press Plc, 2005.

xii.   Nwanze, Ikechukwu. *Random Reflections, Vol. 1*. 2008.

xiii.   Ola Rotimi. *Ovonranwen Nogbaisi*. Benin City: Ethiope Publishing Corporation, 1974.

xiv. Siti Salina, Mustakim, et al. "Teachers' Approach in Teaching Literature." *Malaysian Online Journal of Educational Science*, vol. 2, no. 4.

xv. West African Examination Council. *Syllabuses for 2023.* 2023.

xvi. Yanni, Robert Di. *Literature: Reading Fiction, Poetry, Drama, and Essay.* Boston: McGraw-Hill Companies Inc., 1998.

Highlights

- In-depth analysis of what WAEC, NECO, and JAMB require from candidates in Literature-in-English examinations.
- In-depth discussion of the various genres of literature, including prose, drama and poetry.
- In-depth discussion of literary appreciation and how it enhances the understanding of literary works.
- The best approach to using recommended texts and study materials for Literature-in-English examinations.
- Unseen literature, with sample questions and answers.
- Instructions, tips, practical guides and steps on tackling Literature-in-English exam questions.
- Classroom approach to the teaching and learning of Literature-in-English.
- A glossary of literary terms and principles, especially those that feature regularly in general literary discourse and Literature-in-English examinations.
- WAEC Chief Examiners' reports on the performance of Candidates in the Literature-in-English Examination over the years.
- A selection of essay and objective test questions with answers in Literature-in-English.